Parent & Teacher Guide

This Parent and Teacher Guide is designed to help you support your student's learning. The information presented in this guide is based on the course content at the time of printing. Occasionally, the online version of your course may change slightly, but the tips in the Parent and Teacher Guide are designed to broadly cover the course's content.

This guide is arranged in lesson order. You will find everything you need for each day of the school year.

Copyright © 2018 Lincoln Learning Solutions, Inc. All rights reserved.
This material may not be reproduced, distributed, used to create derivative works, publicly displayed or performed, or otherwise made available to others.

Course Introduction

Welcome to Science 4

Introduction

Welcome to Science 4, by Lincoln Empowered™. Gazing up at the stars, marveling at all of the small parts inside a tulip flower, wondering why that magnet sticks to the refrigerator, or finding a variety of beautiful rocks by digging in the backyard — these are just a few of the ways your student will experience the wonder of the natural world this year. In this course, students will learn the technical and sometimes surprising facts behind the things they see and experience every day. They will expand their understanding of familiar topics in the areas of physics, chemistry, Earth science, ecology, biology, and space science. By studying each of these areas of science every year, students gain a lasting understanding, building on the concepts as more details and complexity are introduced. In addition to these familiar topics, fourth grade students are introduced to technology and engineering concepts, joining their older peers as students of STEM (Science, Technology, Engineering, and Math). These lessons encourage students to become innovative problem-solvers equipped with the skills and knowledge necessary to address twenty-first century issues.

The purpose of this Parent and Teacher Guide is to aid you as you help your student on the path to success. This guide contains an overview of the course content, an introduction to navigating the course online, course expectations, and useful teaching tips and suggestions. Here you will find everything you need to have a successful year.

Course at a Glance

Please guide your student to watch the brief welcome video for their course, which can be found just before the Lesson 1 folder. This engaging video is intended to excite your student and kickstart their learning. It will introduce your student to Professor Hobart, who will guide them on a quick journey through some major topics covered in the course. As your student progresses, Professor Hobart may return to provide encouragement or to simply add a personal touch.

SCIENCE 4
Course Introduction

End of the Year Expectations for Science 4

By the end of the year, and in order to be fifth grade ready, your student will be able to do the following.

Biology	The ability to identify and classify animals and plants based on their observable features; the ability to explain that organisms grow and survive in a particular habitat; the ability to identify behavioral and physical characteristics of animals and plants that have helped them to survive; the ability to explain how changes in an organism's habitat can be helpful or harmful; the ability to describe the life cycles of humans, animals, and plants; the ability to define genetics; the ability to identify physical characteristics in humans, animals, and plants that are passed on through genes; the ability to compare and contrast single-celled and multicellular organisms
Ecology	The ability to explain the relationships between plants and humans in terms of the gases they produce and need to survive; the ability to draw a food web; the ability to identify predator and prey, animal camouflage, and protective traits of plants and to describe how these adaptations aid survival; the ability to explain how humans can cause environmental changes that result in the extinction of plants and animals; the ability to illustrate how matter moves through an ecosystem (death cycles, the carbon cycle, the nitrogen cycle); the ability to recognize the ways that human and natural influences have affected an ecosystem
Agriculture	The ability to show how agricultural commodities progress from production to transportation to retailing to consumption locally and globally; the ability to distinguish between sustainable and non-sustainable resources; the ability to explain how domesticated animals and technological inventions have affected agricultural production; the ability to explain the effect of agriculture on water systems; the ability to explain how unclean water can transmit disease
Natural Resources	The ability to identify resources used to provide humans with energy, food, employment, housing, and water; the ability to identify how humans depend on natural resources for survival; the ability to match natural resources to their geographic origin; the ability to demonstrate understanding that fuels come from natural resources; the ability to identify the negative impacts that the use of fossil fuels has on the environment; the ability to describe the positive effects of plastic in everyday life and the negative effects of plastic on the environment; the ability to identify types of pollution and their sources; the ability to identify items that can be recycled and those that cannot; the ability to describe the impact mining can have on land
Earth Science	The ability to define and give examples of landforms; the ability to label the Earth's layers; the ability to demonstrate understanding of erosion and weathering; the ability to identify the three main types of soil (clay, sand, and loam) and to compare and contrast the effects water has on each; the ability to identify the three layers of soil (topsoil, subsoil, and bedrock); the ability to classify, compare, and contrast rocks and minerals (e.g., as igneous, metamorphic, or sedimentary); the ability to identify fossils as either plant or animal, recognize the period in which the organism lived, and describe the nature of the environment at that time; the ability to categorize Earth's water sources as freshwater or saltwater; the ability to explain the water cycle and basic weather elements (clouds, temperature, precipitation, wind, pressure); the ability to identify the weather elements necessary for the development of a storm; the ability to describe the purpose of weather measurement tools
Space Science	The ability to list the eight planets in our solar system in the correct order; the ability to explain why Pluto is no longer considered a full-size planet; the ability to compare and contrast the characteristics of the planets of our solar system; the ability to locate the Milky Way galaxy and label the solar system on a map; the ability to define the terms *sun*, *star*, *planet*, *universe*, *galaxy*, *moon*, *lunar phase*, *revolve*, *rotate*, and *orbit*; the ability to explain how Earth's rotation and revolution around the sun affect seasons and to describe the motion of the Earth and sun in a 24-hour period
Chemistry	The ability to demonstrate understanding of the properties of matter; the ability to categorize matter as a solid, liquid, or gas; the ability to compare and contrast the properties of solids, liquids, and gases; the ability to define *mass*, *molecule*, and *atom*; the ability to illustrate a water molecule by drawing and labeling the atoms it is composed of; the ability to explain how matter changes when it is heated or cooled; the ability to explain the meaning of the term *conservation of mass*

SCIENCE 4
Course Introduction

Physics	The ability to distinguish between different types of energy and to explain how one type of energy can be converted to another (e.g., kinetic, stored, mechanical, chemical, light, heat); the ability to summarize how sound and vibration are related using scientific vocabulary; the ability to distinguish between substances that are good conductors and those that are good insulators; the ability to describe how light can be refracted, reflected, and absorbed; the ability to create and compare simple, parallel, and series circuits; the ability to explain how magnets work using scientific vocabulary; the ability to describe the properties of waves (amplitude, wavelength) and to classify waves (mechanical, electromagnetic, longitudinal, transverse)
Technology and Engineering	The ability to identify differences between simple and complex machines; the ability to list, compare, and contrast forms of transportation; the ability to identify the impacts of technological developments in transportation on civilization; the ability to identify technologies developed during the sixteenth, seventeenth, and eighteenth centuries; the ability to describe the expansion of civilization as a result of aviation developments; the ability to list the seven steps in the engineering design process, and to explain how the design process can help construct a solution to a given design problem; the ability to identify, compare, and contrast the six types of bridges; the ability to describe how biotechnology has changed the growing of plants and to describe the technologies that have modernized agriculture (GPS, robots, RFID); the ability to identify ways energy conservation helps the planet
Science Skills	The ability to formulate questions, predict, observe, sort, classify, communicate, experiment, and measure; the ability to record observations, make inferences, and look for patterns
Research Skills	The ability to research and describe a topic or question
Scientific Tools	The ability to use scientific tools and to generate ideas for new tools

Materials and Kits

An essential piece for your student's learning is found in the Lincoln Empowered science materials kit for fourth grade. This kit provides many of the tools your student will need in order to complete the activities and experiments in the course. Beyond the items in the kit, you will be asked to utilize common household objects, such as measuring cups, pots or cups, a stove, and a freezer. Your student should have pencil and paper or a notebook available for every lesson, so they will not be listed separately as required materials in the lesson content.

Assessments

There are two types of assessments in Science 4: Assess Its and Mastery Assess Its. Both are graded assessments. Assess Its are shorter assessments with a narrower scope of focus. The purpose of Assess Its is to gauge where your student is on the road to mastery of the targeted content. You can use the result of this formative assessment to reflect on the concepts and skills your student needs to revisit. Assess Its are often completed offline and then submitted for grading.

Mastery Assess Its are longer with a broader scope of focus. They serve as an opportunity for your student to demonstrate their level of mastery of a set of skills and concepts. Mastery Assess Its are typically completed and submitted online, within the course.

Using the Internet

Some lessons will ask your student to use the Internet to search for information. There are a number of kid-friendly search engines available online, which strive to filter out inappropriate content. They include **Kiddle**, **KidRex**, **AskKids**, and **Kidzsearch**.

SCIENCE 4
Course Introduction

Science Notebook

Real scientists keep notebooks, not journals. A notebook is meant to be shared and referenced, while a journal is typically a more personal documentation of ideas. As a "mini-scientist," your student should emulate what scientists do; therefore, keeping a science notebook is key.

In real life, a science notebook can be used as a legal document if it is dated. This type of notebook can establish who gets credit for scientific breakthroughs and discoveries. For primary students, a three-ring binder or a composition book would be an ideal science notebook.

Here are some habits you should practice with your student until they become routine.

- Have the notebook out and open for every lesson.
- Remind your student to write the date at the top of a new page for every lesson. This is a great way for them to practice writing out dates in their full form, and it helps them to learn the appropriate placement of the comma between the date and year (e.g., May 1, 2017). Additionally, it reinforces the concept of documenting scientific "discoveries."
- Write neatly and clearly – scientists do not erase in their notebooks, even if they think their reasoning is off track. They simply use one line to cross out text. This way, they can always reference their initial thoughts, if necessary. Therefore, have your student write legibly, but if a mistake is made, allow them to cross out the text. Again, they are taking on the habits of scientists.
- Teach your student to write vocabulary, important facts, opinions, observations, and questions in their science notebook. They should also include simple drawings that they create while completing course activities. Ask your student to read what they wrote aloud to you, and then talk to them about it.

Understanding How People Learn

Discovery to Understanding

Science is such a fun topic for young students, and it lends itself to learning by discovery. While the lessons in this course will present texts and videos with factual information, the overarching goal is to get students thinking like scientists and making sense of their world. To reach this goal, facts must be brought to life and made real to students. So, get your student out and about, and help them to discover science in a hands-on way. Examples of hands-on learning approaches will often be included in the course activities, but by thinking about how students learn science, you can support your student in reaching their fullest potential. Use the resources that are unique to your student's city or town to make learning fun and exciting. By learning a concept in the following three ways, students are able to achieve a deep and lasting understanding.

1. **Discover Science:** Students are able to discover how things work through demonstrations, reenactments, hands-on displays, or real-life examples. If possible, take your student to a children's museum, science museum, natural history museum, national park visitor's center, zoo, aquarium, farm, or petting zoo. Go on nature walks, exploring your surroundings, collecting samples, and investigating. Grow plants together from seed, observing them as they grow. Cook together in the kitchen, and help your student to observe what happens when different ingredients are combined.

2. **Visualize Science:** Students learn by watching videos, playing games, and viewing pictures. In addition to using the videos provided in this course, check with your local library or search online for science videos made just for kids. *National Geographic Kids* is one source of age-appropriate science videos. You will also find interactive games in this course. If you wish to supplement the content provided in these games, there are many apps and online games that will help young students visualize science. *PBS Kids Science Games* is a good place to start.

SCIENCE 4
Course Introduction

3. **Read about Science:** Students reinforce what they have learned through discovery and visualization by reading. Help your student to find and read books, articles, websites, and magazines on scientific topics. Use flashcards to assist them in memorizing science vocabulary.

Learning Tools

In order to support the development of science vocabulary and concepts, consider these tips:

1. **Science Flashcard Games:** Get creative with flashcards.

     Matching Pairs: Create a set of cards where each card has a clear match. Lay all of the cards out on the table, and work with your student to match the pairs. Once your student is familiar with the pairs, use the cards to play a memory game.

     Sequence Sets: When lessons introduce concepts that represent a cycle of some sort, such as weather patterns or seasons, learning the vocabulary as a set of words in the context of the cycle, rather than individual words, makes learning easier. To create a sequence set, use one card to represent each stage of the cycle your student is studying. Mix them up, and have your student put them in the correct order and explain the cycle to you.

     True or False Sets: Write statements on cards that are true or false. Mix them up and sort them into true and false piles. Be sure to keep the number of cards manageable. Start with four, and work your way up to ten.

2. **A Science Word Wall:** Hang cards with frequently used science terms on a dedicated wall (or refrigerator, closet door, etc.). Consider starting each science lesson by focusing on the word wall.

3. **Graphic Organizers:** These vocabulary displays help students to contextualize new words. Graphic organizers also allow students to integrate the vocabulary into preexisting knowledge. This process increases the likelihood that your student will remember the new vocabulary words. Here is one example you could try:

Helping Your Student

You play an important role in your student's learning, and being able to effectively support the learning process is key. This section will provide you with additional helpful hints, beyond the individual lesson pages, to bring learning to life inside and outside the classroom.

SCIENCE 4
Course Introduction

Did you know? The brain recognizes the five senses in five different areas. It is best for all learners to tap into as many of these areas as they can, simultaneously. This approach is called a multisensory experience for students.

Understanding Attention Span: A good rule of thumb in understanding your student's attention span is to consider their age. Students are generally able to actively concentrate for one minute per age year. Therefore, a fourth grader will only be able to focus on one thing, without a cognitive shift, for about nine to ten minutes. At that point, change the way you present an activity to keep your student engaged. For example, a simple change from reading to completing an activity will help your student to concentrate. You can also watch a video and pause it for a discussion. Alternating modes of learning will help your student stay engaged with the content.

Developmental Characteristics of Fourth Graders: Fourth grade is a challenging yet rewarding year. Fourth grade students are generally more sensitive and intense than they were in third grade. In an academic setting, their intensity translates to interest in learning many subjects, but their sensitivity means they are negatively affected by pressure and punishment. Being aware of these developmental tendencies of nine- and ten-year-old students can help you to be a better educational guide. Here are some tips to keep in mind this year to support your student.

- To help your student reach their potential and avoid defeat, create a low-pressure environment. Redirect your fourth grader with positive feedback and guidance as opposed to negative consequences.
- Watch out for the tendency of your student to be self-critical. Help them maintain a positive self-image and attitude toward learning by providing a great deal of encouragement.
- Create a schedule for your student, and involve them in designing a plan to complete their assignments. Goal setting and planning are skills most fourth graders have not yet developed.

Assess Prior Knowledge

It is always best to assess students' prior knowledge before they are introduced to a new topic. This simply means finding out what students already know (or think they know) about the topic. By knowing what your student knows, you are able to quickly review mastered content, uncover misunderstandings, and learn where you need to slow down and provide better support. Consider these tried and true staples of any educator's classroom.

1. **Ask a focus question:** Focus questions are written in a way that focuses the student's attention solely on the small task ahead and simply asks what they know.
2. **KWL Charts:** Work with your student to complete the chart to the right. K — list what the student knows; W — list what the student wants to know; L — list what the student has learned about a given topic.
3. **3-2-1:** Ask your student to share three things they know about the topic, two things they would like to know, and one question related to the topic.

Know what I *Know*	Wonder what I *Want* to know	Learn what I *Learned*

SCIENCE 4
Course Introduction

Develop Metacognition

Metacognition is a complex word for something that is part of our daily lives. Simply explained, "meta" means after or beyond, and "cognition" means the process of acquiring knowledge. Therefore, metacognition is something we do after we gain knowledge. The process of metacognition is about self-monitoring, self-evaluating, and self-regulating all types of thought.

When students gain knowledge, it is up to teachers and parents to help them build on their knowledge. Helping your student to develop metacognitive skills is essential.

To help build metacognition, ask your student these questions:

- What are you thinking?
- What do you wonder?
- What did you notice?
- What questions do you have?
- What does this remind you of?
- What are you trying to figure out?
- What are you picturing in your head?
- How are you feeling?
- What do you find interesting?
- What other concept does this connect to?

The goal is to eventually move away from asking your student these questions to your student stating them without being prompted. Eventually, your student will say: "I'm thinking, I notice, I wonder…"

The Art of Questioning

To inquire about something is to ask questions about it, to examine or investigate it, or to probe and explore it. A good rule of thumb when guiding your student's learning is to tell less and ask more. While you don't want a student to hit their frustration point, grappling with content actually helps a student to more effectively master that content. To aid them in their learning, consider asking guided questions. This type of open-ended questioning requires more than a one-word answer. Lead your student through the content by posing good questions. A student will retain information longer if they discover the concepts themselves instead of being told.

Here are some questions appropriate for Science 4:

- How would you describe ____?
- What features are unique to ____?
- Which category does ____ fall under?
- How are those two things similar/different?
- What do you think might happen if…?
- What are possible causes of ___?
- What are the effects of ___?

- Do you think ___ is a good idea? Why?
- How does this work?
- What do you notice?
- Why do you think ____ is happening?
- What changes when…?
- What does ___ need in order to work?
- What happens if you take ___ away?

SCIENCE 4
Course Introduction

Empowered™ Courses: What You Need to Know

Lincoln Empowered™ is a unique kind of curriculum. Courses are composed of learning activities called learning objects. A number of learning objects are presented together as lessons. Learning objects are individual pages and activities that provide students with the content and practice they need to master specific learning objectives, or goals, for a course. Students are often asked to demonstrate mastery of learning objectives by completing assessments.

Engagement

Students are engaged through various activities, videos, and simulations. Students may be asked to complete a task on paper, or they may engage with a variety of online activities. TextPoppers, for example, are found within the content as blue, bold text. Students can hover over these words with a mouse or click on them to see definitions of key terms and phrases.

Learning Objects

Ten different types of learning objects exist within Lincoln Empowered courses:

Read Its are the primary learning tools within a course. They contain all of the instructional information students need to demonstrate mastery of the granular learning objectives.

Practice Its are interactive activities that can be accessed online or offline. They provide the opportunity for students to check their understanding of the learning objectives.

Watch Its are learning tools that utilize videos to enhance the learning experience and bring abstract concepts to life for students.

Play Its are content-focused, interactive games that support learning.

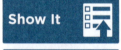

Show Its are activities that provide the opportunity to show mastery of specific learning objectives.

Answer Keys are available to the instructors for all Show Its and Apply Its. They provide correct answers and detailed feedback that can be shared with students.

Assess Its are graded activities that allow students to demonstrate mastery of learning objectives and standards.

Reinforce Its are supplemental activities to assist students who may be struggling. They also offer a great review before taking assessments.

Extend Its provide additional content to extend student knowledge.

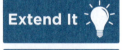

Apply Its are non-graded assessments that cover content from multiple lessons. Apply Its can be cumulative projects that allow students to demonstrate mastery of several learning objectives. Teachers can elect to make these gradable.

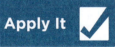

SCIENCE 4
Course Introduction

Course Structure

Each Lincoln Empowered™ course is structured in a similar manner. When you and your student enter a course, you will find a number of topic folders. These topics reflect the key concepts that your student will learn in a specific grade and subject. Each topic folder contains a number of lessons.

Each lesson (e.g., Lesson 1, Lesson 2) represents one day of learning. Lesson folders contain the content, or the learning objects. A set of learning objects is presented to help a student master the content.

The Lincoln Empowered approach to instruction allows students multiple opportunities to learn and master objectives, which leads to mastery of the standards. It is not necessary for a student to complete every learning object. They were created to appeal to different modalities. You will notice that some content repeats, giving students additional exposure to a concept before an assessment. If your student has mastered the concept, move on to the next objective. Work the curriculum to meet your student's needs. There is flexibility in the "Its" that allows for student choice and greater differentiation, which puts you and your student in control of the learning.

Games and Videos

While games (Play Its) and videos (Watch Its) may appear after the content within the course, you may want to consider allowing your student to engage with these items first, especially when you need to grab their attention. This type of engagement builds excitement; it encourages the student to share prior knowledge or ask questions; and it helps to build knowledge for students who are lacking experience in a certain concept. Often, you will hear your student say, "They talked about that in the video," or other statements of excitement.

Course Resources

The first folder in your course is titled "Course Resources." It contains a set of useful resources that will help your student begin the course. Start by reviewing the Supply List and Pacing Guide. Then, view some of the materials you will need throughout the course.

SCIENCE 4
Course Introduction

Tips and Tricks

Documents & Handouts: Throughout the course, you will find many worksheets, stories, and texts provided as PDF files. In some cases, it is best to download these PDFs to your computer so that you can view them in a larger format, while in other situations it will be necessary to print these files.

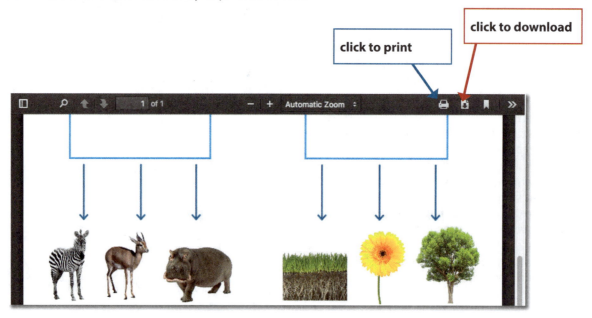

Optimizing Your View: Some PDFs, at first glance, do not seem ideal to read on the computer screen because of their large size. When you encounter these texts, if the content found in the PDF window is too large, click the "Fit to page" icon located at the bottom right of your PDF to adjust the zoom. This will auto adjust your view to your screen.

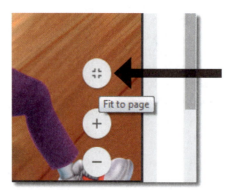

Time to Get Started

You now have all the information you need to have a successful year. So, what are you waiting for? Log in to your course and get started!

SCIENCE 4 PARENT & TEACHER GUIDE

LESSON 1

Topic | Properties of Matter

Learning Objectives

The activities in this lesson will help your student meet the following objectives:

- define the term *matter*
- list objects or materials composed of matter that can be seen
- identify substances composed of matter that cannot be seen

Materials

- balloon
- cup
- dictionary
- empty water bottle
- funnel
- ice cream
- 1/3 cup baking soda
- 1 cup vinegar
- root beer

Define Matter

Activate

1. Have your student open the **Matter of the Universe - Watch It** to view the video.
2. Pause the video at 2:40 and prompt them to explain the difference between mass and weight. Mass is the space something takes while weight is a function of gravity.

Engage

1. As your student reads the **Read It**, have them explain the term *matter* in their own words. Use this opportunity to discuss any misconceptions about the term *matter*.

Demonstrate

1. Now, direct your student to complete the definition activity in the **Show It**. Then, work with them to check their response using the example in the **Show It AK**. Allow them to make any necessary revisions.
2. As an alternative to the **Show It**, have them observe the varying states of matter in a root beer float by completing the following steps:
   a. Fill a cup halfway with root beer and discuss that root beer is a liquid type of matter.
   b. Then, discuss the ice cream's state of matter, which is a solid.
   c. Next, put a scoop of ice cream into the root beer and discuss how the bubbles contain carbon dioxide. Explain to your student that this carbon dioxide is a gaseous type of matter that is not normally visible. However, the ice cream creates bubbles that trap the carbon dioxide, allowing them to see it in the form of bubbles.
3. Last, ask your student, "What did you discover about root beer floats and how they relate to science?"

• • •

Visible Matter

1. While your student reads the **Read It**, invite them to name the examples of visible states of matter presented in the text. (Answers: oxygen gas and helium gas)

1. Now, instruct your student to move on to the **Show It** activity.
2. Finally, check that they listed ten items that are visible matter. You may reference the **Show It AK** for examples.

• • •

Invisible Matter

1. After your student reads the **Read It**, have them verbally name two types of invisible matter from the text.
2. Then, prompt them to question invisible matter by completing the following sentence stem:
   - I really wonder why...

1. Next, direct your student to complete the task in the **Show It**. When they are finished, they can compare their answers to the examples provided in the **Show It AK**.
2. As an alternative to the **Show It**, have them follow the steps to inflate a balloon with carbon dioxide.
   a. Fill a water bottle with 1 cup of vinegar.
   b. Use the funnel to fill the balloon with 1/3 cup baking soda.
   c. Carefully attach the balloon to the top of the water bottle without dropping any baking soda into the vinegar.
   d. Next, lift the balloon to pour the baking soda in the vinegar and observe.
   e. Finally, ask your student, "How is the balloon inflating?" The balloon inflates because the chemical reaction of mixing vinegar and baking soda makes a gas called carbon dioxide.

SCIENCE 4 PARENT & TEACHER GUIDE

LESSON 2

Topic Properties of Matter

Learning Objectives

The activities in this lesson will help your student meet the following objectives:

- explain that all objects and materials in the world are made of matter
- observe matter too small to be seen with the naked eye by using a microscope

Materials

- cooking oil
- microscope
- pin
- ruler
- specimen (such as a droplet of water, a piece of cork, or an onion cell)
- tape
- two balloons

Matter in All Objects

Activate

1. Have your student open the **Introduction: Matter - Watch It** and ask them to make note of the username and password provided on the Discovery Education image. Be sure that they click the link for the video and enter the provided username and password to watch.
2. Then, ask them to name some examples of matter from the video.

Engage

1. As your student reads the **Read It**, ask them to identify the examples of different types of matter presented in the text.

Demonstrate

1. Now, guide your student to complete the activity in the **Show It**. Then, work with them to compare their response with the sample in the **Show It AK**. It is important that they include the word mass in their definition.
2. To provide an alternative to the **Show It**, help them to complete the following activity that tests mass and volume.
   a. Inflate two balloons to the same size and tie them.
   b. Tape the tied end of one balloon to the end of a ruler so that it can dangle. Then, tape the second balloon on the other end of the ruler.
   c. Place the center of the ruler on your student's finger so that they can balance the mass of the balloons.
   d. Next, while your student is still balancing the balloons, dab a drop of cooking oil on one balloon and puncture the oil with a pin. The oil will keep the balloon from popping, but it will slowly release air.

Copyright 2018 © Lincoln Learning Solutions. All rights reserved.

3

e. Instruct them to make observations of the balance of the balloons. The balance will begin to tilt in one direction. It may be hard for your student to keep the ruler from falling, so allow them to adjust as needed.
f. Then, ask them, "What happened to the volume of the balloon that was punctured?" (Answer: The volume decreased and took up less space.)
g. Finally, ask them, "What happened to the balance when the balloon deflated?" (Answer: The balance teetered towards the inflated balloon because it had more mass.)

Using a Microscope

1. While your student reads the **Read It**, emphasize reading the labels of the microscope diagram.
2. Then, allow them to identify these parts on their microscope.

1. Now, instruct your student to move on to the **Show It** activity.
2. Finally, work with them to check their observations with the **Show It AK**.
3. To extend learning, encourage your student to illustrate their observations of cells under a microscope.

SCIENCE 4 PARENT & TEACHER GUIDE

LESSON 3

Topic | Properties of Matter

Learning Objectives

The activities in this lesson will help your student meet the following objectives:

- illustrate before and after pictures of an object composed of matter too small to be seen without magnification
- define the term *properties*
- arrange items from largest to smallest

Materials

- colored pencils
- cotton swab
- dictionary
- drawing paper
- microscope
- specimen (such as a droplet of water, part of a cork, or an onion cell)

Illustrating Observations

Activate

1. Begin by having your student look out a window and name three observations of the outdoors.
2. Then, discuss the importance of paying special attention to details while making observations.

Engage

1. As your student reads the **Read It**, prompt them to describe the before and after images of the onion in the text.

Demonstrate

1. Now, direct your student to complete the microscope activity in the **Show It**.
   a. Encourage them to look at their own cells by rubbing the inside of their cheek with a cotton swab.
   b. Then, wipe the wet end of the cotton swab on the center of the slide, place a drop of water on the sample area, and place a coverslip on top.
   c. Next, follow the remaining steps of the **Show It**.
2. Finally, check that your student illustrated a before and after image of the object.

• • •

Define Properties

1. Have your student open the **Properties of Matter - Watch It** and ask them to make note of the username and password provided on the Discovery Education image. Be sure that they click the link for the video and enter the provided username and password to watch.
2. Then ask them, "What can you use to describe the properties of an object?" (Answer: The five senses can be used to describe the properties of an object. Explain to your student that these properties are properties of matter.)

1. After your student reads the text of the **Read It**, allow them to describe the properties of a chosen object from their learning environment.

1. Now, direct your student to complete the **Show It** activity, and work with them to check their definition with the **Show It AK**.
2. As an alternative to the **Show It**, allow your student to set up a miniature museum exhibit that includes examples of different types of properties such as color, shape, weight, and texture. For each example, instruct them to create a label for the display. Have them use their exhibit to explain and define the term *properties*.

• • •

Property of Size

1. After your student reads the **Read It**, prompt them to explain how properties of matter can be used to categorize objects. Properties of matter can be used to categorize objects by their color, size, shape, etc.
2. Next, have them complete the sorting activity in the **Practice It**.

1. Now, instruct your student to complete the activity in the **Show It**. When they are finished, help them to check their response with the **Show It AK**.
2. Finally, have your student complete the activities in the **Extend It**.

LESSON 4

SCIENCE 4 PARENT & TEACHER GUIDE

| Topic | Properties of Matter |

Learning Objectives

The activities in this lesson will help your student meet the following objectives:

- arrange items from lightest to heaviest
- compare the colors of items
- compare the textures of items

Materials

- basketball
- five small objects
- marble
- triple beam balance

Property of Weight

Activate

1. Have your student open the **Weight - Watch It** and ask them to make note of the username and password provided on the Discovery Education image. Be sure that they click the link for the video and enter the provided username and password to watch.
2. Then ask them, "How does the force of gravity relate to weight?" Explain that weight is determined by the force of gravity. The more gravity a planet has, the more something will weigh.

Engage

1. After your student reads the **Read It**, have them determine if they weigh more on Earth or on the Moon. (Answer: Earth)

Demonstrate

1. Now, instruct your student to complete the activity in the **Show It**. When they are finished, help them to check their answers using the **Show It AK**.
2. As an alternative to the **Show It**, allow your student to find the weight of five objects using the triple beam balance. Then, ask them to line the objects from lightest to heaviest.

Property of Color

 Engage

1. As your student reads the **Read It**, ask them which sense they use to describe an object's color. (Answer: sight)
2. Next, direct your student to complete the activities in the **Practice It**.

 Demonstrate

1. Now, guide your student to complete the **Show It** activity. Then, work them to check their response with the **Show It AK**.
2. As an alternative to the **Show It**, allow your student to group ten objects from their learning environment by their color.

• • •

Property of Texture

 Engage

1. While your student reads the **Read It**, ask them which sense they use to describe an object's texture. (Answer: touch)

 Demonstrate

1. Now, direct your student to complete the activity in the **Show It**.
2. Then, assist them to evaluate their response with the **Show It AK**.
3. To extend learning, have your student go on a texture scavenger hunt for items with the following textures:
   - prickly
   - fuzzy
   - smooth
   - soft
   - slick
   - mushy
   - sharp
4. Then, ask them which textures were easiest to find.

LESSON 5

SCIENCE 4 PARENT & TEACHER GUIDE

Topic | **Properties of Matter**

Learning Objectives

The activities in this lesson will help your student meet the following objectives:

- compare the hardness of items
- contrast the properties of items
- categorize solids, liquids, and gases

Materials

- chalk
- cotton ball
- football
- hard rock
- ping-pong ball

Property of Hardness

Activate

1. Begin by having your student search for three objects of different hardnesses in their learning environment.
2. Then, have them line the objects from softest to hardest. Encourage them to share their thinking in how they determined the hardness of each object.

Engage

1. As your student reads the **Read It**, ask them if they can think of two objects that have different hardnesses. For example, a tree and a piece of paper have different hardnesses.
2. Then, have them complete the activity in the **Practice It**.

Demonstrate

1. Now, instruct your student to complete the **Show It** activity. Then, allow them to compare their response to the example in the **Show It AK**.
2. To extend learning, allow your student to test the hardness of a piece of chalk and a rock. Direct them to scrape the chalk and the rock on a hard surface such as concrete. Ask them to determine which object is harder and have them explain their answer. (Answer: The rock is harder because it does not make a mark on the ground like the chalk.)

• • •

Compare Properties

Engage

1. While your student reads the **Read It**, ask them how the senses are connected to the properties of matter? (Answer: The senses can be used to describe the properties of matter.)
2. Then, allow them time to play the game in the **Ecolibrium-Matter - Play It**.
3. Next, have them sort the properties of the objects in the **Practice It**.

Demonstrate

1. Now, guide your student to complete the chart in the **Show It**.
2. Finally, use the **Show It AK** to help them check their work.

• • •

Identify Forms of Matter

Engage

1. Begin by having your student open the **Qualities of Matter - Watch It** to view the video.
2. When the video ends, prompt them to explain the differences between solids, liquids, and gases.
3. After your student reads the **Read It**, invite them to share other examples of solids, liquids, or gases.

Demonstrate

1. Open the **Assess It** and have your student complete the activity. When they are finished, scan the document or take a photo of it and upload it to the Dropbox. For additional instructions on how to use the Dropbox, click on the paper clip icon in the upper-left corner of the **Assess It**.

LESSON 6

SCIENCE 4 PARENT & TEACHER GUIDE

Topic: Properties of Matter

Learning Objectives

The activities in this lesson will help your student meet the following objectives:

- distinguish examples of matter in each of its forms
- compare and contrast the properties of solids, liquids, and gases

Materials

- baking soda
- colored pencils
- cup
- ice
- orange juice
- resealable plastic bag

Matter Pictures

Activate

1. Begin by having your student open the **States of Matter - Watch It** to view the video.
2. Then, invite them to complete the ice cube melting experiment from the video.

Engage

1. Next, direct your student to move to the **Read It**. As they read, ask them to explain how some forms of matter can change into other forms.
2. Then, have them complete the sorting activity in the **Practice It**.

Demonstrate

1. Now, instruct your student to complete the **Show It** activity. Then, help them check their answers with the **Show It AK**.
2. To provide an alternative activity, allow them to draw and label the images from the **Show It**.

Compare and Contrast Matter

Engage

1. Prompt your student to open the **Solid, Liquid, and Gas - Watch It** to view the video.
2. After the video, ask them, "How can an insect can stand on water?" (Answer: The surface tension of the water holds it up.)
3. Now, have them move on to the **Read It**. Once they complete the reading, have your student explain how they can tell the difference between solids, liquids, and gases.
4. Next, guide them to complete the activity in the **Practice It**.

Demonstrate

1. Now, have your student complete the writing activity in the **Show It**. Ensure they read the expectations of the rubric before they begin writing.
2. When they are finished, encourage them to evaluate their writing with the rubric and reference the **Show It AK** for a sample paragraph.
3. To provide an alternative to the **Show It**, allow your student to compare the phases of matter by making orange soda. Follow the instructions below.
    a. Give your student 2/3 cup orange juice and a teaspoon of baking soda. Ask them to identify the phases of matter for each ingredient. (Answers: Orange juice is a liquid, and baking soda is a solid.)
    b. Next, tell them to stir the baking soda into the orange juice and observe the reaction.
    c. Last, prompt them to identify the phase of matter of the reaction. (Answer: The reaction creates a gas called carbon dioxide.)

LESSON 7

Topic | **Properties of Matter**

Learning Objectives

The activities in this lesson will help your student meet the following objectives:

- label the hydrogen and oxygen atoms in a given picture of a water molecule
- build a model of a water molecule
- arrange water molecule models to demonstrate a change in state from water to ice

Materials

- colored pencils
- different colored marshmallows (two of one color and one of another)
- toothpicks
- water molecule models (or alternative representation)

Label a Water Molecule

Activate

1. Begin by asking your student if they have ever heard of water referred to as H_2O.
2. Explain that the *H* stand for hydrogen, and the *O* stands for oxygen. These are the elements that make up water.

Engage

1. After your student reads the **Read It**, have them explain the difference between atoms and molecules. They may respond by saying that atoms are the smallest pieces of matter. Molecules are a group of atoms bonded together.

Demonstrate

1. Now, instruct your student to label the molecules in the **Show It**. Encourage them to use colored pencils to color code the atoms.
2. Then, allow them to reference the **Show It AK** to check their work.

• • •

Water Molecule Model

1. As your student reads the **Read It**, have them describe the placement of the hydrogen atoms on the oxygen atom for a water molecule. Emphasize that the atoms need to be placed correctly to make a water molecule.

Demonstrate

1. Now, have your student complete the **Show It** activity.
2. Finally, work with them to check their water molecule model using the example in the **Show It AK**.

• • •

Water to Ice

1. Have your student open the **Water & Changing States - Watch It** and ask them to make note of the username and password provided on the Discovery Education image. Be sure that they click the link for the video and enter the provided username and password to watch.
2. When the video ends, prompt them to explain how the molecules in water change into ice as they freeze. (Answer: The molecules slow down and sit closely together to become a rigid form.)
3. Next, direct your student to read the content of the **Read It**. Tell them to pay special attention to the images of water molecules in a liquid and solid state of matter.

Demonstrate

1. Now, have your student move on to complete the activity in the **Show It**.
2. Finally, help them to check their models with the samples provided in the **Show It AK**.

LESSON 8

Topic: Properties of Matter

Learning Objectives

The activities in this lesson will help your student meet the following objectives:

- arrange water molecule models to demonstrate a change from water to steam
- identify the three states of matter

Materials

- pieces of cereal
- pot
- stove
- water
- water molecule models (or alternative representation)

Water to Steam

Activate

1. Begin by asking your student to predict how long it will take to boil a pot of water.
2. Then, help them boil a pot of water to create steam. Have them take note of the time the stove is turned on and the time when the steam begins to rise.
3. Now, ask them to calculate how long it took for the water to boil and compare it to their prediction.

Engage

1. Begin by having your student read the **Read It**. When they finish, have them move their body around like the molecules in water as a liquid form. They should move around at a moderate pace.
2. Then, instruct them to move around like water molecules in a gaseous state. They should move around rapidly.

Demonstrate

1. Now, direct them to the molecule model activity in the **Show It**. Encourage your student to place pieces of cereal on a table to resemble both liquid water and steam.
2. Finally, show them the images in the **Show It AK** and compare them to your student's molecule model.
3. To reinforce learning, have your student draw pictures of their models and label them accordingly.

Matter Molecule Matching

 **Activate**

1. Have your student open the **Phase Changes - Watch It** and ask them to make note of the username and password provided on the Discovery Education image. Be sure that they click the link for the video and enter the provided username and password to watch.
2. Then, prompt them to explain the term *evaporation*, which is presented in the video. (Answer: Evaporation happens when a liquid turn to vapors or gas.)

 **Engage**

1. As your student reads the **Read It**, ask them to explain how shape relates to the phases of matter. Help them to understand that shape relates to the phases of matter by describing its form. Only solids hold a shape, whereas liquids and gases form to the shape that contains them.

 **Demonstrate**

1. Now, instruct your student to complete the matching activity in the **Show It**.
2. Finally, work with them to check their answers using the **Show It AK**.
3. To extend learning, allow your student to complete the water evaporation experiment from the video.
    a. Have them pour water into a shallow dish and mark the water level.
    b. Then, set the dish in a sunny place for a few hours.
    c. Check the water level to see how much water evaporated.

SCIENCE 4 PARENT & TEACHER GUIDE

LESSON 9

Topic | Properties of Matter

Learning Objectives

The activities in this lesson will help your student meet the following objectives:

- describe the arrangement of water molecules as water changes from a solid to a liquid and to a gas
- observe how the properties of a solid change when heat is added
- illustrate the change in a solid when heat is added to it

Materials

- chocolate bar
- colored pencils or markers
- crayon
- microwave
- plastic tray
- sealable container
- three resealable plastic bags

Water Molecule Report

Activate

1. Begin by asking your student to draw a water molecule. Their drawing should show one oxygen atom with two hydrogen atoms attached to it. The hydrogen atoms should be arranged on either side of the oxygen atom.
2. Then, ask your student, "How do you think the molecules change when they are frozen or heated?" Have a discussion with your student and explain that when water molecules are heated, they pull away from each other and spread out. When they are frozen, they pull close to each other.

Engage

1. After your student reads the **Read It**, ask them to explain the phase changes an ice cube goes through when left in the sun.
2. Next, have them read the content of the **Reinforce It** and complete the sorting activity.

Demonstrate

1. Now, instruct your student to complete the **Show It** activity. Then, use the **Show It AK** to make sure your student's work meets the expected criteria. A sample response is also provided in the **Show It AK**.
2. To provide an alternative to the **Show It** activity, give your student three resealable plastic bags and ask them to fill one with a solid, one with a liquid, and one with a gas. Last, ask them to verbally explain the movement of the molecules for the contents of each bag.

Solids and Heat

1. As your student reads the **Read It**, have them share a time that they have seen a solid heated into a liquid. For example, an ice pop left out in the sun will melt into a liquid.

1. Now, help your student to complete the experiment in the **Show It**. Have them create a T-chart, labeling the left side *Before Melting* and ask them to draw a picture of the chocolate bar before melting. This drawing and T-chart will also be used in the next subtopic.
2. After the experiment, allow them time to respond to the prompts in the **Show It**. Then, help them evaluate their responses with the **Show It AK**.

• • •

Illustrate Heat Changes

1. While your student reads the **Read It**, ask them to identify the words in the text used to describe the properties of ice and water.

1. Now, direct your student to complete the **Show It**. Before trying the experiment again, have them refer to the *Before Melting* drawing in the T-chart they began in the previous subtopic. Discuss the properties.
2. Then, have them run the melting experiment again. This time, ask them to draw a picture on the right side of the T-chart and label it *After Melting*. Prompt them to note the properties of the melted chocolate bar.
3. When your student is finished, they can compare their illustrations to the samples provided in the **Show It AK**.
4. To extend learning, allow your student to test different objects, such as a crayon in a car on a sunny day. Be sure they place any test objects in a sealable container so that any melted liquid is contained.

SCIENCE 4 PARENT & TEACHER GUIDE

Topic: Properties of Matter

Learning Objectives

The activities in this lesson will help your student meet the following objectives:

- observe how the properties of a solid change when it is cooled
- explain energy changes in molecules of matter

Materials

- chocolate bar
- gelatin
- microwave
- plastic tray
- refrigerator or freezer
- two bowls

Observe Changes in Matter

Activate

1. Start by helping your student mix the gelatin according to the directions on the package. Then, divide it between two bowls.
2. Next, set one bowl on the counter and the other in the refrigerator. Have your student check the bowls every 10 minutes to see which one sets more quickly.
3. Last, discuss what they discovered about the liquid turning into a solid.

Engage

1. As your student reads the **Read It**, have them predict what would happen when melted chocolate is put in the refrigerator. (Answer: The melted chocolate will become solid again.)

Demonstrate

1. Now, guide your student through the melting and cooling activity in the **Show It**. Have your student create a data table to record their observations. An example is provided below.

	Observations
Properties of chocolate bar	
Properties of melted chocolate bar	
After cooling for 5 minutes	
After cooling for 10 minutes	
After cooling for 20 minutes	

2. Then, work with your student to check their observations. Examples are provided in the **Show It AK**.
3. To extend learning, encourage your student to notice when they observe changes in matter throughout their day. Have them note these observations and discuss them with you.

Explain Changes in Matter

1. While your student reads the **Read It**, have them describe the energy of water molecules when they are hot versus when they are cold.

1. Now, direct your student to complete the **Show It** activity. Encourage them to use the results of their data chart from the previous activity to write their response.
2. Then, help them compare their paragraph to the example in the **Show It AK**.
3. To provide an alternative to the **Show It**, allow your student to act out the energy of the melted and cooled chocolate molecules. They should move quickly for melted chocolate and slowly for cooled chocolate.

SCIENCE 4 PARENT & TEACHER GUIDE

LESSON 11

Topic: Properties of Matter

Learning Objectives

The activities in this lesson will help your student meet the following objectives:

- illustrate examples of how matter can change form as a result of a change in temperature
- perform an experiment to show what matter looks like before and after a change in temperature is applied
- explain the meaning of the term *conservation of mass*

Materials

- bowl
- butter
- camera
- cheese
- colored pencils
- cooking oil
- knife
- microwave
- object, substance, or material to be changed (such as water)
- popcorn kernels
- pot with lid
- source of temperature change (such as freezer or microwave)
- stove

Temperature Changes

Activate

1. Begin by helping your student make popcorn on the stove by following these steps:
   a. Pour 1 tablespoon of cooking oil into a pot and set it to medium-high heat.
   b. Add 2 tablespoons of popcorn kernels to the pot and cover it with the lid.
   c. Listen as the kernels begin to pop. The popping noise will become more frequent and then slow down. When it slows, remove the pot from the stove, but keep the lid on for the remaining kernels to pop. Once it completely stops popping, remove the lid.
   d. Finally, ask your student, "What makes the corn kernels pop and change shape?" (Answer: heat)

Engage

1. As your student reads the **Read It**, have them pay close attention to the way in which heat causes popcorn kernels to pop. Ask them to recall this process when they made popcorn.
2. Then, direct them to complete the sorting activity.

Demonstrate

1. Open the **Assess It** and have your student complete the activity. Ensure that they review the expectations of the rubric before, during, and after they complete the activity.
2. When they are finished, scan the document or take a photo of it and upload it to the Dropbox. For additional instructions on how to use the Dropbox, click on the paper clip icon in the upper-left corner of the **Assess It**.

21

Experiment with Temperature

Engage

1. Have your student read the **Read It** content. When they are finished, have a discussion with them about how an egg doesn't follow the same rules as water when it changes forms of matter. The inside of an egg turns to a solid when both freezing and heating temperatures are applied. Explain that heat causes the proteins in the egg to create a new bond that makes it solidify.

Demonstrate

1. Now, instruct your student to complete the heating and cooling experiment in the **Show It**. Encourage them to use butter for their test object.
2. Finally, work with them to check their response with the example in the **Show It AK**.

• • •

Conservation of Mass

Activate

1. Direct your student to open and view **The Law of Antoine Lavoisier - Watch It** to view the video.
2. When the video ends, have them explain the Lavoisier Law in their own words. They should respond by saying that matter is not created or lost in a reaction.)

Engage

1. As your student reads the **Read It**, discuss the meaning of the word conservation, in which the root words, *conserve*, means to prevent waste or loss.
2. Then, prompt them to explain how the term *conservation of mass* is related to the Lavoisier Law. (Answer: Conservation of mass is related to the Lavoisier Law because objects do not want to lose or waste mass.)

Demonstrate

1. Now, guide your student to move on to the **Show It** activity. When they are finished, allow them to compare their response with the sample provided in the **Show It AK**.
2. To provide an alternative to the **Show It**, have your student test the Lavoisier Law with cheese.
   a. Help them to cut up a piece of cheese and melt it.
   b. Then, ask them to determine if any of the cheese has disappeared.

SCIENCE 4 PARENT & TEACHER GUIDE

LESSON 12

Topic | Properties of Matter

Learning Objectives

The activities in this lesson will help your student meet the following objectives:

- describe the conservation of mass during a physical change
- compare the results of an experiment

Materials

- bowl
- clear or glass measuring cup
- ice cube(s)
- salt
- spoon
- sugar
- triple beam balance
- water

Demonstrate Conservation

Activate

1. Start by having your student weigh and record 1/4 cup salt using a triple beam balance.
2. Then, have them pour 1 cup of warm water into a bowl to measure its weight. They will need to weigh the bowl first to subtract its weight from the total.
3. Next, ask your student, "Do you think the mass will change when the salt dissolves into the water?"
4. Last, have them pour the salt into the bowl with the water and stir it to dissolve the salt.
5. Once the salt has dissolved, have your student weigh the mixture again to see if it has changed. Remind them to subtract the weight of the bowl from the total.
6. Tell them to compare the final weight to the combined weight of the salt and the water from the beginning of the experiment.
7. Discuss how the salt changed into a liquid, but did not lose any mass.

Engage

1. After your student reads the **Read It**, prompt them to explain the law of conservation of mass in their own words. The conservation of mass means that mass is never lost when an object physically changes.
2. Then, ask them if they wonder about anything regarding the conservation of mass.

Demonstrate

1. Now, instruct your student to complete the experiment in the **Show It**. Then, work with them to check their response using the **Show It AK**.
2. To provide an alternative to the **Show It**, allow your student to illustrate their observations of the experiment and verbally explain how they relate to the conservation of mass.

• • •

Copyright 2018 © Lincoln Learning Solutions. All rights reserved.

23

Record Results

 **Engage**

1. As your student reads the **Read It**, have them explain the importance of being a careful scientist when recording information.

 **Demonstrate**

1. Now, direct your student to complete the **Show It** activity.
2. Then, help them to check that their measurements are accurate by reading their measuring cup level.
3. Once your student has completed the **Show It**, collaborate with them to check their work, referencing the **Show It AK** as you go.
4. To extend learning, have your student dissolve 1/4 cup sugar into 1 cup of warm water.
    a. Instruct them to combine the ingredients in a container or liquid measuring cup and record the total measurement.
    b. Then, tell them to stir the mixture until the sugar dissolves.
    c. Next, have them record the measurement of the combined ingredients after the sugar is dissolved.
    d. Finally, ask them what they discovered. They should discover that the total measurement did not change.

LESSON 13

Topic Properties of Matter

Learning Objectives

The activities in this lesson will help your student meet the following objectives:

- list properties of each of the materials used in an experiment
- write a hypothesis to predict what will happen next in an experiment

Materials

- cup
- dish soap
- empty plastic soda bottle
- food coloring
- hydrogen peroxide
- paper bag
- small objects
- water
- yeast

Identifying Properties

Activate

1. Have your student open the **Identifying Properties of Matter - Watch It** and ask them to make note of the username and password provided on the Discovery Education image. Be sure that they click the link for the video and enter the provided username and password to watch.
2. Then, give them a paper bag filled with three small objects. Instruct them to feel an object and describe its properties before pulling it out. Repeat this step until they have described all the objects in the bag.

Engage

1. As your student reads the **Read It**, prompt them to think of more words that describe the properties of a watermelon and water.

Demonstrate

1. Now, instruct your student to complete the activity in the **Show It**.
2. Then, work with them to compare their descriptions with those provided in the **Show It AK**. Encourage them to add any additional descriptions from the answer key to their own list.

• • •

Matter Hypothesis

Engage

1. Have your student open the **Question and Hypothesis - Watch It** to view the video.
2. After your student reads the **Read It**, share with them a common hypothesis sentence starter.
   - If ___(I do this)___, then ____(this)____ will happen.

Demonstrate

1. Now, guide your student to complete the **Show It** activity. Encourage them to use the sentence starter to help them formulate a strong hypothesis.
2. Then, help them to compare their hypothesis with the example in the **Show It AK**.
3. To extend learning, encourage your student to make hypotheses while cooking a meal. They can make predictions before mixing ingredients or before cooking them. For example, they may predict that when they mix vinegar and oil together to make salad dressing, it will mix together when they shake or stir it, but will separate after sitting unshaken.
4. After the food is prepared, have them determine if their hypotheses were correct or incorrect. In the salad dressing experiment, they might now confirm their prediction was correct based on what they observe.

LESSON 14

SCIENCE 4 PARENT & TEACHER GUIDE

Topic | Properties of Matter

Learning Objectives

The activities in this lesson will help your student meet the following objectives:

- list at least three properties of the new material created in an experiment
- describe differences in the properties of given substances before and after they are combined

Materials

- container
- empty plastic soda bottle
- ½ cup hydrogen peroxide
- 1 teaspoon dish soap
- 1 teaspoon yeast
- 3 tablespoons water
- two drops food coloring

Experiment Properties

Activate

1. Begin by playing a game of 20 Questions with your student. Choose an object and say to them, "I am thinking of an object that…" Then describe one of the object's properties.
2. Next, guide your student to ask questions about the object's properties. Explain that they only get to ask 20 questions to get clues in order to guess the object.

Engage

1. As your student reads the **Read It**, prompt them to name other words that can be used to describe the categories of properties in the sorting activity.

Demonstrate

1. Now, guide your student to complete the experiment in the **Show It**. The reaction in this experiment may be messy, so make sure that it is conducted in a place that is easy to clean up.
2. Then, help them compare their observations with the examples listed in the **Show It AK**.

• • •

Contrasting Properties

Engage

1. Have your student open the **Color and Shape - Watch It** and ask them to make note of the username and password provided on the Discovery Education image. Be sure that they click the link for the video and enter the provided username and password to watch.
2. Pause the video at 0:23 for your student to describe the lemon.
3. Next, instruct them to read the content of the **Read It**. Ask your student if they can think of other ways that the properties of apples and oranges are different. For example, oranges have wedges, which is a type of shape that can be used to describe them.

Demonstrate

1. Open the **Assess It** and have your student complete the activity. Ensure that they review the expectations of the rubric before, during, and after they complete the activity.
2. When they are finished, scan the document or take a photo of it and upload it to the Dropbox. For additional instructions on how to use the Dropbox, click on the paper clip icon in the upper-left corner of the **Assess It**.
3. To extend learning, have your student choose an object for the game, 20 Questions. Then, instruct them to use opposite words that describe the properties of the object.
4. The next lesson is a **Mastery Assess It**. Encourage your student to review Lessons 1 through 14 in order to prepare for the assessment.

LESSON 15

Topic: Properties of Matter

Learning Objectives

The activities in this lesson will help your student meet the following objectives:

- not applicable

Materials

- none required

Mastery Assess It 1

1. **Mastery Assess It 1** will cover what your student has learned in Lessons 1 through 14.
2. Click on the **Mastery Assess It 1** icon to begin the online assessment.
3. Have your student read the instructions before they get started. Remind them to take their time and to do their best work.
4. When they are finished and ready for their assessment to be graded, have them click the **Submit** button.

SCIENCE 4 PARENT & TEACHER GUIDE

Topic: Force, Motion and Energy

Learning Objectives

The activities in this lesson will help your student meet the following objectives:

- identify the meanings of the terms *kinetic energy* and *stored energy*
- show how an object can have stored energy and kinetic energy
- identify the difference between stored energy and kinetic energy

Materials

- colored pencils
- drawing paper
- rubber band
- soccer ball or similar type of ball

Kinetic and Stored

 Activate

1. Have your student stand up in a place where they have space to run (preferably outside).
2. Ask them if they are using much energy to stand.
3. Then, tell them to run for about 10 yards and come back to the place they are standing.
4. When they return, ask them if they used more energy standing or running. They should mention that they used more energy running.
5. Explain that they will learn about kinetic and stored energy in this lesson.

1. As your student reads the **Read It**, have them take a rubber band and very carefully pull it back like the bow and arrow being discussed in the content. Tell them to be sure to point it away from their face to ensure safety.
2. Ask them to tell you where there is stored energy in the rubber band. (Answer: The rubber band has stored energy when it has been pulled back.) Also, ask them where kinetic energy is on the rubber band. (Answer: The rubber band has kinetic energy when it is released and moving forward).
3. Then, ask your student to think about standing versus running. Ask them, "Which action uses stored energy and which action uses kinetic energy?" (Answer: Standing uses stored energy and running uses kinetic energy.)
4. Next, have your student view the **Kinetic Energy - Watch It**.
5. Pause the video at 1:58 and discuss the meaning of the following statement with your student. "The bigger an object is and the faster it moves, the more kinetic energy it generates."
6. Have them think of some other times the size of an object may affect its speed and energy. For example, a bowling ball rolling toward the pins at the end of the lane would have more kinetic energy than a ping-pong ball rolling toward the pins. The bowling ball is larger and heavier, and its kinetic energy allows it to knock down the pins.
7. Now, have your student view the **Exploring Potential Energy - Watch It**.

30

Demonstrate

1. Next, direct your student to complete the **Show It**. Help your student think of some new examples that were not provided in the **Read It** or **Watch It** to assist their work.
2. Then have your student compare their answers to the examples provided in the **Show It AK**.
3. To provide an alternative to the **Show It**, encourage your student to draw or act out three examples of kinetic energy and three examples of stored energy.

• • •

Show Kinetic/Stored Energy

Engage

1. Have your student read the **Read It**. Encourage them to discuss with you the difference between stored and kinetic energy.

Demonstrate

1. Next, direct your student to follow the procedure in the **Show It** and answer the questions.
2. Then, have them evaluate their answers in the **Show It AK**.
3. To provide an extension, give your student two balls, one that is smaller and one that is larger than the ball they used for the **Show It** activity. Have them complete the same procedure. Ask them which ball has more kinetic energy and which ball has the least amount of kinetic energy.

• • •

Understand Kinetic versus Stored

Engage

1. As your student reads through the **Read It**, ask them to think about other examples of kinetic versus stored energy.
2. Next, have your student view the **Kinetic vs. Potential Energy - Watch It**.

Demonstrate

1. Now, instruct your student to complete the **Show It** activity.
2. Then, allow your student to compare their answers to the examples in the **Show It AK**.
3. To extend learning, play the "I Spy the Energy" game. While out and about in the car, encourage your student to spot various examples of stored and kinetic energy. For example, "I spy, with my little eye, a dog walking, which is kinetic energy!"

SCIENCE 4 PARENT & TEACHER GUIDE

LESSON 17

Topic: Force, Motion, and Energy

Learning Objectives

The activities in this lesson will help your student meet the following objectives:

- observe differences in speed
- complete a lab report to draw conclusions about an experiment

Materials

- board to make ramp
- books
- measuring tape or ruler
- toy car

Experiment with Speed

Activate

1. Ask your student to order the vehicles below from fastest to slowest.
   - semi truck
   - sports car
   - van
   - motorcycle
2. Then, ask your student why they put the vehicles in that order. Help lead your student to discuss the shape of the object as a factor that might affect its speed.
3. Tell them they will experiment with speed in this lesson.

Engage

1. Begin by having your student try to answer the question in the Introduction section of the **Read It**.
2. Then, have your student read the remainder of the **Read It** content.
3. Next, have your student open the **Moving Things - Watch It** and ask them to make note of the username and password provided on the Discovery Education image. Be sure that they click the link for the video and enter the provided username and password to watch.

Demonstrate

1. Now, have your student complete the **Show It** activity. Have them follow the procedure, and help them set up the books and board if necessary. This lab will require two people to complete, your student and either you or someone else. One person will need to let the car go and another will need to measure the distance it travels. Be sure to follow the same procedure each time to ensure no other variables play a role in the outcome.
2. Then, have your student view the chart in the **Show It AK** to see an example of one way they could have recorded their results.

• • •

Drawing Conclusions

Engage

1. Have your student review the activity they just completed by working through the **Read It** and answering the questions that follow.
2. Encourage your student to try and conduct a different experiment to test the factors that affect speed. For example, they could use different size balls with the ramp, or they could push one car and not the other.

Demonstrate

1. Next, have your student complete the **Show It** by answering the questions based on their lab data.
2. Then, have your student move to the **Show It AK** to view the examples and compare them to their own results. Discuss any differences your student found and have them make any necessary changes.

SCIENCE 4 PARENT & TEACHER GUIDE

LESSON 18

Topic | Force, Motion, and Energy

Learning Objectives

The activities in this lesson will help your student meet the following objectives:

- form a hypothesis comparing the speeds of objects
- observe differences in the speeds of objects

Materials

- board (or similar alternative for creating a ramp)
- books
- golf ball
- ping-pong ball
- timer

Speed and Mass

Activate

1. Ask your student to think about why a person would want to skydive with a parachute. Your student may say that it slows the person down as they fall.
2. Tell your student they will examine how air resistance and mass affect the speed of an object.

Engage

1. Have your student read the **Read It** content. While they are reading, have them write down the terms *mass*, *speed*, and *air resistance* and define each one.
2. When they finish the reading, have your student simulate the paper airplane and the crumpled piece of paper example to visualize how air resistance plays a role in an object's speed.

Demonstrate

1. Have your student formulate their hypothesis for the **Show It**. Consider providing them with the ping-pong ball and golf ball to assist them in their thinking.
2. Next, have your student compare their hypothesis to the example in the **Show It AK**.
3. To extend learning, have your student think of various items that they could drop easily. Then, have them hypothesize which objects will make it to the ground faster. Encourage them to explain their reasoning.

• • •

Observe Speed

Engage

1. While your student reads the **Read It**, ask them to discuss the concept behind why the elephant would hit the ground first.
2. Next, instruct your student to move on to the **Franken Lab Speed - Play It** to play the game.

Demonstrate

1. Now, have your student conduct the lab activity in the **Show It**. Encourage them to create a data table of their choice to showcase their findings.
2. Then, have your student compare their data to the **Show It AK**.
3. To provide an extension, have your student gather other objects to observe speed. Then, ask them to explain how mass and air resistance affect the speed of an object.

LESSON 19

Topic: Force, Motion, and Energy

Learning Objectives

The activities in this lesson will help your student meet the following objectives:

- draw conclusions about an experiment
- make inferences about an object's energy and its speed

Materials

- ball
- bat
- board (or similar alternative for creating a ramp)
- books
- golf ball
- ping-pong ball
- timer

Drawing Conclusions

Activate

1. Ask your student to recall the lab they conducted in Lesson 18. Ask them which ball went down the ramp faster and have them explain why.
2. Provide them with a hypothetical situation with two objects such as a penny and a book. Ask them, "When dropped from high above, which would hit the ground first?"

Engage

1. Next, have your student read through the **Read It** and answer the questions as a review of the lab they did in Lesson 18. If your student needs to set up the lab activity and conduct it again, let them do so now.

Demonstrate

1. Remind your student of the results of their lab activity that included rolling the balls down the slope. Then, have them create a lab report answering the questions found in the **Show It**.
2. Now, have your student examine the examples in the **Show It AK** and compare their lab report answers. If they need to make any changes, let them do so.

Energy and Speed

Engage

1. As your student reads the **Read It**, discuss the amount of energy needed for each task described. For example, baking cookies and jumping on a trampoline require different amounts of energy.
2. Now, have your student open the **Exploring Kinetic Energy-Watch It** where they will explore more about kinetic energy. Ask them to make note of the username and password provided on the Discovery Education image. Be sure that they click the link for the video and enter the provided username and password to watch.
3. When the video ends, discuss the results of the experiment with the two different sized balls falling into the water buckets.

Demonstrate

1. Then, instruct your student to work on the paragraph activity in the **Show It**. When they finish, allow them to compare their paragraph to the sample in the **Show It AK**.
2. As an alternative, take your student outside and give them a bat. Throw a ball to them and ask them to hit the ball with very little force. Then, have them hit the ball as fast as they can. Now, have them explain which hit took more energy and which took less. (Answer: The faster hit took more energy.) Then, have a discussion with them about how energy and speed are related.
3. Next, have your student work through the **Reinforce It**.

SCIENCE 4 PARENT & TEACHER GUIDE

LESSON 20

Topic | Force, Motion, and Energy

Learning Objectives

The activities in this lesson will help your student meet the following objectives:

- distinguish between appropriate scientific terms
- observe the change in motion of an object
- measure the change in motion of an object

Materials

- ball
- key
- meter stick or tape measure
- string
- stop watch
- table
- tape

Distinguish Energy Terms

Activate

1. Begin by taking your student outside and asking them to kick a ball. (They can lightly kick a ball inside if the weather is bad.)
2. Then, ask them to discuss the steps they had to take to kick the ball. For example, ask them to discuss what happens when their foot hits the ball. Where is the energy coming from?
3. Then, tell them they will learn about the different terms used when discussing energy.

Engage

1. As your student reads the **Read It**, have them create a vocabulary photo album.
2. To create the album, have your student write each vocabulary word on a piece of paper. Then, have them write the definition beside the word. Next, they can draw an image depicting the word beside its definition.

Demonstrate

1. Open the **Assess It** and have your student complete the activity. When they are finished, scan the document or take a photo of it and upload it to the Dropbox. For additional instructions on how to use the Dropbox, click on the paper clip icon in the upper-left corner of the **Assess It**.

• • •

Motion

 ## Activate

1. Ask your student if they think they could push their family car and move it. Most likely, your student will say they cannot do this.
2. Then, ask them if they think they would be able to push the car if it was already moving slightly.
3. Finally, ask them which of these scenarios would be easier.
4. Explain to your student that they will learn about the force acting on objects and how friction plays a role in motion.

 ## Engage

1. Have your student read through the **Read It** content. When they are finished, have a discussion about each type of friction.
2. Next, have your student move to the **Ecolibrium Motion - Play It**.

 ## Demonstrate

1. Now, have your student complete the lab activity found in the **Show It**. Encourage them to use key terms such as *kinetic energy* and *force*.
2. When they are finished, have them compare their answer to the example provided in the **Show It AK**.
3. To extend learning, ask your student to observe pushes and pulls as they go about their day. Tell them to pay attention to when friction affects force.

Measuring Changes in Motion

 ## Engage

1. Now, have your student read the **Read It**, and discuss objects that would require a great deal of force to move, such as a large boulder or an airplane.

 ## Demonstrate

1. Next, have your student complete the **Show It**. Help them to recreate the example data table and have them fill it in with their data. You will need to help your student run the stopwatch as they push the key.
2. Finally, have your student view the sample answers in the **Show It AK** to see if their answers are similar.
3. To provide an extension, provide your student with different objects to try and put into motion such as a table, a book, a ball, and a sofa. Ask them to determine which ones were easier to move and why. Be sure that they use the terms *force* and *friction* in their reasoning.

SCIENCE 4 PARENT & TEACHER GUIDE

LESSON 21

Topic: Force, Motion, and Energy

Learning Objectives

The activities in this lesson will help your student meet the following objectives:

- draw conclusions about the relationship between an object's speed and its change in motion
- observe the changes in motion when there is a collision

Materials

- books
- key
- meter stick or tape measure
- stopwatch
- string
- table
- tape
- two toy cars
- two boards to create a ramp

Speed and Motion

Activate

1. Ask your student to share their thoughts on the difference between speed and motion by writing their ideas on a piece of paper.
2. After they complete this lesson, ask them to look back at what they wrote to see if their thinking has changed.

Engage

1. Instruct your student to open the **Read It**, and have them try to answer the question in the Introduction section.
2. Then, have them read through the rest of the content and review the lab they conducted in Lesson 20.
3. Next, have your student move on the **FrankenLab Speed - Play It** and allow them time to play the game.

Demonstrate

1. If your student has not yet completed the activity in the **Show It**, have them do so now. When they are finished, instruct them to write a conclusion on the relationship between an object's speed and its change in motion.
2. Have your student compare their conclusion to the example in the **Show It AK**.
3. Finally, have your student complete the **Extend It**.

Collisions

Engage

1. Direct your student to read the entire **Read It**. As your student reads, have them discuss with you what is happening in the image with the two cars. Ask them, "What does force have to do with the collision?"

Demonstrate

1. Prior to completing the **Show It** activity, have your student hypothesize what will happen. Ask them to write down their prediction.
2. Next, have your student conduct the lab activity in the **Show It** and ask them to record their observations.
3. Then, have your student compare their observations with the example in the **Show It AK**.

SCIENCE 4 PARENT & TEACHER GUIDE

LESSON 22

Topic | Force, Motion, and Energy

Learning Objectives

The activities in this lesson will help your student meet the following objectives:

- predict how an object's energy changes when it collides with another object
- draw conclusions about how a collision affects an object's energy
- identify objects that do contain and do not contain stored electrical energy

Materials

- board (or similar alternative for creating a ramp)
- books
- sticky notes
- toy cars

Energy and Collision

 ## Activate

1. Ask your student to use the following words to describe what is happening when a person pushes a box across the floor and the box hits the wall.
   - kinetic energy
   - force
   - friction
   - collision
2. Then, tell your student they will learn about how energy is transferred during a collision.

 ## Engage

1. While your student is reading the **Read It**, have a discussion about other collision scenarios.

 ## Demonstrate

1. If your student needs to complete the lab again, allow them to do so with the **Show It**. Also, allow them to create other collisions using the ramps.
2. If your student needs to check their prediction, they can take a look at the **Show It AK** example.
3. To provide an alternative to the **Show It**, have your student use their knowledge of energy and collisions to create a presentation explaining everyday collisions, such as kicking a soccer ball.

• • •

42   Copyright 2018 © Lincoln Learning Solutions. All rights reserved.

Experiment and Draw Conclusions

Engage

1. Begin by having your student read the content of the **Read It**. Discuss some of the questions posed throughout the reading.

Demonstrate

1. Now, have your student complete the paragraph in the **Show It** and compare their conclusion to the sample in the **Show It AK**.
2. To extend learning, consider having your student interview a police officer to learn more about collisions and how to prevent real-life car collisions.

• • •

Electrical Energy

Engage

1. After your student reads the **Read It**, have them answer the final question, "Can you think of any additional examples of stored electrical energy?"
2. Then, have your student move to the **FrankenLab Energy - Play It**. Allow them time to play the game.
3. Next, have your student learn more about forms of energy by working through the **Practice It**.

Demonstrate

1. Now, instruct your student to complete the activity in the **Show It**. When they are finished, allow them to review their answers using the **Show It AK**.
2. To provide an alternative to the **Show It**, have your student place sticky notes on items around their learning environment that have stored electrical energy.

LESSON 23

SCIENCE 4 PARENT & TEACHER GUIDE

Topic: Force, Motion, and Energy

Learning Objectives

The activities in this lesson will help your student meet the following objectives:

- explain an example of stored electrical energy
- explain how a flashlight can change its stored energy into another form of energy

Materials

- cell phone
- flashlight

Stored Electrical Energy

Activate

1. Ask your student to name some examples of electrical energy.
2. Tell them that they will learn how electrical energy can be stored.

Engage

1. After reading the **Read It**, have a discussion with your student about the difference between stored energy and energy that is being used.
2. Then, have them turn on a light switch. Ask them to determine when the energy was being stored and when it was being used. (Answer: It is stored when the light switch is off. It is being used when the switch is on.)

Demonstrate

1. Next, have your student use the flashlight and complete the **Show It** activity.
2. Finally, have your student compare their answer to the example in the **Show It AK**. Give your student a chance to make any changes to their paragraph, if needed.
3. To provide an extension, have your student conduct an energy experiment.
   a. Begin by giving your student a device that shows battery life, such as a cell phone or tablet.
   b. Have them turn the device on, but do not allow them to use it for one hour. At the end of the hour, have them check the battery life.
   c. Next, allow your student to use the device for an hour. When they are finished, have them check the battery life again.
   d. Finally, have them compare the battery life of the device when it was on but not in use to when it was on and being used. Ask them to explain what was happening to the energy being used versus the energy being stored.

Changing Stored Energy

Engage

1. After reading the **Read It**, have your student write or draw the energy conversions that happen in a flashlight. (Answer: Chemical energy converts to electrical energy, and electrical energy converts to light energy.)
2. Now, discuss with your student how stored energy has helped to make human lives simpler.

Demonstrate

1. Next, instruct your student to complete the **Show It** activity. If needed, allow them to reference the **Read It**.
2. When they are finished, allow your student to compare their work to the sample in the **Show It AK**. If they need to make any changes, allow them to do so.
3. To provide an alternative to **Show It**, help your student to search the Internet for the phrase, "energy transformation examples." Allow your student to view additional examples of energy conversions, and ask them to explain the conversions they see.

LESSON 24

SCIENCE 4 PARENT & TEACHER GUIDE

Topic: Force, Motion, and Energy

Learning Objectives

The activities in this lesson will help your student meet the following objectives:

- identify objects that contain and do not contain stored mechanical energy
- explain an example of stored mechanical energy
- explain how mechanical energy is converted to another form of energy

Materials

- rubber band
- dowel rods or craft sticks

Mechanical Energy

Activate

1. Before your student begins the lesson, ask them if they think an object that is just sitting on the table has energy. Ask them to explain their thinking.

Engage

1. As your student reads the **Read It**, point out that the total mechanical energy of an object is both the potential or stored energy, along with the kinetic energy. Encourage them to think of some other examples as they read.
2. Next, allow your student to view the **Mechanical Energy - Watch It**.
3. Pause the video at 0:48 and 1:05 and have your student answer the questions.

Demonstrate

1. Direct your student to follow the instructions in the **Show It** and complete the activity.
2. Once they finish placing each object in the columns of their graphic organizer, allow your student to evaluate their answers using the **Show It AK**. Help them to make adjustments to their graphic organizer, if needed.

SCIENCE 4 PARENT & TEACHER GUIDE

Stored Mechanical Energy

Activate

1. Ask your student which of the objects below has the most mechanical energy and why.
   - baseball bat
   - hammer
   - bulldozer
2. Then, tell them they will learn about the stored mechanical energy in objects.

Engage

1. As your student reads the **Read It**, have them describe to you what the image of the cranes is depicting.
2. Then, have your student draw their own picture using a different object to take the place of the crane.

Demonstrate

1. Allow your student to play with the rubber band, and then have them follow the instructions in the **Show It**.
2. Once your student has completed the activity, give them time to compare their answer to sample in the **Show It AK**.

• • •

Changing Mechanical Energy

Engage

1. Have your student begin with the **Read It**. When they finish reading the content, present them with the following scenario.
   - A windmill begins to move when the wind blows. This windmill then generates electricity for the local town.
2. Then, ask your student, "How does the windmill change mechanical energy?" (Answer: The wind has kinetic energy that causes a change in the windmill's motion. This energy is then converted into electrical energy.)

Demonstrate

1. Next, allow your student time to complete the **Show It** and compare their answer to the sample in the **Show It AK**.
2. To provide an alternative to the **Show It**, have your student design an idea for a catapult, including the items they would need in order to make it. Then, have your student create the catapult. When they are finished, have a discussion with them about the different types of energy used in the system.

SCIENCE 4 PARENT & TEACHER GUIDE

LESSON 25

Topic | Force, Motion, and Energy

Learning Objectives

The activities in this lesson will help your student meet the following objectives:

- identify objects that contain stored chemical energy
- explain an example of stored chemical energy

Materials
- baking soda
- cup
- sink
- vinegar

Chemical Energy

Activate

1. Ask your student which of the following items would they most likely want to eat before doing an hour long workout.
   - nutrition bar
   - potato chips
   - glass of fruit punch
2. Tell your student that the nutrition bar is what they should have chosen because it will provide them with the most energy. Ask them if they can explain why this is true.
3. Tell your student they will learn how the stored chemical energy in the bar provides the mechanical energy a person needs to do things.

Engage

1. Direct your student to begin reading the **Read It**. When they are finished, begin a discussion about how the stored chemical energy in an object can be turned into kinetic chemical energy.
2. Next, ask your student if they can think of any other examples of items that might have stored chemical energy.
3. Now, have your student view the **Chemical Potential Energy - Watch It**.

Demonstrate

1. Open the **Assess It** and have your student complete the activity. When they are finished, scan the document or take a photo of it and upload it to the Dropbox. For additional instructions on how to use the Dropbox, click on the paper clip icon in the upper-left corner of the **Assess It**.

• • •

Stored Chemical Energy

Engage

1. Allow your student time to read through the **Read It** to learn more about stored chemical energy.
2. If your student needs a review on the forms of energy, direct them to the **Practice It**. Make sure they pay close attention to the chemical energy tab.

Demonstrate

1. Instruct your student to complete the **Show It** activity. When they are finished, allow them to compare their answer to the example in the **Show It AK**.
2. To provide an extension, help your student to conduct an experiment to see stored chemical energy in action.
    a. Provide your student with some vinegar and baking soda. Have them place 2 to 3 tablespoons of baking soda into the cup, and place the cup into the sink.
    b. Next, have your student take a 1/2 cup of vinegar and pour it into the cup with the baking soda.
    c. As your student watches the reaction take place, hold a discussion regarding the stored chemical energy found in the substances used in this experiment. Help lead them to understand that the baking soda has stored energy, and once it reacts with the vinegar, that stored energy is released.

SCIENCE 4 PARENT & TEACHER GUIDE

LESSON 26

Topic | Force, Motion, and Energy

Learning Objectives

The activities in this lesson will help your student meet the following objectives:

- explain how stored chemical energy is converted to another form of energy
- observe the relationship between the light and heat of a light bulb
- list objects that emit both light and heat

Materials

- flashlight and batteries
- lamp
- light bulb
- thermometer

Changing Chemical Energy

 ### Activate

1. Ask your student to think about the last time they saw a fireworks display. Then ask, "Why are some of the fireworks bigger and brighter than the others?" Your student should mention that there is more potential energy found within the larger fireworks than in the smaller fireworks.
2. Next, explain that they will learn how energy is converted.

 ### Engage

1. Begin by providing your student with a flashlight and batteries. Ask them where they think the energy is stored in the system. (Answer: the batteries)
2. Now, have them read the **Read It**.
3. Next, have your student insert the batteries into the flashlight and turn it on. Ask them to identify what happens to the stored energy when the flashlight on. (Answer: The stored energy in the batteries is converted to electrical energy when the flashlight is turned on. Some of the electrical energy is converted to heat and light energy.)

 ### Demonstrate

1. Instruct your student to complete the **Show It** activity. Example answers are provided in the **Show It AK**.
2. As an extension, help your student to search online to find out how the chemical energy from gasoline (fossil fuel) makes a vehicle move.

• • •

50

Light and Heat

Activate

1. Ask your student to imagine standing near a bonfire or a campfire. Then, ask them which direction they would move if they were too hot. Would they move closer to the fire or farther away from it?
2. Tell your student they will learn about the relationship between light and heat.

Engage

1. Now, allow your student time to read the content of the **Read It**. As they read, allow them to go to a light bulb that is on and place their hand a few inches from it. Discuss what they feel. Then, have them do the same with a light bulb that is not on and discuss what they feel.
2. Next, have your student move on the **FrankenLab Energy - Play It**. Allow them time to play the game.

Demonstrate

1. Direct your student to complete the activity and fill in the chart in the **Show It**.
2. When they are finished, have them review the examples found in the **Show It AK** to compare their data.

Identify Objects

Engage

1. Begin by discussing the question in the Introduction section of the **Read It** with your student. Be sure to have them verbalize their thoughts before they reveal the answer.
2. Then, have them continue reading the remaining content of the **Read It**.

Demonstrate

1. Next, have your student follow the instructions in the **Show It** and complete the activity. They can view sample answers in the **Show It AK**.
2. Discuss your student's list of objects that create both heat and light. Ask them why they chose each item. If time permits, allow them to continue searching their learning environment or allow them to go outside to find additional examples.

SCIENCE 4 PARENT & TEACHER GUIDE

LESSON 27

Topic Force, Motion, and Energy

Learning Objectives

The activities in this lesson will help your student meet the following objectives:

- describe the relationship between light energy and heat energy
- create a device that converts energy from one form to another

Materials

- chocolate
- graham crackers
- lamp with a light bulb
- marshmallow
- plastic wrap
- potato chip can with a plastic lid
- ruler
- scissors
- skewer or metal coat hanger

Understand Light and Heat

Activate

1. Ask your student to think about a time they felt warmth. Where was it coming from? Was the object that was giving off heat also producing light or was it dark? Your student most likely will say that the object had some sort of light.
2. Explain to your student that they will learn about objects that give off both light and heat.

Engage

1. Have your student read the **Read It** content. When they are finished, discuss more examples of objects that produce light and give off heat.
2. The **Practice It** reviews the forms of energy. Direct your student's attention to the light energy tab.

Demonstrate

1. Next, have your student complete the procedure in the **Show It** and then answer the questions that follow.
2. Give your student time to compare their work to the example provided in the **Show It AK**.
3. To provide an extension, have your student look around their learning environment for sources of heat and light energy.

• • •

52   Copyright 2018 © Lincoln Learning Solutions. All rights reserved.

Solar Oven

Engage

1. Begin by having your student answer the question in Introduction of the **Read It**.
2. Then, have them read through the rest of the **Read It** content. Have a discussion with your student about the potato chip can solar oven. Ask them to describe, in their own words, how the oven works. Prompt them to discuss the energy conversion that takes place to cook the food.

Demonstrate

1. Allow your student plenty of time to complete the procedure in the **Show It**. You may need to help them create the solar oven using the materials listed. Have them use a marshmallow (saving the hot dog for the next lesson) for their summary of the experiment.
2. Then, have your student compare their summary to the example in the **Show It AK**.
3. To extend learning, encourage your student to try cooking other food items in their solar oven. For example, they could melt chocolate and a marshmallow to make a s'more.

SCIENCE 4 PARENT & TEACHER GUIDE

LESSON 28

Topic | Force, Motion, and Energy

Learning Objectives

The activities in this lesson will help your student meet the following objectives:

- test a solar oven made from a potato chip can and plastic wrap
- draw conclusions about the ways in which energy is changed from one form to another

Materials

- homemade solar oven
- hot dog
- wooden skewer

Solar Oven Test

Activate

1. Ask your student if they have ever heard the saying, "The sidewalk is so hot you could fry an egg on it!" Then, ask them how the sidewalk becomes hot.
2. Tell them they will learn how the sun is able to cook things from the heat it produces.

Engage

1. Instruct your student to read the **Read It**. Discuss why a solar oven has the ability cook food.

Demonstrate

1. Now, have your student complete the **Show It** using the solar oven they made in Lesson 27. This time, have them try cooking a hot dog.
2. Before they begin, have them write down a prediction about what will happen to the hot dog. After the experiment, have them compare their prediction to the actual results.
3. Finally, have your student review the example answers in the **Show It AK**. Your student should have similar results.
4. To provide an extension, have your student cook various items and record their results for each item. Then, ask them to write a conclusion on the effectiveness of cooking food in a solar oven.

• • •

Energy Conversions

Engage

1. As your student reads through the **Read It**, have them create a bubble map like the one shown below to help them organize each type of energy discussed in the content. Have your student write *Types of Energy* in the center circle and label each outer circle with a type of energy. Finally, have them draw a picture and write a description of the energy type.

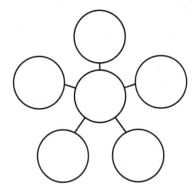

2. Now, have your student open the **Energy Transformation - Watch It** to learn about how the movement of water can be transferred into electrical energy. Ask your student to make note of the username and password provided on the Discovery Education image. Be sure that they click the link for the video and enter the provided username and password to watch.
3. Next, direct your student to move to the **Play It** and play the game.

Demonstrate

1. Now, instruct your student to complete the **Show It** activity.
2. Then, have them compare their answer to the example in the **Show It AK**.
3. To provide an extension, have your student go outside on a sunny, warm day. Ask them to think about how their arm feels before and after being in the sun. If it is not sunny, have them try the same thing with a lamp or heater. Be sure to tell them not to touch it directly.

SCIENCE 4 PARENT & TEACHER GUIDE

LESSON 29

Topic: Force, Motion, and Energy

Learning Objectives

The activities in this lesson will help your student meet the following objectives:

- examine musical instruments to identify the parts which vibrate to produce sound waves
- design and build a musical instrument to create vibration and sound energy

Materials

- empty tissue box
- metal bowl
- rubber bands
- spoon or fork
- two musical instruments

Musical Instruments

Activate

1. Give your student a metal bowl and a spoon or fork. Then, have them gently hit the utensil off the bowl.
2. Ask them what would happen if they hit the bowl harder or softer. Your student may mention that the noise would be louder or softer.
3. Tell them they will learn how musical instruments make sounds.

Engage

1. Next, have your student read about each type of instrument in the **Read It**.
2. Allow them to create a foldable graphic organizer to help them organize the differences between the three types of instruments. Direct your student to place the name of the instrument on the front of the flap. Under the flap, instruct them to add an example image and description of the instrument. Reference the image below for guidance.

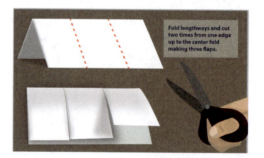

3. Now, have your student open the **Sound to Ear - Watch It** to get a better idea of how the human ear receives sounds and transfers them to the brain. Ask them to make note of the username and password provided on the Discovery Education image. Be sure that they click the link for the video and enter the provided username and password to watch.

Demonstrate

1. Next, have your student complete the **Show It** activity. They may use the images provided in the **Show It** if they do not have access to musical instruments.
2. The **Show It AK** provides example answers for the guitar and the drum.
3. To provide an alternative to the **Show It**, ask your student to draw their instruments and label the parts. Instruct them to show where the sound waves would be located when the instrument is played by circling the parts that produce sound waves.
4. Extend your student's learning the next time they listen to their favorite music. Have a discussion with them about what is happening as the sound is transferred to their ears.

• • •

Build an Instrument

Engage

1. As your student read through the **Read It**, ask them to answer the question posed at the end of the content: How can you compare rubber bands on a homemade instrument to the strings of a violin?

Demonstrate

1. Give your student an empty tissue box and rubber bands before they begin the **Show It**. Then, help them to follow the instructions to build a musical instrument.
2. After they have created their instrument, have them answer the questions in the **Show It**.
3. Now, allow them to compare their work to the example in the **Show It AK**.
4. To provide an extension, have your student create other instruments to make music and hear different sounds. For ideas, help them search the Internet using the search phrase, "homemade musical instruments."

SCIENCE 4 PARENT & TEACHER GUIDE

LESSON 30

Topic — Force, Motion, and Energy

Learning Objectives

The activities in this lesson will help your student meet the following objectives:

- explain how a musical instrument changes energy from one form to another
- observe differences in sounds

Materials

- empty tissue box
- rubber bands

Instruments and Energy

 Activate

1. Ask your student to name some instruments they know. Have them tell you which instrument has the highest pitch and which has the lowest. If your student is unsure about pitch, do a quick Internet search to hear the difference between a flute and a tuba.

1. Next, instruct your student to read each section of the **Read It**. Using the Part of Your Ear section, have your student draw a diagram of the steps of how sound is perceived as it reaches the ear.

    sound waves → cochlea → inner ear → auditory part of brain

2. Then, have your student play the **Cosmic Trail-Physical Science - Play It**.

1. Allow your student to use the instrument they created in Lesson 29 to help them answer the question in the **Show It**.
2. Although answers will vary, allow your student to review the answer provided in the **Show It AK**.

Vibrations and Sounds

Engage

1. Instruct your student to read the **Read It**.
2. Using the image below, have your student use their finger to trace the direction sound travels through the ear.

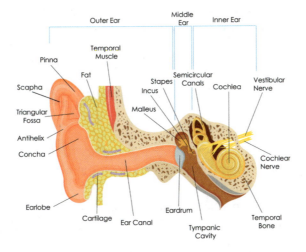

EAR

3. Next, have your student move on to the **Beaker's Big Buzz-Sound - Play It** and allow them time to play the game.
4. Next, direct your student to the **Practice It** and have them review the sound energy tab.

Demonstrate

1. Now, have your student complete the **Show It**. If your student wants to continue learning about sound, swap out the rubber bands on their instrument with thicker or thinner bands to see how the sounds changes.
2. Then, have your student use the **Show It AK** to compare their responses with the samples provided.
3. To extend learning, take your student to a concert or symphony, either in person or virtually. Encourage them to listen to the different instruments involved in the performance.

SCIENCE 4 PARENT & TEACHER GUIDE

LESSON 31

Topic | Force, Motion, and Energy

Learning Objectives

The activities in this lesson will help your student meet the following objectives:

- observe how sound causes vibration
- observe how the pitch of sound changes

Materials

- glasses
- metal bowl
- spoon
- string
- two empty tin cans
- water

Model Waves

Activate

1. Ask your student to go into a room and close the door. Then, go on the other side of the wall and try to talk to your student.
2. Ask them if they can understand what you are saying.
3. Tell them that they will learn how sound waves can travel through many types of materials.

Engage

1. As your student reads the **Read It**, have them recall the Activate activity when they could hear you through the solid door or wall. Even if the sound was muffled, reinforce the concept that sound can travel through states of matter.
2. Then, ask your student to recall a time they noticed sound traveling through water. Examples may include while they were under water at a swimming pool.

Demonstrate

1. Fill the metal bowl with water. Then, present the bowl and spoon to your student and direct them to follow the steps of the procedure in the **Show It**.
2. After your student has written their observation, have a brief discussion about what they observed. Be sure to mention the vibration of the sound waves.
3. To provide an extension, have your student make their own telephone by taking two empty tin cans and poking holes in the bottoms as shown in the image below. Then, place a string between the cans and attach them. Use the system with your student, and have them explain to you how it works.

60

Copyright 2018 © Lincoln Learning Solutions. All rights reserved.

Pitch

 Activate

1. Tell your student to talk in a high-pitch, squeaky voice. Then, have them talk in a very low, deep voice. Have them keep the same volume each time they speak.
2. Next, have them say hello in a very loud voice. Then, have them say hello very softly, as a whisper. This time, make sure they keep the same pitch in their voice.
3. Then, have a discussion with your student about the differences between a high and low voice and a loud or soft voice.
4. Tell them they will learn about the term *pitch* and how it is important in making sound waves.

 Engage

1. As your student works through the **Read It**, have them pay close attention to the section about the ways in which pitch can vary based on the amount of water placed in a glass. Your student will be working with this concept in the **Show It**.
2. Next, direct your student to view the **Pitch and Volume - Watch It**. Pause the video and discuss the difference between pitch and volume. Then, be sure that your student pays close attention to the water glass demonstration so that they can set up their own experiment.

 Demonstrate

1. Next, give your student the materials listed in the **Show It**. Then, have them follow the instructions and complete the activity.
2. Direct your student to the **Show It AK** to check the observations.
3. To provide an extension, allow your student to fill additional glasses with various levels of water. Encourage them to make music using the different pitches that each glass creates. Consider helping your student to search the Internet for videos of making music with water glasses.

LESSON 32

SCIENCE 4 PARENT & TEACHER GUIDE

| Topic | Force, Motion, and Energy |

Learning Objectives

The activities in this lesson will help your student meet the following objectives:

- explain how sound and vibration are related
- identify the definitions of the scientific terms *reflect*, *refract*, and *absorb* based on how they relate to light

Materials

- black piece of paper
- flashlight
- clear glass cup
- mirror
- straw
- water
- white piece of paper

Sound and Vibration

 Activate

1. Begin by asking your student to explain what they know about pitch and volume. They should mention that pitch is the highness or lowness a sound, and volume is the loudness and softness of a sound.
2. Next, ask them to place two fingers on their throat. Have them whisper and then yell. Ask them to share which sound is soft and which sound is loud.
3. Tell your student they will learn about the connection between sound and vibration.

 Engage

1. Now, prompt your student to read through the content of the **Read It**.
2. After reading, ask them to explain the relationship between vibration and sound. (Answer: Sound is created by vibration. When an object vibrates, it makes a sound.)
3. Then, have them play the **FrankenLab-Sound - Play It** to review what they have learned about sound.

 Demonstrate

1. Open the **Assess It** and have your student complete the activity. Make sure they review the expectations of the rubric before and after writing.
2. When they are finished, scan the document or take a photo of it and upload it to the Dropbox. For additional instructions on how to use the Dropbox, click on the paper clip icon in the upper-left corner of the **Assess It**.

• • •

Behavior of Light Waves

Activate

1. Begin by having your student shine a flashlight on a mirror, and ask them what happens as the light hits the mirror. Your student should say that the light bounces or reflects off the mirror.

Engage

1. Now, have your student view the **Magic Mirror on the Wall - Watch It**. When the video ends, ask them to explain how people see different colors.
2. As your student reads the **Read It**, pause and discuss each type of light behavior mentioned in the reading.

Demonstrate

1. Have your student complete the matching activity in the **Show It**. When they are finished, allow them to compare their answers to the **Show It AK**. Have them make any changes necessary.
2. To provide an alternative to the **Show It**, have your student show what they know about reflection, refraction, and absorption by completing the following explorations:
   a. Provide your student with a transparent glass of water and a straw. Have them look through the glass from the side and explain to you why the straw appears to be split in half. They should say it is because the light is traveling slower through the water than the air, which makes the light refract.
   b. Next, have your student take a piece of white paper and a piece of black paper outside. Have them place both pieces of paper in the sunlight. After approximately 15 minutes, ask them to feel each piece of paper and discuss which feels warmer and why. The black paper should feel warmer because the black color absorbs the light and the white color reflects it.
   c. Then, have your student find objects around their learning environment that reflect their image, such as a television when it is off. Ask them to explain why they can see their image. They can see their image because certain surfaces reflect light, and this reflection allows them to see their image.
3. Finally, have your student complete the **Reinforce It**.

LESSON 33

Topic: Force, Motion, and Energy

Learning Objectives

The activities in this lesson will help your student meet the following objectives:

- perform an experiment to observe how light is refracted
- illustrate the colors formed by refracted light

Materials

- cardboard
- clear glass cup
- colored pencils, crayons, or markers
- drawing paper
- hose
- prism
- scissors
- tape
- water

Observe Refraction

Activate

1. Start by having your student open the **Light Reflection - Watch It** and ask them to make note of the username and password provided on the Discovery Education image. Be sure that they click the link for the video and enter the provided username and password to watch.
2. Then, prompt them to explain the difference between *reflection* and *refraction*. Reflection is when light bounces off an object. Refraction is the bending of light rays.

Engage

1. As your student reads the **Read It**, allow them to observe their pencil through a glass cup of water. Encourage them to describe what they notice about the shape of their pencil. They should notice that their pencil looks like it is bending.
2. Then, instruct them to open the **FrankenLab-Light - Play It** to play the game.

Demonstrate

1. Now, guide your student to complete the refraction experiment in the **Show It**.
2. Then, work with them to check their responses using the **Show It AK**. Have them clarify their observations, if necessary.

Illustrate Colors

Engage

1. Direct your student to open the **I See the Light - Watch It** to view the video.
2. Then, pause the video at 1:56 for your student to explain how wavelengths are connected to light refraction. When light is refracted, the colors are separated out or spread apart.
3. Next, have them read the content of the **Read It**. Then, ask your student to apply what they know and try to explain what causes a rainbow.

Demonstrate

1. Now, instruct your student to complete the **Show It** activity and remind them to think of the refraction experiment from the previous subtopic as they illustrate their drawing.
2. Finally, help them check their illustration with the **Show It AK**.
3. To extend learning, have your student stand outside with the sun behind them and spray water from a hose. If the hose does not have a spray handle, have them use their thumb to fan out the water. They may need to move the hose slightly to get the right angle, but instruct them to look for a rainbow or light refraction in the water.
4. If the weather does not allow for this activity, have your student visit the child-safe search engine *KidRex* and search the phrase "rainbow with water hose video" to watch videos of this activity.

LESSON 34

SCIENCE 4 PARENT & TEACHER GUIDE

Topic | Force, Motion, and Energy

Learning Objectives

The activities in this lesson will help your student meet the following objectives:

- test the angle of reflection of light
- draw conclusions about the relationship between reflected light and angles

Materials

- analog clock
- flashlight or laser pointer
- masking tape
- mirror

Angle of Reflection

Activate

1. Begin by having your student point out an angle on an analog clock. The two hands form an angle. The space between the two hands is called an angle.
2. Direct them to look around their learning environment to find other examples of angles such as a book, door, or window.

Engage

1. As your student reads the **Read It**, have them explain the term *law of reflection* in their own words. The law of reflection means that the angle of light reflected from an object is the same angle as the light that entered the object.
2. Then, emphasize the terms *incident* and *reflected ray* from the text. Instruct your student to point out the terms in the diagram and explain what they mean. The incident ray is the light hitting the object, while the reflected ray is the light ray bouncing off the object.

Demonstrate

1. Now, guide your student through the angle of reflection experiment in the **Show It**. Encourage them to draw a diagram to accompany their written observations.
2. The **Show It AK** explains the results of the experiment.

Reflected Light and Angles

Engage

1. Have your student open the **Inside the Pinball Machine - Watch It** and ask them to make note of the username and password provided on the Discovery Education image. Be sure that they click the link for the video and enter the provided username and password to watch.
2. Then, ask them to explain how the pinball machine showed how light travels. Light hit the prism and color waves refracted. In order to get the colors to their designated target, the mirrors needed to be angled so the colors bounced off in the right direction.
3. Next, tell your student to read the content of the **Read It**.

Demonstrate

1. Now, instruct your student to complete the activity in the **Show It**, and help them evaluate their response with the **Show It AK**.
2. As an alternative to the **Show It**, work with your student to find the angle at which two people must stand to see each other in the same mirror.
   a. Move your student to a room with a mirror fastened to the wall.
   b. Position a yard of masking tape (approximately 36 inches) on the ground in the center of the mirror.
   c. Stand beside your student on the opposite side of the tape and slowly move outward until you both see each other in the mirror.
   d. Then, discuss the angles of each person's position according to the line of tape. Ask them, "Are the angles equal?"

LESSON 35

Topic | Force, Motion, Energy

Learning Objectives

The activities in this lesson will help your student meet the following objectives:

- observe how color affects temperature
- draw conclusions about the relationship between an object's color and its ability to absorb light

Materials

- dark-colored bowl
- light-colored bowl
- thermometer
- water

Color and Heat Experiment

Activate

1. Ask your student to share a time they were very hot while standing in the sun. Prompt them to remember the color of their clothing. Was it light or dark?
2. Discuss how wearing light-colored clothes can keep a person cooler on a hot day.

Engage

1. While your student reads the **Read It**, ask them if they have ever tried walking barefoot on a black, paved road in the summer? Have a discussion about the temperature of the pavement in this scenario.
2. Then, instruct them to review the information in the **Practice It**.

Demonstrate

1. Now, help your student complete the experiment in the **Show It**. Have them create a data table to record the temperatures. A sample data table has been provided below.

	Before Direct Sunlight	After Direct Sunlight
light-colored bowl		
dark-colored bowl		

2. Finally, allow your student to compare their results with the examples in the **Show It AK**.

Draw Conclusions Color and Heat

Engage

1. After your student reads the **Read It**, discuss the ways in which scientists can make rules or generalizations based on experiments.
2. Ask them to verbally explain a rule or generalization they could conclude from the color and heat experiment. Your student may respond by saying that darker objects will have higher temperatures.

Demonstrate

1. Open the **Assess It** and have your student complete the activity. Be sure they read the expectations of the rubric before they begin writing.
2. When they are finished, scan the document or take a photo of it and upload it to the Dropbox. For additional instructions on how to use the Dropbox, click on the paper clip icon in the upper-left corner of the **Assess It**.
3. To extend learning, on a sunny day, have your student test the temperature of various surfaces by carefully touching them with the back of their hand. Then, have them determine which common surfaces have similar temperatures.

SCIENCE 4 PARENT & TEACHER GUIDE

LESSON 36

Topic Force, Motion, and Energy

Learning Objectives

The activities in this lesson will help your student meet the following objectives:

- describe how heat energy is transferred through the process of conduction
- label pictures using the terms *conduction*, *convection*, *sound energy*, *radiation*, and *electricity*
- distinguish between substances that are good conductors of heat versus good insulators

Materials

- bread
- butter
- colored pencils
- drawing paper
- glue
- hot water
- knife
- metal spoon
- mug
- plastic spoon
- scissors
- toaster
- "Conductors and Insulators" activity page

Conduction

Activate

1. Begin by asking your student, "How can you move heat?" Discuss that heat can be moved (transferred) to other objects such as a pot on the stove.

Engage

1. While your student reads the **Read It**, emphasize that conduction is the process of transferring heat to objects.
2. Then, ask them to name some other ways that conduction is used in their daily lives. Conduction is used to cook their meals.

Demonstrate

1. Now, instruct your student to complete the **Show It** activity. Then, help them to check their response with the **Show It AK**.
2. As an alternative to the **Show It**, have them toast a piece of bread and then spread butter on it. Ask them to explain how heat is transferred between the toaster, the bread, and the butter. They may respond by saying that heat is transferred from the toaster to the bread. Then, the heat is transferred from the toast to the butter.

• • •

70

SCIENCE 4 PARENT & TEACHER GUIDE

Understand Energy Terms

Engage

1. As your student reads the **Read It**, prompt them to verbally use the terms *conduction*, *convection*, *sound energy*, *radiation*, and *electricity* in sentences. Use the following examples, if needed:
   - The process of conduction caused the marshmallow to soften over the campfire.
   - Boiling water is an example of convection because the hot water rises and the cooler water moves to the bottom.
   - Sound energy comes from music.
   - The heat from a fire is called radiation.
   - Electricity is used to power many devices such as the television, a computer, and kitchen appliances.

Demonstrate

1. Now, guide your student to complete the activity in the **Show It**. Then, allow them time to check their answers with the **Show It AK**.
2. To provide an alternative to the **Show It**, invite your student to create a booklet of the terms from the **Read It**. Have them draw pictures to represent each term, and encourage your student to use labels to illustrate the meaning of each term. Ask them to use everyday examples to represent the terms.

• • •

Conductors and Insulators

Engage

1. Prompt your student to open the **Currently Electrical - Watch It** to view the video.
2. Then ask them, "Why are electrical wires covered in plastic?" Plastic insulates metal wires and keeps energy from passing through.
3. After your student reads the **Read It**, tell them to search their learning environment for examples of insulators and conductors.

Demonstrate

1. Now, direct your student to complete the T-chart activity in the **Show It**.
2. Then, direct them to the **Show It AK** to check their answers.
3. To extend learning, invite your student to test a metal and plastic spoon to see if they are conductors of heat. Tell them to complete the following steps:
   a. Pour hot water into a mug.
   b. Place the metal and plastic spoon in the cup.
   c. Wait five minutes and then touch the handles of each spoon.
4. Ask your student what they discovered through this experiment. They should respond by saying that the metal spoon is a conductor because the water cause it to get hot.

LESSON 37

Topic: Force, Motion, and Energy

Learning Objectives

The activities in this lesson will help your student meet the following objectives:

- predict what will happen after inverting a bottle of hot water over one of cold water
- predict what will happen in an experiment involving a bottle of hot water with red food coloring being inverted over a bottle of cold water with blue food coloring

Materials

- blue food coloring
- coffee mug
- colored pencils
- clear quart container or jar
- dropper
- freezer
- spoon
- water

Hypothesize about Convection

Activate

1. Start by having your student open the **Conduction and Convection - Watch It** to view the video.
2. Then, have them explain the difference between conduction and convection. Conduction is when a solid object is heated by a source. Convection is when heat transfers to a liquid through a current.

Engage

1. After your student reads the **Read It**, ask them to explain how molecules move in the convection process. Molecules move rapidly in the convection process and can transfer heat energy.

Demonstrate

1. Now, instruct your student to complete the activity in the **Show It** and reference the **Show It AK** to evaluate their hypothesis. Explain to them that they will perform the experiment in another lesson.
2. To provide an alternative to the **Show It**, allow your student to illustrate their hypothesis. Encourage them to use their knowledge of the convection process to add scientific information to their illustration.

Make a Prediction

Engage

1. Have your student work through the **Read It**. After reading the content, ask them to tell you the difference between a hypothesis and a prediction. Allow them to look up the definition of both words.
2. Then, have a discussion about the subtle difference between *hypothesis* and *prediction*. Let them know that a hypothesis proposes a possible explanation based upon prior knowledge and observations. A prediction is a guess of what might happen based on prior knowledge. For example, a hypothesis is that plants need sunlight to grow, whereas a prediction would be that a plant will grow if put in the sunlight.

Demonstrate

1. Now have your student move on to the **Show It** activity to make a prediction. When they are finished, they can compare their prediction to the example in the **Show It AK**.
2. To provide an alternative to the **Show It**, have them predict what will happen when they put hot drops of colored water into cold water. Then, instruct them to complete the following steps to test their prediction.
   a. Fill a jar halfway with cold water and set it in the freezer for 15 minutes.
   b. Fill a coffee mug a quarter full with hot water and mix in 10 drops of blue food coloring.
   c. Take the jar from the freezer and set it on the table. Allow the water to settle.
   d. Fill the dropper with hot blue water.
   e. Put the dropper in the jar so the tip is at the bottom.
   f. Release two drops of blue water at the bottom of the jar and remove the dropper.
   g. Observe what happens to the blue drops of water. They should rise to the top of the cold water and disperse on the surface.
   h. Continue adding the hot blue water to the cold water using two drops at a time to observe the convection process.

SCIENCE 4 PARENT & TEACHER GUIDE

LESSON 38

Topic | Force, Motion, and Energy

Learning Objectives

The activities in this lesson will help your student meet the following objectives:

- illustrate the results of a convection experiment
- summarize the results of experiments

Materials

- blue food coloring
- crayons, markers, or colored pencils
- playing card or piece of cardboard
- glue
- poster board
- red food coloring
- two empty bottles
- water

Illustrate Convection Results

Activate

1. Start by helping your student to stand on chair to feel the air close to the ceiling of the room.
2. Then, ask them if they can feel a difference in the temperature when they climb down from the chair. If not, explain that the air near the ceiling of a room will usually be warmest because hot air rises.

Engage

1. After your student reads the **Read It** content, have them explain why air gets cooler in the evening. They may mention that when the sun sets, it no longer heats the earth, so the warm air rises because it is less dense. Cool air gets pulled down closer to the earth.

Demonstrate

1. Now, help your student complete the experiment in the **Show It** and allow them time to illustrate the results.
2. Then, have them repeat the experiment by swapping the cold and hot bottles of water. Place the cold water bottle in the sink and invert the hot bottle on top. Instruct your student to illustrate their results for both experiments.
3. Finally, reference the **Show It AK** to evaluate their illustration.

• • •

Summarize Experiment Results

Engage

1. While your student reads the **Read It**, emphasize how density is connected to convection. When they finish the reading, ask them to explain how density affects convection. In the convection process, molecules in warm water move faster and spread apart, making them less dense and allowing them to rise above the molecules of the cool water.

Demonstrate

1. Now, direct your student to complete the activity in the **Show It**. Be sure that they read the expectations of the rubric before they begin writing.
2. Then, work with them to evaluate their paragraphs with the **Show It AK**.
3. To extend learning, invite your student to create a science board to display their scientific process for the convection experiment that began in Lesson 37. They can use the hypothesis that they wrote in Lesson 37 and the illustrated results and summary from Lesson 38 for the display. Instruct them to display the following components on their board for the convection experiment.
   - title of experiment
   - hypothesis
   - procedure
   - results
   - summary
4. Encourage your student to type each component so that their science board is neat and easily legible. Then, help them to make a design plan on the board and layout each component before they glue them down. Allow your student to decorate the board by adding appropriate borders or images that relate to the experiment.

SCIENCE 4 PARENT & TEACHER GUIDE

LESSON 39

Topic Force, Motion, and Energy

Learning Objectives

The activities in this lesson will help your student meet the following objectives:

- identify heat energy being transferred from one place to another through convection
- illustrate how convection currents result when hot and cold weather systems meet

Materials

- colored pencils, crayons, or markers
- national weather forecast from newspaper or online source
- "Draw Convection Currents" activity page

Weather Patterns

 ### Activate

1. Begin by having your student look at a national weather forecast from a newspaper or an online source. Look for images of maps with cold and hot fronts, if possible.
2. Ask your student what they notice. They should notice hot or cold symbols, snow or rain, or heat waves.

 ### Engage

1. As your student reads the **Read It**, ask them to explain why hot air rises. Hot air rises because it is less dense.
2. Then, have them identify the cold and warm fronts on the map in the text.

 ### Demonstrate

1. Now, instruct your student to complete the **Show It** activity, and help them check their answers with the **Show It AK**.
2. To provide an alternative to the **Show It**, invite them to create a map that includes a cold and warm front using the appropriate symbols.

• • •

Draw Convection Currents

Engage

1. Have your student open the **Winds and Air Masses - Watch It** and ask them to make note of the username and password provided on the Discovery Education image. Be sure that they click the link for the video and enter the provided username and password to watch.
2. Then, ask them to explain how warm and cold air circulate. They should respond by saying that, as warm air rises, cold air replaces it until it heats up and rises.
3. Next, instruct your student to read the content of the **Read It**. When they are finished, ask them, "How is convection connected to weather?" (Answer: Convection is connected to weather because the circulation of warm and cold air causes storms and other weather conditions.)

Demonstrate

1. Now, direct your student to complete the activity in the **Show It**.
2. Finally, have them reference the **Show It AK** to check their answers.
3. To extend learning, encourage your student to watch the weather forecast on the news and pay special attention to the warm and cold fronts.

SCIENCE 4 PARENT & TEACHER GUIDE

LESSON 40

Topic | Force, Motion, and Energy

Learning Objectives

The activities in this lesson will help your student meet the following objectives:

- describe a real-life weather event caused by convection currents
- explain the transfer of energy in a simple circuit from a battery, through wires, to a light bulb
- label a diagram of a simple circuit

Materials

- none required

Weather Events

Activate

1. Start by asking your student to look out a window and describe the weather. Is it rainy, sunny, or cloudy? What is the temperature? Is it warm, cold, or freezing?

Engage

1. After your student reads the **Read It**, ask them to explain how convection currents are part of the weather. Convection currents cause changes in temperatures and movement of clouds.

Demonstrate

1. Open the **Assess It** and have your student complete the activity. Ensure that they review the expectations of the rubric before and after they write their paragraph.
2. When they are finished, scan the document or take a photo of it and upload it to the Dropbox. For additional instructions on how to use the Dropbox, click on the paper clip icon in the upper-left corner of the **Assess It**.

• • •

Circuits

Activate

1. Have your student open the **Circuits - Watch It** to view the video.
2. Then, pause the video at 1:59, and ask your student to explain the circuit diagram.

Engage

1. After your student reads the **Read It**, discuss how the circuit needs to be a complete loop in order for electricity to flow.

Demonstrate

1. Now, instruct your student to complete the task in the **Show It**, and reference the **Show It AK** to check their response.
2. To provide an alternative to the **Show It**, allow your student to draw a diagram to demonstrate the flow of energy through a circuit.

Label a Circuit

Engage

1. As your student reads the **Read It**, guide them to read the labels of the diagram and explain their functions.
2. Then, direct them to open the **FrankenLab-Circuit - Play It** to play the game.

Demonstrate

1. Now, have your student move on to the **Show It** to label the diagram.
2. Then, work with them to check their answers using the **Show It AK**.
3. To extend learning, invite them to identify the path of the flow of electricity in their learning environment. Discuss the location of the main breaker box for the building.

SCIENCE 4 PARENT & TEACHER GUIDE

LESSON 41

Topic | Force, Motion, and Energy

Learning Objectives

The activities in this lesson will help your student meet the following objectives:

- draw a labeled diagram to show the three main parts of a simple direct current circuit
- construct a simple direct current circuit

Materials

- alligator clips or tape
- battery
- battery holder or paper clips
- light bulb or buzzer
- wire or foil

Parts of a Circuit

Activate

1. Start by having your student go on a scavenger hunt for items in their learning environment they can use to make a circuit. If they cannot find all the parts, allow them to name what other items they would need.

Engage

1. As your student reads the **Read It**, ask them to name the three main items they would need to make a simple circuit to light a light bulb. (Answer: battery, wire, light bulb)

Demonstrate

1. Now, have your student move on to the **Show It** activity.
2. Then, help them check their diagram with the sample provided in the **Show It AK**.

Simple Circuit

Engage

1. As your student reads the **Read It**, ask them how electrons are related to a circuit. Electrons flow along the path of a complete circuit.
2. Then, instruct your student to open the **Ecolibrium-Current Electricity - Play It** to play the game.

Demonstrate

1. Now, help your student make a circuit by following the steps in the **Show It**.
2. Then, use the **Show It AK** and work with your student to check their results.
3. To extend learning, have your student list the types of household objects that use electricity. Possible answers may include the refrigerator, microwave, toaster, hair dryer, lamps, television, etc.

LESSON 42

Topic: Force, Motion, and Energy

Learning Objectives

The activities in this lesson will help your student meet the following objectives:

- redesign an already constructed simple direct current circuit to create a parallel circuit
- compare simple and parallel circuits

Materials

- alligator clips or tape
- battery
- battery holder or paper clips
- light bulbs or buzzers
- wire or foil

Parallel Circuit

Activate

1. Start by asking your student to explain what the term *parallel* means. *Parallel* means two lines or objects that travel side by side. They have the same distance between them and never intersect.

Engage

1. While your student reads the **Read It**, prompt them to explain the path of electrons in the parallel circuit. Encourage them to use their finger to trace the path on the parallel circuit shown in the reading.
2. Then, ask your student what they would have to do to change a simple circuit to a parallel circuit. They may respond by saying they would need to connect another loop that includes a resistor to the first loop.

Demonstrate

1. Now, move to the **Show It** and guide your student to convert a simple circuit to a parallel circuit. Have them rebuild their simple circuit from Lesson 41 to create a parallel circuit.
2. Then, use the **Show It AK** to review the steps for creating a parallel circuit.

• • •

Compare Simple and Parallel

 **Engage**

1. As your student reads the **Read It**, ask them to explain the similarities and differences between a simple and parallel circuit. They both have a battery or source of energy. In the simple circuit, the energy flows in one pathway. In a parallel circuit, the energy is directed into two pathways. If one pathway is broken in a parallel circuit, the energy still has one complete pathway to flow. In a simple circuit, if the pathway is broken, the energy flow stops.

 **Demonstrate**

1. Now, instruct your student to complete the Venn diagram in the **Show It**. Then, help them check their responses with the **Show It AK**.
2. To extend learning, allow your student to experiment with their parallel circuit. Guide them to test one wire at a time by lifting one end to see if the any of the light bulbs turn off. Then, have them determine the closed loops in the parallel circuit by showing the paths that keep at least one light bulb on at a time.

LESSON 43

SCIENCE 4 PARENT & TEACHER GUIDE

Topic Force, Motion, and Energy

Learning Objectives

The activities in this lesson will help your student meet the following objectives:

- redesign a previously created parallel circuit to create a series circuit
- compare simple, parallel, and series circuits

Materials

- alligator clips or tape
- battery
- battery holder or paper clips
- colored pencils
- light bulbs or buzzers
- wires or foil
- "Compare Circuits" activity page

Series Circuit

Activate

1. Have your student open the **Series and Parallel Circuits - Watch It** and ask them to make note of the username and password provided on the Discovery Education image. Be sure that they click the link for the video and enter the provided username and password to watch.
2. Then ask them, "What is the advantage of using a parallel circuit?" Your student may respond by saying that parallel circuits continue to give multiple loads (light bulbs) electricity even if one load is disconnected.

Engage

1. After your student reads the **Read It**, ask them to explain the difference between a simple and series circuit. The only difference between a simple and series circuit is that the series circuit has multiple resistors (light bulbs) in the same loop.

Demonstrate

1. Now, help your student to complete the series circuit activity by following the instructions in the **Show It**.
2. Then, use the **Show It AK** to check that the steps for creating the series circuit were followed properly.

• • •

Compare Circuits

Engage

1. As your student reads the **Read It**, ask them to explain how the three types of circuits are similar. For example, they all have a battery or source of energy.

Demonstrate

1. Now, instruct your student to complete the "Compare Circuits" activity page in the **Show It**.
2. Then, use the **Show It AK** and allow your student to compare their work to the example answer.
3. To provide an alternative to the **Show It**, allow your student to illustrate and label the three types of circuits in a brochure.

SCIENCE 4 PARENT & TEACHER GUIDE

LESSON 44

Topic | Force, Motion, and Energy

Learning Objectives

The activities in this lesson will help your student meet the following objectives:

- redesign a simple circuit as a series or parallel circuit to demonstrate that energy is transferred in multiple ways
- illustrate the differences between how energy is converted in a simple circuit and in a series or parallel circuit

Materials

- alligator clips or tape
- battery
- battery holder or paper clips
- light bulbs or buzzers
- wires or foil

Redesign a Circuit

 ## Activate

1. Begin by having your student open the **Simple and Complex - Watch It** to view the video.
2. When the video ends, ask them to explain the meaning of a complex circuit. A complex circuit is a combination of parallel and series circuits in the same circuit.

1. As your student reads the **Read It**, ask them how they might change a series circuit to a parallel circuit. They may respond with the following steps:
   a. First, remove one of the resistors and one wire.
   b. Then, make a simple circuit with the remaining resistor.
   c. Next, attach the first resistor with two wires so it makes a secondary loop.
2. Last, tell them to review the information in the **Reinforce It**.

 ## Demonstrate

1. Now, help your student to redesign the simple circuits in the **Show It**.
2. Then, use the **Show It AK** to be sure that the steps for redesigning the circuits were followed properly.
3. To extend learning, have your student redesign a parallel circuit to a series circuit.

• • •

Draw a Diagram

Engage

1. While your student reads the **Read It**, instruct them to pay special attention to the symbols used in a circuit diagram.
2. Then, have them open the **FrankenLab-Circuit - Play It** to play the game.

Demonstrate

1. Open the **Assess It** and have your student complete the activity. Ensure they review the expectations of the rubric before they draw their diagram.
2. When they are finished, scan the document or take a photo of it and upload it to the Dropbox. For additional instructions on how to use the Dropbox, click on the paper clip icon in the upper-left corner of the **Assess It**.
3. To extend learning, encourage your student to draw an electrical plan for their bedroom. Tell them to include three objects that need electricity, and explain the circuits that can be used to power them.

LESSON 45

SCIENCE 4 PARENT & TEACHER GUIDE

Topic | Force, Motion, and Energy

Learning Objectives

The activities in this lesson will help your student meet the following objectives:

- arrange magnets in such a way as to illustrate attraction and repulsion of their poles
- demonstrate the effect of magnetism

Materials

- two bar magnets
- "Experiment with Magnetism" activity page

Magnets

Activate

1. Ask your student if they have ever heard the saying, "opposites attract."
2. Once your student answers, explain that this saying is true for magnets, and they will learn more about magnets in this lesson.

Engage

1. Now, have your student read the content of the **Read It**.
2. Next, direct them to view the **Marvelous Magnets - Watch It**.
3. When the video ends, ask your student to recall some of the items from the video that use magnets such as credit cards and some trains.
4. Encourage your student to carry a magnet around their learning environment and try to find other things that are magnetic, similar to the experiment shown in the video.

Demonstrate

1. Then, instruct your student to test two magnets by completing the **Show It** activity and writing their observations.
2. Now, allow your student to review the example answers in the **Show It AK** and compare their findings.
3. To provide an extension, have your student conduct some research about Earth's poles. Have them discuss how the poles work and what they affect.

• • •

Copyright 2018 © Lincoln Learning Solutions. All rights reserved.

87

Magnetism Experiment

Engage

1. As your student begins to read the **Read It**, have them discuss with you how magnets work. Allow them to explore with the bar magnets as they read the final paragraph of the **Read It**.

Demonstrate

1. Now, have your student move to the **Show It**. Allow them to continue to explore with the magnets to create an experiment and then answer the questions in the "Experiment with Magnetism" activity page.
2. If your student is struggling to complete the activity, have them use the "I notice" and "I wonder" prompt.
   - For example, if they notice that the magnets can attract between sheets of paper, they can say what they notice. "I notice the magnets attract between paper and I wonder if I can test..."
3. After working through the prompt, have them complete the activity page to go along with their experiment.
4. Once your student completes the **Show It**, have them evaluate their observations by checking the sample answers in the **Show It AK**.

SCIENCE 4 PARENT & TEACHER GUIDE

LESSON 46

Topic | Force, Motion, and Energy

Learning Objectives

The activities in this lesson will help your student meet the following objectives:

- explain how magnets work
- compare and contrast the positive and negative charges of a battery with the north and south poles of a magnet

Materials

- battery
- calculator or remote control
- colored pencils
- magnets
- "Compare and Contrast Batteries and Magnets" activity page

Explain Magnetism

Activate

1. Have your student get out a piece of paper and fold it in half to create two columns. Ask them to label one side *magnetic* and the other *not magnetic*.
2. Then, have them list items in each column that correspond with the column titles. Remind your student to think about the magnetic substances they learned in Lesson 45.

Engage

1. As your student reads the **Read It**, have them pay close attention to the image with the magnetic filings surrounding the magnet. Ask your student why they think the filings lined up in this form.
2. Next, have your student view the **Magnetism - Watch It**.
3. Pause the video at 2:39 and discuss with your student what was meant by "various materials can be magnetized." Explain that these materials are not magnetic, but they can become magnetized when a permanent magnet comes near.
4. Next, allow your student time to play the game in the **Ecolibrium-Magnets - Play It**.

Demonstrate

1. Instruct your student to move to the **Show It** and follow the directions to complete the activity. When they are finished, they can compare their paragraph to the example provided in the **Show It AK**.
2. Alternatively, have your student use the word bank in the **Show It** to create a comic strip explaining how magnets work.
3. To reinforce learning, encourage your student to teach you about magnets. Have them create a short worksheet with five questions. After you completing those questions, prompt your student to check your work.

• • •

89

Batteries

1. Present your student with the following objects:
   - cell phone
   - flashlight
   - watch
   - remote control
   - computer
2. Then, ask your student to brainstorm what is common to all of these objects. Prompt them, if necessary, to suggest that each item uses energy to work.
3. Tell them they will learn about batteries.

1. Begin by having your student read the **Read It**. Give your student a battery and point out the negative and positive ends. Have them draw the battery and include the negative and positive symbols where they belong.

1. Then, instruct your student to complete the worksheet in the **Show It**. If needed, allow them to go back to the **Read Its** in this lesson to review the similarities and differences between batteries and magnets.
2. Finally, allow your student to compare their answers to the samples provided in the **Show It AK**.
3. To provide an extension, have your student get an object that requires batteries such as a calculator or remote control.
   a. Have them observe how the batteries are placed in the device.
   b. Then, have them take the batteries out.
   c. Ask your student to correctly place the batteries back into the device and explain how they did it. They should state that the positive side of the battery must go where the plus sign is shown on the device. The negative side goes where the minus sign is shown on the device.
   d. Then, ask them to connect the battery placement to what they read about the way electrons flow in batteries.
4. The next lesson is a **Mastery Assess It**. Encourage your student to review Lessons 16 through 46 in order to prepare for the assessment.

LESSON 47

Topic Force, Motion, and Energy

Learning Objectives

The activities in this lesson will help your student meet the following objectives:

- not applicable

Materials

- none required

Mastery Assess It 2

1. **Mastery Assess It 2** will cover what your student has learned in Lessons 16 through 46.
2. Click on the **Mastery Assess It 2** icon to begin the online assessment.
3. Have your student read the instructions before they get started. Remind them to take their time and to do their best work.
4. When they are finished and ready for their assessment to be graded, have them click the **Submit** button.

LESSON 48

Topic: Waves and Technology

Learning Objectives

The activities in this lesson will help your student meet the following objectives:

- give examples of everyday waves
- define the terms *amplitude*, *wavelength*, *transverse wave*, and *longitudinal wave*

Materials

- colored pencils
- dictionary
- dominoes

Mechanical and Electromagnetic

Activate

1. Start by having your student stand up 20 dominoes in a line about a finger space apart.
2. Then, tell them to nudge one domino on one end of the line so that it falls onto the next domino.
3. Next, ask them to describe what happened. They should respond by saying that when the first domino was nudged, it bumped the next, which continued the cycle down the line until all of the dominoes were all knocked over.
4. Last, prompt them to explain how the fall of the domino line is like a wave. The fall of the domino line is like a wave because it is like a surge of movement in one direction that crashes at the end.

Engage

1. After your student reads the **Read It**, ask them how mechanical and electromagnetic waves are different? Mechanical waves transfer energy through matter, while electromagnetic waves travel through empty space, air, or solid materials.

Demonstrate

1. Now, have your student move on to the T-chart activity in the **Show It**. Allow them to reference the text in the **Read It** for examples.
2. Then, allow your student to compare their work to the sample in the **Show It AK**.

• • •

Define Wave Terms

Engage

1. Instruct your student to open the **Characteristics of a Wave - Watch It** to view the video. When they are finished, have them share something they learned about waves from the video.
2. Then, as they read the **Read It**, prompt them to explain each of the terms in their own words. Help them to clarify the meanings of the terms if they are having any difficulties.

Demonstrate

1. Now, direct your student to complete the definition activity in the **Show It**. Then, help them check their responses with the **Show It AK**.
2. Alternatively, allow them to make a booklet where they draw an image for each term from the **Show It**. Tell them to label each image and give a verbal explanation of the terms.

SCIENCE 4 PARENT & TEACHER GUIDE

LESSON 49

Topic Waves of Technology

Learning Objectives

The activities in this lesson will help your student meet the following objectives:

- list examples of transverse waves and longitudinal waves
- describe the amplitude and wavelength of a transverse wave
- describe the amplitude and wavelength of a longitudinal wave

Materials

- Slinky®

Researching Waves

 Activate

1. Begin by having your student open the **Wave Motion - Watch It** to view the video.
2. Then, ask them to act out the movement of a small and large wave.

 Engage

1. After your student reads the **Read It**, prompt them to explain the difference between transverse and longitudinal waves. Transverse waves move in an up and down motion as they move forward, like the movement of shaking out a blanket. Longitudinal waves move in a line as if traveling through a tube.

 **Demonstrate**

1. Now, direct your student to complete the **Show It** activity.
2. Then, work with them to compare their list with the sample in the **Show It AK**. Encourage them to add examples to their lists from the answer key.
3. To provide an alternative to the **Show It**, allow your student to use a Slinky to demonstrate the movement of a transverse and longitudinal wave.
   a. Have them stretch the Slinky out on a smooth surface while someone else holds the other end. During the investigation, both people will always hold on to the Slinky.
   b. For a transverse wave, have your student shake one end back and forth while the other end stays held in place. The up-and-down motion will travel as a wave along the Slinky.
   c. For the longitudinal wave, have your student pull some of the Slinky together at one end and then release the part they pulled together while still holding the end. They will observe the wave of compressed parts move along the Slinky.

Traverse Waves

Engage

1. As your student reads the **Read It**, have them explain the crests and troughs in a transverse wave. Crests are the high points of the wave, and troughs are the low points. Crests and troughs are used to measure the wavelength.

Demonstrate

1. Now, instruct your student to complete the T-chart in the **Show It**. Allow them to reference the text in the **Read It** for detailed information.
2. Finally, help them check their work with the **Show It AK**.
3. To provide an alternative to the **Show It**, allow them to draw and label a diagram that illustrates the amplitude and wavelength of a transverse wave.

• • •

Longitudinal Waves

Engage

1. While your student reads the **Read It**, ask them to explain how the wavelength is measured in longitudinal waves. The wavelength of a longitudinal wave is measured by the distance between two compressions.

Demonstrate

1. Now, guide your student to complete the T-chart in the **Show It**. Then, assist them to evaluate their lists with the **Show It AK**.
2. To provide an alternative to the **Show It**, have your student return to the Slinky and demonstrate changes in longitudinal wave amplitudes.

LESSON 50

SCIENCE 4 PARENT & TEACHER GUIDE

Topic | Waves and Technology

Learning Objectives

The activities in this lesson will help your student meet the following objectives:

- describe an experiment involving a Slinky that shows transverse and longitudinal waves
- illustrate wave patterns

Materials

- balloon
- music
- plastic disposable cup
- salt
- scissors
- Slinky®

Slinky Experiment

1. Start by helping your student create a vibration cup by completing the following the steps.
   - Give your student a plastic cup.
   - Cut off the neck of a balloon and discard it. Then, stretch the top part of the balloon over the cup so it looks like a drum.
   - Set the vibration cup near a speaker, and play music to observe what happens.
   - Sprinkle salt on top of the stretched balloon. Then, play the music and observe again.
   - Now, turn the volume of the music higher and observe the salt.
2. Finally, ask your student what they discovered about sound vibrations. They should share that they noticed the salt dance from the sound waves of the music. The louder the music, the higher the salt bounced.

1. As your student reads the **Read It** content, allow them to manipulate the Slinky to create some theories about modeling transverse waves and longitudinal waves.

1. Now, have your student move on to the experiment in the **Show It**.
2. Then, reference the **Show It AK** to help them compare their responses with the sample answers.
3. To extend learning, allow your student to move the Slinky in response to the amplitude of music.

• • •

Illustrating Wave Patterns

Engage

1. Prompt your student to open the **Wave Energy - Watch It** to view the video. Ask them to explain which part of a wave changes based on its frequency. The wavelength changes based on the energy of the wave.
2. Then, direct them to read the content of the **Read It**. Encourage them to pay close attention to the diagrams and their labels.

Demonstrate

1. Now, instruct your student to draw the diagrams in the **Show It** and reference the **Show It AK** to check their work.
2. To extend learning, take your student to a local lake or body of water to observe the waves. Invite them to describe some of the waves they see. If this is not possible, try a virtual trip to view waves.

SCIENCE 4 PARENT & TEACHER GUIDE

LESSON 51

Topic | Waves and Technology

Learning Objectives

The activities in this lesson will help your student meet the following objectives:

- describe how waves move objects
- define the terms *sclera, cornea, iris, pupil, lens, retina, photoreceptors* (rods and cones), and *optic nerve*
- explain the three factors required for vision

Materials

- blanket
- colored pencils
- glue
- piece of paper
- push pin
- round container
- straw
- tape
- tray
- water
- wax paper

How Waves Move

Activate

1. Have your student open the **Investigating Waves - Watch It** and ask them to make note of the username and password provided on the Discovery Education image. Be sure that they click the link for the video and enter the provided username and password to watch.
2. If time permits, allow your student to perform the activity from the video. Have them make waves in a tray of water with a straw to see how the paper responds.

Engage

1. While your student reads the **Read It**, prompt them to explain why an object does not move with waves. An object does not move because the energy travels through the wave and does not cause the object to travel.

Demonstrate

1. Open the **Assess It** and have your student complete the activity. Make sure they review the expectations of the rubric before and after writing.
2. When they are finished, scan the document or take a photo of it and upload it to the Dropbox. For additional instructions on how to use the Dropbox, click on the paper clip icon in the upper-left corner of the **Assess It**.

• • •

98

Copyright 2018 © Lincoln Learning Solutions. All rights reserved.

Vision Terms

Activate

1. Guide your student to open the **Sight - Watch It** to view the video.
2. Pause the video at 2:14 and have your student explain how their eyes see an object. Light reflects off of an object and into their eyes. As the light goes through their pupil, it forms a upside down image on the retina. Their brain then helps them to see the image correctly.

Engage

1. Next, instruct your student to read the text of the **Read It**. As they read about each part of the eye, have them point to the corresponding part on the diagram. Encourage them to use the labels to help them find each part.

Demonstrate

1. Now, direct your student to complete the **Show It** activity. Reference the **Show It AK** and help them check their answers.
2. To provide an alternative to the **Show It**, have your student create a lift-the-flap diagram of the human eye, with a flap for each part.
    a. They can glue or tape pieces of paper to the diagram to make the flaps.
    b. Have them write the name of the part on the top of the flap and its definition under the flap.

• • •

How Vision Works

 **Engage**

1. As your student reads the **Read It**, ask them to list the parts of the eye in the order in which light passes through them as the eye sees an object. Your student should respond by listing the parts of the eye in the following order:
    - cornea
    - iris
    - pupil
    - lens
    - retina
    - cones and rods
    - optic nerve

 **Demonstrate**

1. Now, instruct your student to complete the activity in the **Show It**. Then, allow your student to compare their paragraph with the sample provided in the **Show It AK**.
2. To provide an alternative, have your student make a pinhole camera by completing the following steps.
    a. Give your student a round container, and instruct them to make a hole with the push pin in the bottom center of the container.
    b. Cut a piece of wax paper and tape it to cover the top of the container.
    c. Direct your student to take their camera under a blanket. Then have them position the pinhole end of the round container outside of the blanket.
    d. Have them look through the wax paper side of the container.
    e. Ask them what they notice. They should see that the objects are upside down.
    f. Discuss how a pinhole camera is similar to the eye. It takes in light through the lens and creates an upside down image.

LESSON 52

SCIENCE 4 PARENT & TEACHER GUIDE

Topic: Waves and Technology

Learning Objectives

The activities in this lesson will help your student meet the following objectives:

- experiment with vision and light
- draw conclusions about how light affects vision
- list ways in which patterns are used to transfer information from one place to another

Materials

- black construction paper
- flashlight
- fork
- shoebox
- spoons

Shoebox Light Experiment

Activate

1. Ask your student, "How do you see at night?" They should respond by saying that they use lights, lamps, or flashlight.
2. Discuss how the iris in their eye opens up the pupil to take in as much light as possible.

Engage

1. While your student reads the **Read It**, ask them if they have any questions about the experiment. Explain that they will complete the experiment in the **Show It**.

Demonstrate

1. Now, guide your student to complete the experiment in the **Show It**.
2. Then, allow your student to compare their observations to the samples provided in the **Show It AK**.
3. To continue the experiment, complete the following the steps:
   a. Have your student cover the enlarged hole with black construction paper.
   b. Then, ask them to poke another small hole in the construction paper where the flashlight can shine through.
   c. Next, place another object in the box without your student seeing it. Instruct them to try to identify the object by shining a flashlight into the small hole.
   d. If they are unable to identify the object, allow them to remove the piece of black construction paper.

• • •

Interpret Light Experiment

Engage

1. As your student reads the **Read It**, discuss how scientists complete experiments to find rules or generalizations about nature.
2. Ask them, "What rule or generalization can you make for the light experiment you conducted in the previous subtopic?" They may respond by saying, "Objects in the dark cannot be seen."

Demonstrate

1. Now, instruct your student to complete the **Show It** activity. Then help them evaluate their responses using the example in the **Show It AK**.
2. To extend learning, invite them to design another experiment that tests how light affects vision.

• • •

Patterns and Signals

Engage

1. After your student reads the **Read It**, ask them which type of communication pattern would they prefer to use: sound, light, or electronic. Have them explain their choice.

Demonstrate

1. Now, direct your student to complete the activity in the **Show It**. Assist them in comparing their responses with the examples in the **Show It AK**.
2. To provide an alternative to the **Show It**, send rhythms back and forth with your student by clicking spoons together.
    a. Sit in a room away from your student.
    b. Take turns playing a rhythm with the spoons.
    c. After the rhythm is played, the other person should try to repeat it.

SCIENCE 4 PARENT & TEACHER GUIDE

LESSON 53

Topic | Waves and Technology

Learning Objectives

The activities in this lesson will help your student meet the following objectives:

- describe how a device can quickly transfer information over long distances in the form of electrical signals
- list modern ways in which information is transferred over long distances
- compare ways people communicated before electricity was discovered to modern ways people communicate

Materials

- buttons
- glue
- Morse code chart
- noodles

Electric Telegraph

Activate

1. Begin by visiting the search engine *Kiddle* at **www.kiddle.co** to search for a student-friendly Morse code chart.
2. Next, write a sentence using Morse code, and have your student decode it using the chart.
3. Then, allow them to write a secret message to you in Morse code.

Engage

1. While your student reads the **Read It**, ask them if they have seen telephones that are still connected to wires such as those used in stores.

Demonstrate

1. Now, guide your student to complete the activity in the **Show It**. Then work with them to evaluate their paragraph with the example in the **Show It AK**.
2. To provide an alternative to the **Show It**, have them create a sign using Morse code to write their name. Instruct them to use buttons as dots and pieces of noodles for the lines.
3. Then, instruct them to explain how using Morse code helped to quickly transfer information over long distances. They should explain that the electric telegraph was a device that transmitted electric currents. Operators used the electric telegraph to send message by Morse code to people in distant places.

103

Methods of Transferring Info

1. As your student reads the content of the **Read It**, have them share their experiences with the forms of modern communication presented in the text.

1. Now, direct your student to read the **Show It** instructions and complete the activity. When they are finished, they can compare their list to the sample in the **Show It AK**.
2. To provide an alternative to the **Show It**, allow your student to make a poster that illustrates modern forms of communication. Instruct them to label each form of communication.

• • •

Comparing Info Transfer

1. Once your student reads the **Read It**, ask them to explain the differences in communication before and after electricity.

1. Open the **Assess It** and have your student complete the activity. Help them to understand the expectations of the rubric before they begin writing. When they are finished, help them review their work to make sure they have met the rubric expectations.
2. When they are finished, scan the document or take a photo of it and upload it to the Dropbox. For additional instructions on how to use the Dropbox, click on the paper clip icon in the upper-left corner of the **Assess It**.
3. The next lesson is a **Mastery Assess It**. Encourage your student to review Lessons 48 through 53 in order to prepare for the assessment.

LESSON 54

Topic: Waves and Technology

Learning Objectives

The activities in this lesson will help your student meet the following objectives:

- not applicable

Materials

- none required

Mastery Assess It 3

1. **Mastery Assess It 3** will cover what your student has learned in Lessons 48 through 53.
2. Click on the **Mastery Assess It 3** icon to begin the online assessment.
3. Have your student read the instructions before they get started. Remind them to take their time and to do their best work.
4. When they are finished and ready for their assessment to be graded, have them click the **Submit** button.

SCIENCE 4 PARENT & TEACHER GUIDE

LESSON 55

Topic Earth and Space

Learning Objectives

The activities in this lesson will help your student meet the following objectives:

- define the term *planet* as described by the International Astronomical Union
- list the planets of the solar system in the correct order
- explain why Pluto is no longer considered a full-sized planet

Materials

- ball
- index cards
- light bulb
- sidewalk chalk
- toy car
- "KWL Chart" activity page
- "Pluto Paragraph" activity page

Define Planet

 ### Activate

1. Show your student the following items:
   - a ball
   - a toy car
   - a light bulb
2. Then, ask your student to list some characteristics that make these items unique. For example, a ball is usually round, and a car has wheels.
3. Explain to your student that all items must meet specific criteria in order to be classified a certain way. For example, a toy car would not be classified as a ball because it does not have the criteria that makes it a ball.
4. Tell your student that they will learn about the criteria an object in space must meet to be considered a planet.

 ### Engage

1. Have your student read the first paragraph of the **Read It**. Ask them to think about the ways in which people learned about planets before technology was available to view them.
2. Then, have your student read the remaining content of the **Read It**.
3. Next, have them view the **Planets of the Solar System - Watch It**.

 ### Demonstrate

1. Now, have your student complete the **Show It** activity. When they are finished, they can compare their work to the sample answer in the **Show It AK**.
2. To extend your student's knowledge about the criteria of planets, have them conduct research and compare the composition of stars and planets. Encourage them to create a Venn diagram to organize the results of their research. They should place the similarities in the center circle and the differences in the outer circles. An empty Venn diagram is provided below.

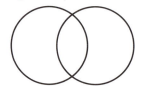

• • •

106 Copyright 2018 © Lincoln Learning Solutions. All rights reserved.

Order of the Planets

 ## Activate

1. Ask your student if they can name their family members from the youngest to the oldest.
2. Explain that it is important to know the order of things, and they will learn about the order of the planets in the solar system.

1. As your student engages in the **Read It**, ask them to identify the planet on which they live. Then ask them where it falls in the order of planets in the solar system.
2. Next, direct your student to view **The Planets - Watch It.**
3. Pause the video at 0:28, and ask your student to observe a difference between the first four planets and the last four planets in the image.
4. As the video discusses the planets, have your student write down some facts about each planet on index cards.
5. Next, have your student move to the **Beakers Big Buzz Planets - Play It** and allow them time to play the game.

 ## Demonstrate

1. Now, have your student complete the **Practice It**. Let them practice ordering the planets as many times as they like until they feel confident in remembering the correct order.
2. Next, have your student complete the **Show It**. They may need help creating their own acronym for ordering the planets.
3. Finally, have them check their answer with the **Show It AK**.
4. To reinforce your student's knowledge of planetary order, take them outside and give them some sidewalk chalk. Ask them to draw the sun and then the planets in the correct order.

Pluto

Activate

1. Ask your student to tell you what they know about Pluto.
2. Then, ask them how they might learn more about it. They may mention searching the Internet, asking an expert, etc.

Engage

1. Begin by having your student read the content of the **Read It**.
2. Once they complete the reading, ask them to name the steps a researcher completes to answer a question.
3. Next, have your student view the **Watch It** titled, **Is Pluto a Planet?**

Demonstrate

1. Then, have your student complete the **Show It** activity. Your student may need help conducting research and constructing their paragraph.
2. Once your student completes the **Show It**, use the **Show It AK** to ensure that their paragraph includes the reasons why Pluto is no longer considered a planet.

SCIENCE 4 PARENT & TEACHER GUIDE

LESSON 56

Topic | Earth and Space

Learning Objectives

The activities in this lesson will help your student meet the following objectives:

- compare and contrast characteristics of the four inner planets and the four outer planets
- design and label a poster of a planet

Materials

- construction paper
- crayons or colored pencils
- glue
- index cards
- large paper
- markers
- scissors
- "Venn Diagram of the Planets of the Solar System" activity page
- "Taking Notes" activity page

Compare and Contrast Inner and Outer Planets

Activate

1. Ask your student to tell you what makes up the solar system.
2. Then, ask them what they would like to learn about Earth's nearest neighbors in the universe.

Engage

1. While your student reads the **Read It**, pause after each planet and discuss what they learned.
2. Next, have them view the **Inner and Outer Planets - Watch It**.

Demonstrate

1. Now, have your student complete the Venn diagram in the **Show It**. Then have them compare their answers to the samples in the **Show It AK**.
2. To help reinforce this concept, create a game to play with your student. Begin by writing the following information on index cards:

   - names of all eight planets
   - rocky
   - solid
   - gaseous
   - large in size
   - small in size
   - has many moons
   - has rings

3. Next, write the terms *inner planets* and *outer planets* on separate pieces of paper. Place these pages on separate ends of a table or on the floor at opposite ends of the room.
4. Set a timer for one minute, and ask your student to place all of the index cards under the correct category of *inner planets* or *outer planets*.

• • •

Planet Poster

 **Engage**

1. Allow your student to read the **Read It** content to help them understand how they will conduct research. Your student does not need to complete the activity page now. They will do so in the **Show It** where additional instructions are provided.
2. Next, have your student view **Racking up the Miles - Watch It**.
3. To review the content, allow them time to play the game in the **Ecolibrium-Astronomy - Play It**.

 **Demonstrate**

1. As additional practice, have your student review the planets using the **Practice It**.
2. Finally, have your student move to the **Show It**. They may need help organizing their thoughts to plan out their poster. Be sure they complete the "Taking Notes" activity page.
3. Then, have your student compare their poster to the criteria listed in the **Show It AK**.
4. To extend this concept, have your student present their poster to a family member and persuade them to visit the planet.

SCIENCE 4 PARENT & TEACHER GUIDE

LESSON 57

Topic | **Earth and Space**

Learning Objectives

The activities in this lesson will help your student meet the following objectives:

- define the term *star*
- define the term *sun*
- label a map of the solar system to illustrate the galaxy

Materials

- crayons or colored pencils
- dictionary
- flashlight
- scissors

Define *Star*

Activate

1. Prior to this lesson, have your student go outside and view the stars in the sky. If viewing the stars is not possible, ask your student if they have ever looked in the sky at night and saw many stars.
2. Ask them if they are able to count all the stars they see. Then, ask if they notice any differences in the stars they see. Are some brighter than others? Do they see different colors? If your student is unable to view the stars, ask them what they can recall.
3. Then, tell your student that they will learn more about stars in this lesson.

Engage

1. Now, have your student read the **Read It**. Ask them to pay close attention to the section of the reading that discusses the Sun appearing to be larger than other stars because it is closer to Earth.
2. Now, do an experiment with your student. Get the flashlight, and ask them to stand about 12 feet away from you. Shine the flashlight in their direction, and have them move closer and closer to the flashlight.
3. Ask your student to explain what happens.

Demonstrate

1. Next, have your student complete the **Show It** activity and compare their answer to the **Show It AK**.
2. To provide an alternative to the **Show It**, have your student view different types of stars by searching the Internet. Ask them to look at the size and color differences.

Define *Sun*

 Activate

1. Ask your student to draw a picture of the Sun using crayons.
2. Ask them why they chose the color they used. Most likely, they chose yellow.
3. Tell your student they will learn more about Earth's closest star, the Sun.

 Engage

1. Next, have your student view the **Cosmic Galaxies - Watch It**.
2. Then, have them read about the Sun in the **Read It**.
3. Ask your student to think about the many things the Sun provides for people on Earth. They may say that the Sun provides warmth, and it helps plants live through photosynthesis.

 Demonstrate

1. Let your student review using the **The Solar System - Practice It**.
2. Have your student complete the **Show It** and then check their answer in the **Show It AK**.
3. As an alternative to the **Show It**, give your student a sheet of paper. Instruct them to cut out a circle about 8 inches in diameter to represent the Sun. They can color it yellow.
4. Next, have them write as many facts about the Sun as they can on the circle. When they are finished, they can hang the picture on a wall or the refrigerator.

• • •

Label the Solar System

 Engage

1. As your student reads through the **Read It**, discuss with them the size the Milky Way galaxy.
2. Next, have your student watch **The Solar System - Watch It**.
3. Then, have your student engage in the **Nueva's Cross Country Chase-Solar System - Play It**.
4. Finally, complete the **Planet Order from the Sun - Practice It** and review key concepts introduced in the lesson.

 Demonstrate

1. Open the **Assess It** and have your student complete the activity. When they are finished, scan the document or take a photo of it and upload it to the Dropbox. For additional instructions on how to use the Dropbox, click on the paper clip icon in the upper-left corner of the **Assess It**.

SCIENCE 4 PARENT & TEACHER GUIDE

LESSON 58

Topic | **Earth and Space**

Learning Objectives

The activities in this lesson will help your student meet the following objectives:

- define the term *universe*
- define the term *galaxy*
- use a map to identify the Milky Way galaxy and other galaxies

Materials

- colored pencils or crayons
- dictionary or glossary
- hanger
- scissors

Define *Universe*

Activate

1. Begin by asking your student to tell you what they know about the sun. They may mention that it is a star and planets revolve around it.
2. Next, ask them if they think any of the stars they see in the night sky could be like Earth's sun.
3. Tell them they will learn that Earth's solar system is not all that makes up the universe.

Engage

1. While your student reads through the **Read It**, discuss what is meant in the text when it states, "The universe could go on forever." Also, help them to understand the number trillion.
2. Now, have your student view the **Space - Watch It**.
3. Have a discussion with your student about the advancement of astronomical discoveries over the last few hundred years.

Demonstrate

1. Now, have your student work on the activity in the **Show It**. Then, compare their work to the example answer in the **Show It AK**.
2. To provide an alternative to the **Show It**, have your student create a list of objects that are found within our universe. Their list may include planets, stars, galaxies, and asteroids.

Define *Galaxy*

Engage

1. Begin by having your student read the content of the **Read It**.
2. Next, open the **Cosmic Galaxies - Watch It** and allow them time to view the video.

Demonstrate

1. Now, instruct your student to open the **Show It** and complete the activity.
2. Then, have your student compare their definition to the sample in the **Show It AK**.

Label Galaxies

Engage

1. Have your student read through the **Read It**. Encourage them to compare the galaxies discussed.

Demonstrate

1. Next, have your student label the galaxies in the **Show It**. They can refer to the **Read It** if they need help.
2. Then, have your student compare their answers to the **Show It AK**.
3. To reinforce the information about galaxies, your student can make a mobile with differently shaped galaxies.
    a. Have them draw the galaxies and label them.
    b. Next, attach their drawings to a string and hang them from a hanger.

LESSON 59

Topic: Earth and Space

Learning Objectives

The activities in this lesson will help your student meet the following objectives:
- compare and contrast refracting and reflecting telescopes
- define the term *moon*

Materials
- dictionary or glossary

Types of Telescopes

Activate

1. Ask your student if they have ever looked through a pair of binoculars. If so, ask them, "How did the objects appear?"
2. Then, ask them if they can think of something astronomers might use to help them see objects in space. If your student is having a difficult time recalling the word *telescope*, remind them that Galileo used this tool to view Jupiter's moons and the craters on Earth's moon.
3. Explain that they will learn about telescopes in this lesson.

Engage

1. As your student reads through the **Read It**, have them pause at some of the more difficult words. Help your students to define the new terms.
2. Ask your student if they can think of another everyday object that uses the types of lenses that are in the refractor telescope. Examples may include eye glasses and a magnifying glass.
3. Next, have your student view the **Now I See It - Watch It**. Then, have a discussion with your student about the objects that astronomers can view using telescopes that could not be seen without them.
4. Then, have your student play the game in the **Ecolibrium Space Exploration - Play It**.

Demonstrate

1. Next, direct your student to complete the Venn diagram in the **Show It**. They can compare their answers to the sample in the **Show It AK**.
2. To expand your student's knowledge of telescopes, help them search the Internet for images from the Hubble Space Telescope.

● ● ●

Define *Moon*

Activate

1. Ask your student if they have ever heard the quote, "One small step for man, one giant leap for mankind."
2. Tell your student that this quote is from the astronaut, Neil Armstrong. He said these words as he took his first steps on the Moon. Remind them that Armstrong was the first human to ever set foot on the Moon's surface.

Engage

1. While your student reads the content of the **Read It**, ask them to explain, in their own words, why a moon is called a natural satellite.
2. Now, have your student view the **Planets and Moons - Watch It**. As your student watches the video, have them note the size of Earth and its moon as compared to the size of the outer planets and their moons.

Demonstrate

1. Next, have your student complete the **Show It** to define the term *moon*.
2. When they finish, allow them to compare their definition to the example in the **Show It AK** and revise their definition, if necessary.
3. To extend learning, have your student create a list of similarities and differences between Earth and its moon.

SCIENCE 4 PARENT & TEACHER GUIDE

LESSON 60

| Topic | Earth and Space |

Learning Objectives

The activities in this lesson will help your student meet the following objectives:
- define the term *lunar phase*
- label the eight lunar phases

Materials
- ball
- dictionary or glossary
- lamp without a shade
- 16 index cards

Lunar Phase

 ### Activate

1. Prior to the lesson, have your student view the current phase of the Moon. Help them to search the Internet for images of the current Moon phase or allow them to look into the night sky.
2. Have them draw the current Moon phase on a sheet of paper.
3. Next, ask them to think about where the Moon gets its light.

 ### Engage

1. As your student reads the content of the **Read It**, have them try to recall times that they have seen various Moon phases in the sky.
2. Next, have them view the **Watch It** titled **Our Solar System**.
3. Then, allow your student time to engage with the **Nuevas Cross Country Chase Earth and Moon - Play It** to learn more about the Earth and its moon.

 ### Demonstrate

1. Have your student complete the **Show It** and review their answer with the **Show It AK**.
2. To provide an alternative to the **Show It**, consider having your student complete an experiment to model the different phases of the Moon. Follow the steps below.
   a. Begin by giving your student a ball and going in to a dark or dimly lit room.
   b. Turn on a lamp.
   c. Explain that the ball represents the Moon, and the lamp represents the sun.
   d. Have your student hold the ball while facing the light. Ask them to turn the ball counter clockwise. The light from the lamp will reflect off of the ball.
   e. Ask your student to observe how the different parts of the ball are lit as they rotate.
   f. Have your student shout out the phase of the Moon as they are moving the ball around the lighted lamp.

• • •

Eight Lunar Phases

Engage

1. As your student reads the **Read It**, have them compare their drawing of the current Moon phase from the Activate section to the images in the text. Ask them to determine the name of the current phase of the Moon based on their drawing.
2. Next, have your student view the **Man in the Moon - Watch It**.
3. Then, move to the **Ecolibrium Astronomy - Play It**, and allow your student time to play the game.

Demonstrate

1. Now, have your student work on labeling the phases of the Moon in the **Show It**.
2. Then, have them check their answers with the **Show It AK**.
3. To help reinforce the phases of the Moon, create a game with your student.
    a. Provide them with 16 index cards.
    b. Have them draw each phase of the Moon on an index card.
    c. Next, direct them to write the name of each of the Moon phase on separate index cards.
    d. Mix the cards and have your student place the pictures in order and then match the name of the phase to each picture.

SCIENCE 4 PARENT & TEACHER GUIDE

LESSON 61

Topic: Earth and Space

Learning Objectives

The activities in this lesson will help your student meet the following objectives:

- define the term *revolve*
- define the term *rotate*
- perform an experiment to show the Earth's rotation

Materials

- ball
- flashlight

Revolve Definition

Activate

1. Ask your student to demonstrate the terms *rotation* and *revolution* using their body. Your student should spin in a circle to demonstrate *rotation*, and move around an object to demonstrate *revolution*.
2. Then, ask your student to think of these terms in relationship to Earth's movements. Have them decide which of these movements would cause day and night and which would cause the seasons to change.
3. Discuss with them they will learn about these movements in this lesson.

Engage

1. Next, move to the **Read It** and have your student read through the content.
2. Now, have your student open and view the **Our Place in Space - Watch It** to learn more about gravity in space and how it affects Earth's rotation. Encourage them to try the experiment with the globe and flashlight presented in the video.

Demonstrate

1. Next, have your student complete the **Show It** activity and then compare their definition to the example in the **Show It AK**.
2. To extend learning, encourage your student to identify the current season. Then, have them draw a picture to show how Earth is currently positioned in relationship to the Sun.

•••

Rotate Definition

Engage

1. As your student reads the **Read It**, have them discuss with you the difference between the terms *rotation* and *revolution*.
2. Next, have your student view the **Blast Off Into Space - Watch It**.
3. Now, have them play the **Ecolibrium-Earth's Movement - Play It**.

Demonstrate

1. Have your student complete the **Show It** by defining the term *rotate*. Then, allow them to compare their definition to the example in the **Show It AK**.
2. To provide an alternative to the **Show It**, have your student draw Earth and the Sun. Ask them to label the sides of the Earth to show which one has daylight and which one is night.
3. To expand your students knowledge, have them conduct research and compare Earth's rotation time to the amount of time it takes the other planets to rotate.

• • •

Rotation of Earth

Activate

1. Ask your student to explain how Earth revolves and rotates.

Engage

1. Then, have your student read through the **Read It**. Discuss the content with them.
2. Next, have them open and view the **As the World Turns - Watch It**.

Demonstrate

1. Now, have your student complete the **Show It** activity using the materials listed. Then, have them answer the questions after completing the procedure.
2. Finally, allow your student to compare their observations to the sample provided in the **Show It AK**.

LESSON 62

Topic: Earth and Space

Learning Objectives

The activities in this lesson will help your student meet the following objectives:

- describe the motion of the earth in relationship to the sun during a twenty-four hour period
- define the term *orbit*
- draw an example of Earth's true shape and compare it to a sphere

Materials

- dictionary or glossary
- play dough

Motion of Earth

Activate

1. Ask your student to tell you where the sun rises and sets each day. If they have not yet observed this, take time one day to watch the sunrise and sunset with your student.
2. Explain that the sun will always rise in the east and set in the west due to Earth's movement, which they will learn about in this lesson.

Engage

1. As your student works through the **Read It**, pause and have them briefly define both *rotation* and *revolution* aloud for you. Then, compare their response to the definitions within the text.
2. Then, allow your student time to play the game in the **Cosmic Trail-Solar System - Play It**.

Demonstrate

1. Open the **Assess It** and have your student complete the activity. Help them to understand the expectations of the rubric before they begin writing. When they are finished, help them to review their work to ensure they have met the rubric expectations.
2. When they are finished, scan the document or take a photo of it and upload it to the Dropbox. For additional instructions on how to use the Dropbox, click on the paper clip icon in the upper-left corner of the **Assess It**.

Orbit Definition

 Activate

1. Tell your student that it takes 365.25 days for Earth to make one complete orbit.
2. Have them tell you what they think the word *orbit* means.

 Engage

1. While your student is reading the **Read It**, ask them to infer which planet would have the longest orbit around the Sun and which would have the shortest orbit.

 Demonstrate

1. Now, have your student complete the **Show It** activity. When they are finished, allow them time to compare their definition to the example in the **Show It AK**. Ask them to make revisions, if necessary.
2. To extend your student's learning, have them work through the **Solar System - Practice It** and identify the orbit of each planet. Consider allowing them to draw the Sun in the center of a piece of paper and draw the orbits of each planet around the Sun. Then, have them label the length of each orbit.

Ellipse

 Activate

1. Have your student take some play dough and roll it in the shape of Earth.
2. Tell them they will learn the true shape of Earth in this lesson, and it may surprise them.

 Engage

1. After your student reads the **Read It**, have them take their play dough shape they created in the Activate section and adjust it based on what they learned from the reading.

 Demonstrate

1. Next, have your student complete the **Show It** activity. Have a discussion with them about the differences in the shapes they drew.
2. Then, have them compare their drawing to the samples in the **Show It AK**.

SCIENCE 4 PARENT & TEACHER GUIDE

LESSON 63

Topic | Earth and Space

Learning Objectives

The activities in this lesson will help your student meet the following objectives:

- explain how Earth's tilt and revolution around the Sun cause the seasons
- describe how the tilt and revolution of the Earth cause the seasons

Materials

- dry erase board and marker
- lamp without a shade
- marker
- pencil
- Styrofoam® ball

Earth's Seasons

 ### Activate

1. Ask your student what their favorite season is and why they like it. Have them use words to describe this season such as warm, cold, green, etc.
2. Then, ask them what they think causes the seasons to change. Try to lead your student to recall what they learned in earlier lessons and to use the word *revolution* in their response.

1. Have your student begin by reading the **Read It**. Be sure to pause and explain that the Southern Hemisphere, which is below the equator, experiences the opposite season as the Northern Hemisphere.
2. Next, ask your student to imagine that it is summer in the Northern Hemisphere. Then, ask them what season a person in the Southern Hemisphere would be experiencing? (Answer: winter)
3. Then, have your student view the **Rotation and Revolution of Earth - Watch It**. Pause at 2:15 and have a discussion about leap year with your student.

1. Next, have your student simulate seasons by completing the **Show It** activity. Encourage your student to check the **Show It AK** to see what they should have observed.
2. To help reinforce this concept, use a dry erase board or piece of paper and ask your student to represent the specific seasons.
   a. Have them draw the Sun on the left side of the paper, and then draw four Earth pictures on the right side.
   b. For their Earth pictures, instruct them to show how Earth would be titled to face the Sun in different ways for each season. For example, the Northern Hemisphere of Earth would be tilted toward the Sun for summer, away from the Sun for winter, and in between for spring and fall.

• • •

One Year Around the Sun

Engage

1. As your student reads the **Read It**, discuss the different positions of the Earth with them. Pretend you are the Sun and they are the Earth. Have your student bend at the waist (the equator) and begin to revolve around you, explaining which season they are experiencing in each position.
2. Next, have your student view the **Off Kilter - Watch It**.

Demonstrate

1. Now, have your student complete the paragraph activity in the **Show It**. Ask them to compare their work to the example provided in the **Show It AK**.
2. To help your student expand their knowledge of the seasons, have them conduct research to determine several plants and animals that rely on the change of seasons for their life cycle.
3. The next lesson is a **Mastery Assess It**. Encourage your student to review Lessons 55 through 63 in order to prepare for the assessment.

LESSON 64

Topic: Earth and Space

Learning Objectives

The activities in this lesson will help your student meet the following objectives:

- not applicable

Materials

- none required

Mastery Assess It 4

1. **Mastery Assess It 4** will cover what your student has learned in Lessons 55 through 63.
2. Click on the **Mastery Assess It 4** icon to begin the online assessment.
3. Have your student read the instructions before they get started. Remind them to take their time and to do their best work.
4. When they are finished and ready for their assessment to be graded, have them click the **Submit** button.

SCIENCE 4 PARENT & TEACHER GUIDE

LESSON 65

Topic: Earth's Elements and Landforms

Learning Objectives

The activities in this lesson will help your student meet the following objectives:

- define the term *landform*
- match pictures of landforms to their names and definitions

Materials

- dictionary or glossary
- index cards
- map of the United States

What is a Landform?

 ### Activate

1. Begin by having your student view the **Geographers - Watch It**.
2. Pause the video at 0:23, and ask your student to answer the question about what they see outside. They can draw their answers or discuss them with you.

1. Have your student read the content of the **Read it**. Then, ask them to recall what they leaned in the **Watch It** about the ways in which mountains and valleys are formed.

 ### Demonstrate

1. Have your student complete the **Show It** activity. When they are finished, have them compare their definition to the sample in the **Show It AK**.
2. To provide an alternative to the **Show It**, have your student draw and label a picture of a landform. Then, instruct them to add a caption below the picture that defines a landform.

• • •

Identifying Landforms

Engage

1. While your student reads the **Read It**, have them identify any landforms that they live near.
2. Next, have your student view the **United States Landforms - Watch It**. As they view the video, ask them to locate each landform discussed on a map of the United States.
3. Now, have your student engage with the **Nuevas Cross Country Chase-Land - Play It**.

Demonstrate

1. Then, have your student complete the **Show It** activity by matching each landform to its picture.
2. Next, have your student evaluate their answers using the **Show It AK**.
3. To help reinforce the different landforms, create a memory game to play with your student.
   a. Begin by creating index cards with images of the various landforms discussed in this lesson.
   b. Then, write the names of each landform on separate index cards.
   c. Next, turn all the cards face down to play the memory matching game.

SCIENCE 4 PARENT & TEACHER GUIDE

LESSON 66

Topic Earth's Elements and Landforms

Learning Objectives

The activities in this lesson will help your student meet the following objectives:

- create representations of different landforms
- research a chosen landforms
- build a landforms in a box

Materials

- art supplies
- paint
- paper plate
- paper towels
- salt dough or modeling clay
- shaving cream
- shoe box

Modeling Landforms

Activate

1. Have your student use their hands to demonstrate different landforms that they can recall. They can use motions such as putting their hands upward to make a mountain or laying them flat to demonstrate a plain.
2. Explain to your student that they will learn about different landforms and model them in this lesson.

Engage

1. As your student reads the content of the **Read It**, have them identify the similarities and differences between the different landforms. Encourage them to use a Venn diagram or T-chart to compare and contrast.

Demonstrate

1. Then, have your student create models of landforms by completing the **Show It** activity.
2. After your student has created each landform, have them refer to the **Show It AK** to see if their representations are accurate.
3. To provide an alternative to the **Show It**, your student can use other objects around their learning environment, such as food, to represent different landforms. Encourage your student to find food items with points or peaks, rounded tops, flat surfaces, etc.

• • •

A World of Landforms

Engage

1. After your student reads the **Read It**, have them complete the activity at the end of the reading by sorting the landforms.
2. Next, have your student view the **Landforms of the United States - Watch It**.
3. Talk with your student about some of their favorite landforms that were presented in the video.
4. Then, have your student move on to the **Nueva's Cross Country Chase-Mountains - Play It**, and allow them time to play the game.

Demonstrate

1. Have your student complete the activity in the **Show It**.
2. Next, ask them to review the **Show It AK** to see a sample response.
3. To extend the learning, encourage your student to identify landforms they observe when riding in the car or on their next airplane trip.

• • •

Landform-in-a-Box

Engage

1. Now, have your student read the **Read It** about landforms.

Demonstrate

1. Then, help your student to create their landform based on the information in the **Show It**. Review the expectations of the rubric with your student before, during, and after they complete the activity.
2. To help extend this concept, encourage your student to create various landforms using the clay or dough. Challenge them to see how many different types of landforms they can create.

SCIENCE 4 PARENT & TEACHER GUIDE

LESSON 67

Topic | Earth's Elements and Landforms

Learning Objectives

The activities in this lesson will help your student meet the following objectives:

- label map symbols for basic landforms
- label Earth's layers

Materials

- clear drinking glass
- corn syrup
- physical map
- vegetable oil
- water

Label Map Symbols

Activate

1. Ask your student to draw a symbol that would represent lightning on a weather map.
2. Then, ask them to explain why having symbols for things has relevance when looking at a map.
3. Tell your student they will learn about the landform symbols used on a map.

Engage

1. Have your student begin by reading the **Read It**. Pause them before they reach the map legend.
2. Then, ask your student if they can infer what each symbol on the map represents before they look at the legend for the map.

Demonstrate

1. Next, have your student label the landforms in the **Show It** and check their work with the **Show It AK**.
2. To extend learning, give your student a paper map that shows landforms or search for one online. Have them look at the legend and find all the landforms shown on the map.

• • •

SCIENCE 4 PARENT & TEACHER GUIDE

Earth's Layers

Activate

1. Begin by showing your student a clear drinking glass. Pour in the vegetable oil, then water, then corn syrup and allow the liquids to settle. Ask your student why the liquids separate. Lead them to think of the term *density* and explain that the liquid on the top is less dense than the others.
2. Next, explain that, just like these substances, the Earth has formed into layers based on the density of each layer.

Engage

1. Now, have your student read the content of the **Read It**.
2. A great way to organize information about each layer of Earth is to have your student create a foldable. Use the following instructions and reference the image below to see an example of a completed foldable.
   a. Place one sheet of paper on top of another sheet.
   b. Slide the top sheet up so that you can see a half-inch of space on the bottom sheet.
   c. Then, fold over the top portion of the two sheet together so that they stack above the two bottom flaps. This fold will create four flaps in total.
   d. Next, have your student label the top flap with the term *crust*, Then, have them write the following terms on the tops of the remaining flaps: *mantle*, *outer core* and *inner core*.
   e. Instruct your student to write down some key notes under each flap as they read the text.

3. Next, have your student view the **Watch It** titled **What's Under Your Feet**.

Demonstrate

1. Have your student complete the activity in the **Show It**. When they are finished, allow them to evaluate their answers using the **Show It AK**.
2. To provide an alternative to the **Show It**, ask your student the following questions:
   a. Which of Earth's layers is the only one that humans can study directly? (Answer: crust)
   b. Which of Earth's layers is made of iron and nickel? (Answer: core)
   c. Where on Earth is the crust the thickest? Where would it be the thinnest? (Answer: top of a mountain; bottom of the ocean)
   d. Which of Earth's layers causes the plates move? (Answer: mantle)

LESSON 68

SCIENCE 4 PARENT & TEACHER GUIDE

Topic | Earth's Elements and Landforms

Learning Objectives

The activities in this lesson will help your student meet the following objectives:

- define the term *erosion*
- define the term *weathering*
- define the terms *weathering* and *erosion*

Materials

- dictionary or glossary
- rock

Carried Away

Activate

1. Ask your student if they have ever placed a stick or object in a moving body of water such as a stream. What happened to the object? Your student should answer that the object kept moving with the water.
2. Explain that they will learn how water and wind move objects through the process of erosion.

Engage

1. Have your student read the **Read It** content. After the reading, have a discussion with them about all the ways erosion can occur.
2. Next, move to the **Weathering and Erosion - Watch It** and allow your student time to watch the video.
3. Pause the video at 1:40, and discuss the difference between *weathering* and *erosion*. Ask your student to name examples of each term.
4. Pause the video at 2:42, and ask your student if they have ever seen any type of erosion near their home.

Demonstrate

1. Now, have your student move to the **Show It**. Once they complete the activity, have them compare their definition to the sample provided in the **Show It AK**.
2. To provide an alternative to the **Show It**, take your student on an erosion hunt. Visit a hiking trail or river and help your student to search for the ways erosion is taking place. Have your student take a notebook to sketch some of their observations. Then, ask them to provide an explanation as to the type of erosion they discovered.

• • •

Breaking Down Matter

1. Before beginning the **Read It**, have your student take a piece of paper and create a T-chart. Ask them to label one side *Mechanical Weathering* and the other side *Chemical Weathering*.
2. While your student reads through the content, ask them to place each example of weathering from the text under the correct type of weathering on their T-chart.

1. Next, have your student complete the **Show It** activity, and ask them to compare their response to the sample definition in the **Show It AK**.
2. To provide an extension to this lesson, have your student observe weathering by conducting a simple lab activity.
    a. Have your student take a rock and rub it against some concrete. They will begin to see the rock breaking into smaller pieces or dust.
    b. Explain to them that they have just weathered the rock.

• • •

Define *Weathering* and *Erosion*

1. Have your student read the **Read It**. Ask them if they had ever heard of the Dust Bowl, which is an example of large scale erosion. If they have not, help your student to search the Internet to find more information.
2. Then, allow your student time to engage with the **Ecolibrium-Erosion - Play It**.

1. Next, have your student complete the **Show It** activity and compare their answers to the samples in the **Show It AK**.
2. To provide an alternative to the **Show It**, instruct your student to create a Venn diagram. A blank diagram has been provided below.
    a. Ask your student to label one side of the diagram as *Weathering* and the other side as *Erosion*.
    b. Have them think of similarities between weathering and erosion to place in the middle and differences to place below each term.

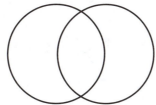

3. Finally, have your student complete the **Reinforce It** to review what they have learned about weathering and erosion.

LESSON 69

SCIENCE 4 PARENT & TEACHER GUIDE

Topic: Earth's Elements and Landforms

Learning Objectives

The activities in this lesson will help your student meet the following objectives:

- compare and contrast the processes of erosion and weathering
- observe the process of water erosion

Materials

- black garden soil
- clay
- cracker
- cup
- plastic tray
- sand
- water

A Destructive Team

Activate

1. Ask your student to tell you about a time they played on a team or worked with someone else to accomplish something. Ask them to think about what they did to reach the end result and what the other person (or people) did.
2. Explain that teamwork also happens in nature. In this lesson, they will learn how weathering and erosion are a team that, by working together, can tear down mountains.

Engage

1. As your student reads the content of the **Read It**, help them act out weathering and erosion. Choose one person to act as weathering by breaking something, such as a cracker, into smaller pieces. The other person will act as erosion by blowing the broken pieces gently across the table.
2. Next, have your student view the **Landform and Destructive Forces - Watch It**.
3. After the video, have your student think about some of the main agents that cause destruction.

Demonstrate

1. Now, have your student work to complete the **Show It** activity.
2. Next, allow your student to compare their answers to the sample provided in the **Show It AK**.
3. To help extend your student's learning, have them research some famous erosion sites such as the Grand Canyon or Carlsbad Caverns in New Mexico.

Soils That Stand Up to Erosion

Engage

1. Have your student work through the **Read It** to learn about the composition of soil.
2. It may be helpful to have your student create a foldable to organize the ingredients of soil.

Demonstrate

1. Then, help your student to gather the materials listed in the **Show It**, and work with them to follow the procedure.
2. Next, have your student use their observations to answer the questions at the end of the **Show It**.
3. Now, direct your student to compare their observations to the samples provided in the **Show It AK**.

SCIENCE 4 PARENT & TEACHER GUIDE

LESSON 70

Topic Earth's Elements and Landforms

Learning Objectives

The activities in this lesson will help your student meet the following objectives:

- compare and contrast the effects water has on different types of soil
- write a multi-paragraph report on either volcanoes or earthquakes
- define the term *rock*

Materials

- art supplies
- cup
- magnifying glass
- plastic tray
- three types of soil (sand, garden soil, and clay)
- water

How Much Erodes?

Activate

1. Ask your student to go outside, dig up some soil, and investigate it under a magnifying glass.
2. Then, have a discussion with them about what they observe.

Engage

1. Have your student begin with the **Read It**, which describes the different components of soil.

Demonstrate

1. As directed in the **Show It**, have your student use the information from the lab they completed in Lesson 69 to write a paragraph stating the results of the experiment. If your student needs to run the lab activity again, allow them to do so.
2. Then, have them compare their paragraph to the sample in the **Show It AK**.

• • •

Earthquakes and Volcanoes

Activate

1. Begin by allowing your student to view a volcanic eruption on the Internet.
2. Then, ask them to think about the different ways a volcano can be destructive, and ask them how they would feel if they lived near one.
3. Next, ask your student to imagine an earthquake if they have never experienced one. Ask them how they think they would feel in an earthquake.
4. Explain to your student that they will learn about volcanoes and earthquakes and what they have in common.

Engage

1. Next, have your student begin to read the content of the **Read It**.
2. When your student is finished reading the section on earthquakes, have them view the **Shake It Up - Watch It**.
3. Review the different scales that are used to measure earthquakes.
4. Then, have your student continue reading the **Read It** through the section about volcanoes.
5. Now, have your student view the **Volcanoes Go Boom - Watch It**.
6. Pause the video at 1:43, and ask your student if they can infer why this area is called the Ring of Fire.
7. Next, allow your student time to engage with the **Disaster Strikes Volcano - Play It** and the **Ecolibrium-Disasters - Play It**.

Demonstrate

1. As a review, have your student view the **Earthquakes - Watch It** and complete the **Reinforce It**.
2. Next, open the **Assess It** and have your student complete the activity. Help them to understand the expectations of the rubric before they begin writing. When they are finished, help them to review their work to make sure they have met the rubric expectations.
3. When they are finished, scan the document or take a photo of it and upload it to the Dropbox. For additional instructions on how to use the Dropbox, click on the paper clip icon in the upper-left corner of the **Assess It**.

What Exactly Is a Rock?

 Activate

1. Have your student go outside and find a few rocks. Then, start a discussion with them about some similarities and differences between the rocks they found.
2. Tell your student they will learn about rocks and their composition.

 Engage

1. Once your student has finished reading the content of the **Read It**, have a discussion with them about what they learned.
2. Then, have them create a list of the characteristics of a rock.
3. Ask your student to think of another example, other than a fruit salad, to explain the difference between a rock and a mineral.

 Demonstrate

1. Next, have your student complete the **Show It** activity and compare their definition to the sample in the **Show It AK**.
2. To provide an alternative to the **Show It**, have your student find a rock in order to create a pet rock. Allow them to decorate their rock to look like an animal, insect, monster, or anything your student can imagine.
3. Then, have them answer the following questions about their pet rock.
   a. How does the rock feel? For example, is the rock is cold, rough, or smooth?
   b. What color is your rock? Is it more than one color?
   c. Explain why it looks the way it does. Has it be weathered?
   d. Describe its habitat.

SCIENCE 4 PARENT & TEACHER GUIDE

LESSON 71

Topic | Earth's Elements and Landforms

Learning Objectives

The activities in this lesson will help your student meet the following objectives:

- compare and contrast the properties of rock samples
- compare and contrast the hardness of mineral samples

Materials

- ceramic tile
- iron nail
- magnifying glass
- paper clip
- penny
- rock and mineral samples
- steel knife or glass plate

Properties of Rocks

Activate

1. Begin by asking your student, "Where do you think the rocks outside come from?"
2. Explain that they will learn more about rocks and their differences in this lesson.

Engage

1. After your student reads the content of the **Read It**, ask them to think about which rock property is the most helpful in identifying a rock. Try to lead them to realize that, on their own, none of the rock properties provide enough information to be useful for identification. However, when all the properties are considered together, rocks can be identified.
2. Now, have your student open the **Rocks are Different - Watch It** and ask them to make note of the username and password provided on the Discovery Education image. Be sure that they click the link for the video and enter the provided username and password to watch.
3. Next, have your student move to the **Ecolibrium-Rocks - Play It**, and allow them time to play the game.

Demonstrate

1. Have your student use the rock samples to complete the chart in the **Show It**. If your student is struggling to find the information about each type of rock, encourage them to use their observation skills and discuss their ideas aloud with you.
2. Then, have your student use the **Show It AK** to view the examples provided. Keep in mind that if they did not use the same rocks as the examples, they will have different answers.
3. To extend learning, encourage your student to conduct research to learn more about the rocks they chose for the **Show It** activity. Have them search for answers to the following questions.
   a. Where did the rock form? (Did it originate in a volcano, water, or another area?)
   b. What type of rock is it? (sedimentary, metamorphic, igneous)
   c. How did the rock form? (erosion, melting, heat and pressure)

Mineral Hardness

 **Activate**

1. Present your student with a penny, a paper clip, and two of the rock samples used in the previous subtopic. Have them try to rub the first rock with the paper clip and then the penny. Then, have them do the same with the other rock.
2. Have your student explain what they observe. They may mention that they noticed the penny was scratched or the rock started to crumble when they used the paper clip.

 **Engage**

1. As your student reads the **Read It**, have them think about why it is important to know the hardness of a mineral.
2. Now, have your student open the **Minerals - Watch It** to view the video.

 **Demonstrate**

1. Have your student obtain the minerals and conduct the hardness test described in the **Show It**.
    a. First, have your student examine each sample with a magnifying glass in order to identify a smooth area to scratch.
    b. After they test the mineral, have them use the magnifying glass again to observe whether or not a scratch occurred on the mineral in the same area.
    c. Have them repeat the test to confirm their results. Once their results are confirmed, have them move on to the next mineral.
2. After they complete all of their testing, have them check their findings in the **Show It AK**.
3. To help extend your students knowledge, instruct them to research the minerals they tested to see how they are used in daily life.

LESSON 72

Topic: Earth's Elements and Landforms

Learning Objectives

The activities in this lesson will help your student meet the following objectives:

- define the term *igneous*
- define the term *metamorphic*
- define the term *sedimentary*

Materials

- art supplies
- dictionary or glossary
- poster board
- rock and mineral samples

Igneous Rocks

Activate

1. Ask your student to try and define the term *ignite*. If they need help, have them try to use it in a sentence. Let them know that it has to do with fire or extreme heat.
2. Then, ask them if they can determine what the word *igneous* means. They may infer that it comes from the word *ignite* and that it also has to do with heat or fire.
3. Explain to your student that they will learn about a type of rock called igneous rocks in this lesson.

Engage

1. As your student reads the **Read It**, discuss some key words such as *magma* and *lava*.
2. Instruct your student to make a T-chart with one side labeled *Intrusive Igneous Rocks* and the other side labeled *Extrusive Igneous Rocks*. Ask them to list the names of the rocks from the reading under the correct type of igneous rock on their T-chart.
3. Have a brief discussion about the similarities and differences between intrusive igneous rocks and extrusive igneous rocks.
4. Now, have your student open the **Igneous Rock - Watch It** and ask them to make note of the username and password provided on the Discovery Education image. Be sure that they click the link for the video and enter the provided username and password to watch.

Demonstrate

1. Have your student complete the activity in the **Show It**. Allow them time to compare their definition with the sample in the **Show It AK**.
2. To extend learning, have your student research intrusive and extrusive igneous rocks to learn more.

• • •

Metamorphic Rocks

Engage

1. Have your student read the content of the **Read It**. Pause them after the introduction and ask if they can think of anything else that goes through metamorphosis like the butterfly.
2. Then, have your student finish the reading to learn about metamorphic rocks.
3. Now, direct your student to the **Metamorphic Rock - Watch It** to view the video.

Demonstrate

1. Next, have your student define the term *metamorphic rock* in the **Show It**. They can compare their response to the sample in the **Show It AK**.
2. To provide an alternative to the **Show It**, have your student create a poster to represent the metamorphic rocks: gneiss, slate, marble, and quartzite.
   a. Along the left side of a poster board, have your student draw or print and glue a picture of the parent rock that has been put under extreme heat and pressure to be changed.
   b. Then, have your student draw an arrow from each parent rock and either draw or print and glue a picture of the metamorphic rock that formed from each parent rock.
   c. Finally, direct your student to place an arrow from each metamorphic rock and have them describe whether it is foliated or nonfoliated. For example: granite → gneiss → foliated

• • •

Sedimentary Rocks

Engage

1. As your student reads through the **Read It**, have them create a foldable with three flaps as shown in the image below.
   a. On the top of each flap, direct them to write the name of each type of sedimentary rock (clastic, chemical, organic).
   b. Under the flap, have them write a description of each rock type.

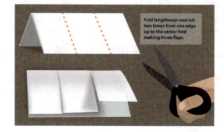

Demonstrate

1. Open the **Assess It** and have your student complete the activity. When they are finished, scan the document or take a photo of it and upload it to the Dropbox. For additional instructions on how to use the Dropbox, click on the paper clip icon in the upper-left corner of the **Assess It**.

SCIENCE 4 PARENT & TEACHER GUIDE

LESSON 73

Topic | Earth's Elements and Landforms

Learning Objectives

The activities in this lesson will help your student meet the following objectives:

- compare and contrast properties of rock samples
- define the term *mineral*

Materials

- dictionary or glossary
- rock and mineral samples
- "Compare and Contrast Rocks" activity page

Compare and Contrast Rocks

Activate

1. Ask your student to tell you what they know about the three types of rocks.
2. Then, have your student view the **Three Types of Rocks - Watch It**.

Engage

1. While your student is reading the content of the **Read It**, help them to complete the "Compare and Contrast Rocks" activity page.
2. Next, have your student view the **Amazing Rock Cycle - Watch It**.
3. Ask your student the following questions after they watch the video.
   a. Which type of rock begins with the process of weathering and erosion? (Answer: sedimentary)
   b. Is there a specific pattern to the rock cycle? (Answer: No. Any type of rock can be turned into another type of rock by the processes that forms them.)
4. Then, have your student play the game in the **Antigua's New Exhibit-Minerals - Play It**.

Demonstrate

1. Next, move to the **Show It**. Help your student gather the rocks listed in the content. Then, instruct them to follow the directions in the **Show It** and complete the Venn diagram.
2. Afterward, have them compare their answers to the example provided in the **Show It AK**.
3. To extend learning, have your student demonstrate the rock cycle by acting it out. They can begin with any type of rock, but have them show the formation of each type as they go through the cycle.

• • •

What is a Mineral?

 Activate

1. Begin by showing your student an image of a lab-generated emerald and a natural emerald. Search the Internet using the phrases *lab-generated emerald* and *emerald mineral*. Ask them if they can tell the difference.
2. Explain to your student that one is a real mineral while the other is not.
3. Tell them they will learn about the characteristics that define a mineral.

 Engage

1. Next, have your student read the **Read It**. When they are finished, have a discussion with them about how a jeweler would be able to tell a real emerald from a lab-generated emerald.
2. Then, have them view the **Mineral Mystery - Watch It**.
3. Ask your student how the tests described in the video would help them identify a mineral if they came across two minerals of the same color. They may respond by saying that one mineral might have a different streak or hardness compared to the other.

 Demonstrate

1. Now, direct your student to complete the **Show It** and compare their definition to the example in the **Show It AK**.
2. Alternatively, gather four minerals that are similar in color. Ask your student what they could to identify each mineral.

SCIENCE 4 PARENT & TEACHER GUIDE

LESSON 74

| Topic | Earth's Elements and Landforms |

Learning Objectives

The activities in this lesson will help your student meet the following objectives:

- compare and contrast properties of mineral samples
- explain the difference between rocks and minerals
- identify common uses of rocks and minerals

Materials

- dry erase board and marker
- index cards
- rock and mineral samples
- "Properties of Minerals" activity page

Properties of Minerals

Activate

1. Ask your student to define the term *mineral* and discuss some of the properties that help identify minerals.
2. Next, open the **Watch It** titled **The Reveal Show - Watch It**, and allow your student time to watch the video.

Engage

1. Then, direct your student to the **Read It**. As they read the text, discuss the different mineral properties with them.

Demonstrate

1. Then, have your student complete the "Properties of Minerals" activity page in the **Show It**.
2. Once they complete the activity, your student can compare their chart to the sample observations in the **Show It AK**.

● ● ●

Rock and Mineral Differences

Activate

1. Provide your student with a rock and mineral sample. Ask them to identify any differences they see between the two samples.
2. Then, explain that they will learn the difference between a rock and mineral in this lesson.

Engage

1. Allow your student to read through the **Read It** content. Give them the opportunity to discuss the differences between rocks and minerals with you as they read.
2. To reinforce learning, have your student use the information from the Venn diagram in the **Read It**. Instruct them to write each characteristic on an index card. Mix the cards and have your student categorize the characteristics as those belonging to a rock, a mineral, or both.

Demonstrate

1. Have your student use the word bank in the **Show It** to complete the paragraph activity.
2. Your student can use the **Show It AK** to ensure their response includes the appropriate details about the differences between rocks and minerals.
3. Alternatively, have your student present a rock and a mineral to a family member and explain the difference between them.

Uses of Rocks and Minerals

Activate

1. Ask your student to think about their morning routine.
2. Then, have them create a list on the dry erase board to show all the items they use during their routine. For example, their list may include an alarm, toothpaste, cereal, etc.
3. Next, ask your student to think of some minerals they use while completing their morning routine.
4. If your student struggles to complete the previous step, explain that they will learn about where people use minerals in daily life.

Engage

1. Begin by having your student read the **Read It**. As they read about the everyday uses of minerals, ask them to share the ways in which they use each mineral personally.
2. Now, have your student view the **You're Surrounded - Watch It**.
3. Pause the video at 1:30, and ask your student to brainstorm ideas about the materials and minerals that were used to build their home.

Demonstrate

1. Open the **Assess It** and have your student complete the activity. When they are finished, scan the document or take a photo of it and upload it to the Dropbox. For additional instructions on how to use the Dropbox, click on the paper clip icon in the upper-left corner of the **Assess It**.
2. To extend your student's learning, have them choose items around their learning environment. Encourage them to research the minerals that are used to make the items. For example, the glass window is made from silica, which comes from the mineral quartz.

SCIENCE 4 PARENT & TEACHER GUIDE

LESSON 75

Topic: Earth's Elements and Landforms

Learning Objectives

The activities in this lesson will help your student meet the following objectives:

- define the term *fossil*
- label fossils as animal, plant, or sea life

Materials

- dictionary or glossary
- index cards
- modeling clay

Define *Fossil*

Activate

1. Ask your student, "How do scientists know that dinosaurs once lived on Earth if dinosaurs have never been seen?" Help to lead your student to think about the many types of dinosaur fossils that have been discovered.
2. Explain that they will learn about fossils in this lesson.

###

1. While reading the **Read It** content, your student will learn about various types of fossils. As they read, have them use index cards to create flashcards by writing the type of fossil on one side and the description on the other side.
2. Next, have your student view the **Fossils Are Amazing - Watch It**.
3. Pause the video at 1:38, and ask your student to think back to what they learned about sedimentary rocks. Ask them why they think fossils only form in this type of rock.
4. If time permits, encourage your student to follow the procedure in the video to cast their own fossils.
5. Then, have your student engage with the **Ecolibrium-Fossils - Play It**.

Demonstrate

1. Now, have your student move to the **Show It** and complete the activity. Be sure that they compare their definition to the sample in the **Show It AK**.
2. To extend learning, encourage your student to research fossils online. Discuss the results of their research.

• • •

Kinds of Fossils

Engage

1. Have your student look at the different fossil images as they read through the **Read It**.
2. Next, allow your student time to play the game in the **Antigua's New Exhibit-Pterodactyl - Play It**.

Demonstrate

1. Now, have your student work through the **Show It** activity and identify the fossils.
2. Then, have them compare their answers to the **Show It AK**.
3. To extend learning, visit the nearest natural history museum with your student and view the fossils from around the world.

SCIENCE 4 PARENT & TEACHER GUIDE

LESSON 76

Topic: Earth's Elements and Landforms

Learning Objectives

The activities in this lesson will help your student meet the following objectives:

- describe the nature of the environment at the time a fossil was created
- describe how rock layers depict changes in a landscape over time
- define the term *soil*

Materials

- construction paper
- dictionary or glossary
- three plastic cups
- three types of soil
- three pinto beans
- water

When Fossils Were Created

Activate

1. Ask your student to think about five big events that have happened in their life. Examples may include losing their first tooth, their first day of school, etc. Have them place the events in order from the first that occurred to the last.
2. Explain to your student that Earth's history is also broken into big events using the geologic scale, which they will learn about in this lesson.

Engage

1. As your student begins to read the **Read It**, have them analyze the two different time scales. Then have a discussion about what they notice and what they wonder about each scale.
2. Next, open the **Ancient Life - Watch It** and allow your student time to watch the video. Afterward, discuss the importance of studying fossils.

Demonstrate

1. Now, have your student move on to the **Show It**. If they struggle to complete the activity, help them to search the Internet for more information about the trilobite.
2. Then, have your student compare their paragraph to the sample provided in the **Show It AK**.

Rock Layers

## Activate

1. Take some papers or books and stack them on top of each other. Then, ask your student which paper or book was placed on the table first. They should identify the book or paper on the bottom of the pile. Encourage them to discuss their thoughts out loud.
2. Explain that, in nature, the same processes occurs. The oldest layer of rock is located at the bottom, while newer layers are stack on top.

## Engage

1. While your student reads the **Read It**, discuss with them how layers of rock can help scientists to discover the events that occurred in a certain area. Help them to understand that each new layer of rock indicates a new environment.
2. Next, have your student study the image of the rock layers at the end of the text. Ask them to try to place names of the rock layers in order, from oldest to youngest.

Demonstrate

1. Have your student complete the paragraph in the **Show It**. Be sure that they review the rubric before they begin writing so that they understand the expectations.
2. When your student is finished writing, have them compare their work to the expectations outlined in the rubric. They may also compare their paragraph to the sample in the **Show It AK**.
3. To help reinforce this concept, have your student create five rock layers using construction paper.
   a. Instruct your student to cut five different colors of construction paper into 3-inch strips.
   b. Then, have your student lay the strips on top of each other and staple the ends.
   c. They can bend the paper in the middle to see the various layers, from the oldest layer on the bottom to the youngest layer at the top.

● ● ●

Define Soil

1. Ask your student to identify some ways in which soil is important to their life. Try to lead them to think about how it provides people with food, which humans could not live without.

1. Ask your students to keep the importance of soil in mind as they read the content of the **Read It**.
2. Then, have your student move to the **What's Under Your Toes - Watch It**.
3. Now, allow them time to engage with the **Ecolibrium-Soil - Play It**.

1. Next, ask your student to move to the **Show It** and define the term soil. They can compare their definition to the sample in the **Show It AK** to check for accuracy.
2. To extend learning, have your student conduct the following experiment.
    a. First, gather three plastic cups. Make sure the cups are all the same type.
    b. Then, place three different types of soil in each cup. Soil types may include potting, topsoil, and rocky soil.
    c. Next, have them place a pinto bean about an 1 to 2 inches into the soil. Then, ask them to water the beans with about ¼ cup of water.
    d. Place all three cups on a windowsill and have your student observe them throughout the next week. Ask them to predict in which soil the bean plant will grow the fastest.
    e. Finally, have them create a presentation to explain how the components of soil affected the growth of the plant.

SCIENCE 4 PARENT & TEACHER GUIDE

LESSON 77

Topic — Earth's Elements and Landforms

Learning Objectives

The activities in this lesson will help your student meet the following objectives:

- identify the three layers of soil (topsoil, subsoil, bedrock)
- describe the similarities and differences between the three layers of soil

Materials

- colored pencils
- scissors

Label Three Layers of Soil

Activate

1. Take your student outside and allow them to dig a small hole in an area that can be disturbed. They should only dig about a six inches into the ground.
2. As they dig, ask them what they observe about the soil.
3. Explain that they will learn about the different layers of soil in this lesson.

Engage

1. While your student is reading through the **Read It**, ask them if they recall seeing layers of soil as they dug into the ground.
2. Now, have your student open and view the **What is Soil - Watch It**. Ask them to make note of the username and password provided on the Discovery Education image. Be sure that they click the link for the video and enter the provided username and password to watch.

Demonstrate

1. Have your student complete the activity in the **Show It** and then evaluate their answers using the **Show It AK**.
2. To provide an alternative to the **Show It**, have your student create a foldable to help them organize the information about the layers of soil. They can use the image below as a guide.
    a. On the top of the first flap, instruct them to write the word *topsoil* and draw a picture of it.
    b. On each of the remaining flaps, ask them to write the words *subsoil* and *bedrock* and draw images of each soil layer.
    c. Under each flap, instruct your student write at least three to four facts about each soil layer.

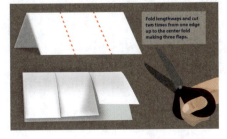

Copyright 2018 © Lincoln Learning Solutions. All rights reserved.

Compare Layers of Soil

 ## Engage

1. Have your student read the content of the **Read It**. Once they finish, ask them, "Why do you think the layers of soil are named in this way?" Help to guide your student to look at the prefix for the first two layers of soil to determine their answer.

 ## Demonstrate

1. Next, have your student complete the activity in the **Show It**. They may need to reference the **Read It** to gather the information they need to write their paragraph.
2. Then, encourage them to compare their paragraph to the sample in the **Show It AK**.
3. To provide an alternative to the **Show It**, have your student answer the following questions.
    a. Which soil layer is the youngest? Why? (Answer: Topsoil is the youngest soil layer because the topsoil is made of weathered parts of the bedrock layer.)
    b. Which soil layer contains humus? (Answer: topsoil)
    c. Which soil layer contains minerals such as iron oxide that make it appear reddish orange? (Answer: subsoil)
    d. In which soil layer do plant roots grow? (Answer: topsoil)

LESSON 78

SCIENCE 4 PARENT & TEACHER GUIDE

Topic: Earth's Elements and Landforms

Learning Objectives

The activities in this lesson will help your student meet the following objectives:

- identify the three main types of soil: clay, sand, and loam
- explain the uses of one type of soil (clay, sand, or loam)
- define the term *evaporation*

Materials

- dictionary or glossary
- marker
- plastic cup
- water

Identify Types of Soil

Activate

1. Ask your student to tell you what they know about soil.
2. Then, ask them if they know how many types of soil there are.
3. Explain that they will learn about three types of soil in this lesson.

Engage

1. Have your student read about clay, sand, and loam in the **Read It**.
2. Then, ask them to think about the type of soil outside of their learning environment.

Demonstrate

1. Now, have your student complete the **Show It** activity and then evaluate their answers in the **Show It AK**.
2. To provide an alternative to the **Show It**, have your student go outside and collect a soil sample. Have them spread it out on a piece of paper and examine the components. Encourage them to look closely and see if they can identify more than one type of soil.
3. To extend your student's learning, arrange for them to speak with a local farmer about the importance of soil and how the type of soil dictates where they plant certain crops.

Explain Uses of Soil

Engage

1. Begin by having your student read the Introduction in the **Read It**. Ask them to think about other differences between soil in a rain forest and soil in the desert.
2. Then, have them finish working through the content of the **Read It**.

Demonstrate

1. Open the **Assess It** and have your student complete the activity. Be sure that they review the expectations of the rubric before and after writing.
2. When they are finished, scan the document or take a photo of it and upload it to the Dropbox. For additional instructions on how to use the Dropbox, click on the paper clip icon in the upper-left corner of the **Assess It**.

• • •

Define *Evaporation*

Activate

1. Ask your student to recall the last time they saw a puddle after a rainstorm. Then, ask them, "What do you think happens to the water after the storm?"
2. Tell them they will learn about the process of evaporation.

Engage

1. Next, have your student read the **Read It**. Discuss other places where water evaporates, such as oceans, lakes, etc.

Demonstrate

1. Have your student complete the **Show It** activity and then compare their definition to the sample in the **Show It AK**.
2. To provide an alternative to the **Show It**, have your student observe evaporation.
   a. Have them set a plastic cup filled with water near a window.
   b. Tell them to use a marker and draw a line on the cup to show the water level.
   c. Then, be sure they observe and mark the water line each day.
   d. Finally, ask them to explain the process of evaporation.

SCIENCE 4 PARENT & TEACHER GUIDE

LESSON 79

Topic Earth's Elements and Landforms

Learning Objectives

The activities in this lesson will help your student meet the following objectives:
- define the term *condensation*
- define *precipitation*

Materials
- art supplies
- cup
- dictionary or glossary
- plastic wrap
- water

Define *Condensation*

Activate

1. Ask your student to imagine a boiling pot of water on the stove. Ask them, "What happens to the water?"
2. Next, ask them to think about what would happen to the water if they put a lid on the top of the pot.
3. Explain that they will learn about the term *condensation* and how it relates to evaporation.

Engage

1. After your student reads the Introduction in the **Read It**, have them pause to recall a time when they experienced dew on the grass. Ask them to suggest where this water came from if it never rained.
2. Then, allow them to continue to read the remainder of the **Read It** content.
3. Next, have your student open and view the **Evaporation and Condensation - Watch It**.
4. Pause the video at 3:35, and ask your student to suggest what will happen to the water in the glass with the plastic on the top.
5. Then, allow your student read more about the water cycle in the **Practice It**.

Demonstrate

1. Next, have your student complete the **Show It** activity. When they are finished, they can compare their definition to the sample provided in the **Show It AK**.
2. To provide an alternative to the **Show It**, have your student discuss what happens when a bathroom mirror gets foggy after someone takes a shower.

• • •

Define *Precipitation*

Activate

1. Ask your student to give you some examples of the forms of precipitation. They may mention rain, snow, etc.
2. Then, ask them where this precipitation comes from. How do they know when it is going to rain?

Engage

1. Begin by having your student open and view the **Rain, Please Go Away - Watch It**.
2. Ask them to list the different forms of precipitation they learn about. (Answers: rain, snow, sleet, hail)
3. Next, have them move to the **Read It**. Once they finish the reading, ask your student to explain to you why they are drinking the same water that dinosaurs drank.

Demonstrate

1. Next, have your student define *precipitation* in the **Show It** and compare their definition to the example in the **Show It AK**.
2. To provide an alternative to the **Show It**, have your student fold a piece of paper into four squares.
   a. Ask them to label each square with a different type of precipitation.
   b. Then, have them draw or use art supplies, such as cotton balls, paint, or glitter, to represent the types of precipitation.

LESSON 80

Topic: Earth's Elements and Landforms

Learning Objectives

The activities in this lesson will help your student meet the following objectives:

- define the term *collection*
- define the terms *ocean, sea, lake, river, pond, swamp, glacier,* and *groundwater*
- label the four parts of the water cycle

Materials

- bucket
- colored pencils
- dictionary or glossary
- index cards
- map of the world
- napkin
- plate
- poster board

Define Collection

Activate

1. Show your student three items: a bucket, a plate, and a napkin. Ask them which item is the best for storing water. They will most likely say the bucket.
2. Explain to your student that Earth also has places for storing water. Ask them where they think Earth's water buckets are located.
3. Then, tell your student that they will learn where water can be stored on Earth before it evaporates back into the atmosphere.

Engage

1. Allow your student to read the Introduction in the **Read It** and then ask them to pause. Have a discussion with them about some of the major impacts a flood or drought would cause to the area in which they live.
2. Then, have your student continue reading through the remainder of the **Read It**.

Demonstrate

1. As your student is writing their definition in the **Show It**, encourage them to use a real-life example in their second sentence.
2. Then, have your student compare their definition to the sample in the **Show It AK**.
3. To provide an alternative to the **Show It**, have your student research the area in which they live in order to identify some places water is collected. These areas may include lakes, ponds, streams, etc.

Define *Water Resources*

Activate

1. Provide your student with a map of the world, and have them point out some places where water is collected.
2. Tell them they will learn about the resources from which water originates.

Engage

1. Have your student read through the content of the **Read It**.
2. Then, ask your student to identify the bodies of water discussed in the content that are sources of freshwater.
3. Next, allow your student time to engage with the **Nuevo's Cross Country Chase-Water - Play It**.

Demonstrate

1. Now, have your student define each water resource in the **Show It** and then compare their definitions to the examples in the **Show It AK**.
2. To provide an extension to this lesson, discuss the importance of water conservation with your student.
   a. Ask them to create a poster that explains why water conservation is important. Have them list several ways to conserve water on their poster.
   b. Then, ask them to hang the poster in their home so that they can educate other family members about water conservation and encourage them to help conserve water.

• • •

Label the Water Cycle

Engage

1. While your student reads the content of the **Read It**, have them draw or act out the water cycle.
2. To help your student practice the concepts in the **Read It**, follow these steps.
   a. Place the terms in the chart below the water cycle image on index cards.
   b. Create additional index cards for each heading.
   c. Lay out the heading cards on a table, and have your student place the remaining cards under the correct heading.
3. Then, allow your student time to play the game in the **Ecolibrium Water Cycle - Play It**.
4. Your student can review using the **Practice It**.

Demonstrate

1. Next, have your student complete the **Show It**.
2. Then, have them check their answers using the **Show It AK**.
3. To extend learning, give your student a resealable bag and ask them to fill it 1/4 of the way with water. Seal the bag and tape it to the window or door where they can visibly watch a miniature water cycle.

LESSON 81

| Topic | Earth's Elements and Landforms |

Learning Objectives

The activities in this lesson will help your student meet the following objectives:

- explain the water cycle
- identify the various uses of water

Materials

- none required

Explain the Water Cycle

Activate

1. Have your student recall the steps of the water cycle. Ask them to imagine what might happen if water never condensed into clouds, never came back to the earth as precipitation, or never evaporated from the ground.

Engage

1. Have your student read through the content of the **Read It**.
2. After the reading, help your student to search the Internet for a song about the water cycle and have your student sing along.
3. Next, have your student view the video in the **The Water Cycle - Watch It**.

Demonstrate

1. Open the **Assess It** and have your student complete the activity. Be sure that they review the expectations of the rubric before and after writing.
2. When they are finished, scan the document or take a photo of it and upload it to the Dropbox. For additional instructions on how to use the Dropbox, click on the paper clip icon in the upper-left corner of the **Assess It**.

• • •

Uses of Water

**Activate**

1. Have your student create a list of all the ways they use water throughout the day. Try to help them think of less obvious ways they use water, such as brushing their teeth and washing clothes.

**Engage**

1. As your student reads the **Read It**, ask them to think about how much water humans use indirectly. Examples include the following:
   - Factories use water to make the products people use each day.
   - Farmers use water to nourish the crops that people eat.
2. Now, have your student view the **Water is Everywhere - Watch It**.

**Demonstrate**

1. Next, have your student complete the **Show It** activity by labeling the uses of water.
2. Then, allow your student to check their responses with the **Show It AK**.
3. To extend learning, contact a local water treatment facility and arrange for your student to visit. Prior to the visit, have your student think of three to five questions to ask an employee. For example, "How is the water cleaned?"

LESSON 82

Topic: Earth's Elements and Landforms

Learning Objectives

The activities in this lesson will help your student meet the following objectives:

- define the term *atmosphere*
- define the term *respiration*
- define the term *photosynthesis*

Materials

- colored pencils
- dictionary or glossary
- poster board

Define *Atmosphere*

Activate

1. Ask your student if they have ever heard someone say, "I am under so much pressure!"
2. Tell them that while this saying is a figure of speech, all people are truly under a lot of pressure from the atmosphere above the earth.
3. Explain that they will learn about Earth's atmosphere and its different parts.

Engage

1. Direct your student to read through the content of the **Read It**.
2. Ask them to list each layer of Earth's atmosphere on a piece of paper.
3. Then, discuss any questions they may have about the content.

Demonstrate

1. Next, have your student move to the **Show It** and follow the instructions to complete the activity.
2. Assist your student to check their definition with the **Show It AK**.
3. To provide an alternative to the **Show It**, instruct them to make a flip book with five sections like the one shown below. Have them complete the following steps:

   a. Have them fold a piece of paper in half lengthwise, and then use a pencil to divide one side into five sections.
   b. Instruct them to cut along the lines to the fold, which should create five flaps that open up like doors.
   c. Next, ask your student to write the name of each layer of the atmosphere on the front of the flap and draw a few things that are unique to that layer.
   d. Inside each flap, have the student write two facts they learned about the layer of atmosphere.

Define *Respiration*

1. Ask your student to take a deep breath in and then out. Then, ask them to tell you what they were breathing in when they took the deep breath.
2. Tell them they will learn about respiration.

1. Direct your student to the **Read It** and have them read the content.
2. After the reading, ask your student to recall a time when they had to hold their breath under water. Ask them, "Why did you need to come back up for air? Why don't fish need to come up for air?"

1. Now, direct your student to complete the **Show It** activity. Afterward, they can compare their response to the sample in the **Show It AK**.
2. To extend your student's learning, have them research the seven main parts of the respiratory system in humans. Then, have them explain to you why each part is important.

• • •

Define *Photosynthesis*

1. Ask your student what it means when someone says that, by planting a tree, they are providing oxygen for people.
2. Explain that, in this lesson, they have learned about the oxygen they breathe in. Now they will learn about the carbon dioxide they breath out and what happens to it.

1. While your student reads through the **Read It**, ask them to identify whether humans are producers are consumers.
2. Then, have your student view the **Watch It** titled **The Process of Photosynthesis**.

1. Next, instruct your student to complete the activity in the **Show It**. Then, have them compare their definition to the example in the **Show It AK**.
2. To extend learning, have your student use colored pencils to create a poster that explains photosynthesis and present it to a family member.

LESSON 83

Topic: Earth's Elements and Landforms

Learning Objectives

The activities in this lesson will help your student meet the following objectives:

- explain the relationship between plants and humans
- categorize Earth's water resources as either freshwater or saltwater

Materials

- five 8 oz. cups
- ice cube tray
- salt
- water

Plant and Human Relationship

Activate

1. Ask your student why a plant would need humans and animals to help it survive.
2. Next, explain to your student that they will learn about the human and plant relationship.

Engage

1. After your student finishes reading the **Read It**, ask them to suggest why the destruction of the rain forests is having an impact on the amount of oxygen and carbon dioxide in the atmosphere.

Demonstrate

1. Now, have your student move to the **Show It** and complete the paragraph activity.
2. Then, help your student compare their response to the sample provided in the **Show It AK**.
3. To provide an alternative to the **Show It**, work with your student to plant a tree or a plant. Then, have your student discuss with you how this activity will help provide more oxygen in the atmosphere.

Earth's Water Resources

Engage

1. While your student reads through the **Read It**, discuss some of the differences between saltwater and freshwater bodies of water.

Demonstrate

1. Assist your student to create a three-columned chart for the **Show It** activity. Then, have them categorize each water resource.
2. Then, direct them to the **Show It AK** to evaluate their answers.
3. To extend your student's learning, have them create their own experiment to compare freshwater and saltwater. Consider having them choose either the freezing or floating activity below.
    a. For freezing, have your student complete a process similar to the following:
        i. Using an ice cube tray, have them place salt in five ice cube slots, using a pinch of salt for the first one, then ⅛ teaspoon, then ¼ teaspoon, then ½ teaspoon, and 1 teaspoon.
        ii. Add water to fill the five slots of the ice cube tray where salt has been added. (Note: The salt may not dissolve in the slot with the full teaspoon of salt, but encourage your student to try anyway.)
        iii. Now, prompt them to place the tray in the freezer and observe in which slot the water freezes fastest.
        iv. Then, discuss how the amount of salt makes a difference regarding freezing.
    b. For floating, have your student use the same amounts of salt listed for the freezing activity, but place the salt in 8 ounce cups of water.
        i. Then, have them drop plain ice cubes into the saltwater solutions.
        ii. They should notice that the ice cube will rest higher to the top of the water in the saltier solutions.

SCIENCE 4 PARENT & TEACHER GUIDE

LESSON 84

| Topic | Earth's Elements and Landforms |

Learning Objectives

The activities in this lesson will help your student meet the following objectives:

- illustrate one of Earth's water resources
- match the terms *cloud, temperature, humidity, precipitation, wind* and *pressure* to corresponding pictures
- illustrate types of precipitation

Materials

- art supplies
- drawing paper or poster board

Label Water Resources

Activate

1. Help your student to find a map of their hometown before starting the lesson.
2. Ask them to identify some of the main bodies of water near their home such as rivers, lakes, and ponds.
3. Help your student to brainstorm the ways in which these bodies of water are used within their community. Examples may include fishing and boating.

Engage

1. Have your student read through the **Read It** content. When they are finished, begin a discussion with them about the importance of the bodies of water mentioned in the text.
2. Next, have your student view the video in the **Aqua on the Earth - Watch It**.
3. Pause the video at 1:42 and ask them to try to answer the question posed. How did the Great Lakes form?
4. Then, allow your student to finish watching the video.
5. Next, have your student view the **Wet + Land = Wetland - Watch It**.

Demonstrate

1. Now, instruct your student to complete the **Show It** activity. You may need to help them think of a body of water they would like to use for their poster.
2. Have your student compare their work to the sample in the **Show It AK**.
3. To help expand your student's knowledge on bodies of water, take a trip to the nearest body of water and have them observe and sketch what they see. Then, have a discussion with your student about the ways in which this body of water is important to the local community.
4. For extra practice, have your student complete the crossword puzzle in the **Extend It**.

Define Weather Element Terms

 **Activate**

1. Ask your student if they have heard anyone mention the term *humidity*. Ask them how they feel when the weather is very humid.
2. Explain that they will learn about the terms used when discussing weather.

 **Engage**

1. As your student reads the **Read It**, ask them if they recall hearing any of the terms used to discuss weather. Where have they heard these terms before?
2. Now, open the **Weather Tools 2 - Watch It** and allow your student time to view the video.

 **Demonstrate**

1. Instruct your student to complete the **Show It** activity by matching the terms to each picture.
2. Then, have your student evaluate their answers using the **Show It AK** and make any necessary corrections.
3. To provide an alternative to the **Show It**, have your student watch a weather forecast. Then, instruct them to write down some of the weather terms they heard the meteorologist say. Discuss any new terms with your student.

• • •

Illustrate Precipitation

 **Engage**

1. Begin by having your student read the **Read It**. Discuss the types of precipitation they have observed. Have they seen all the forms of precipitation mentioned in the text?
2. Now, have your student view the different types of precipitation in the **Types of Precipitation - Watch It**.
3. Next, have your student move to the **Nueva's Cross Country Chase-Weather and Water Cycle - Play It**.
4. Then, allow your student time to engage with the **Disaster Strikes - Play It**.

 **Demonstrate**

1. Now, have your student create the graphic organizer in the **Show It**. Allow them to be creative.
2. Next, have your student compare their sentences about weather elements to the samples in the **Show It AK**.
3. To extend your student's learning, have them keep a log of the type of precipitation and cloud cover that occurs over the course of a week.

SCIENCE 4 PARENT & TEACHER GUIDE

LESSON 85

Topic | Earth's Elements and Landforms

Learning Objectives

The activities in this lesson will help your student meet the following objectives:

- distinguish among other weather-related vocabulary terms
- identify weather elements necessary for the development of a storm

Materials

- none required

Weather Vocabulary

Activate

1. Have your student discuss a few terms they hope they never hear when it comes to weather where they live. Terms may include *hurricane*, *flood*, or *tornado*.
2. Ask your student to recall whether or not they have experienced damage to their home due to a weather-related incident.
3. Explain that they will learn about weather-related terms.

Engage

1. Begin by having your student read the Introduction in the **Read It**. Then, discuss more recent weather-related events that were severe and caused damage.
2. Now, have them view the **Floods - Watch It**.
3. When your student is finished watching the video, ask them to conduct research to learn more about the Johnstown flood.
4. Then, ask them to explain the events that can cause flooding.

Demonstrate

1. Next, instruct your student to complete the **Show It** by matching the term with the definition.
2. Then, have your student evaluate their answers using the **Show It AK**.

• • •

Weather Elements on a Map

Engage

1. As your student reads the **Read It**, discuss the terms presented in the text and when a meteorologist may use them in their forecast.
2. Then, ask your student if they have ever used the weather forecast to help them decide what to do on a particular day.
3. Now, have your student move to the **Weather - Watch It** and view the video.
4. Pause the video at 3:32 and ask your student which direction the weather appears to be moving across the United States.
5. Then, allow your student time to play the game in the **Disaster Strikes-Weather Terms - Play It**.

Demonstrate

1. Next, have your student view the weather map in the **Show It** and complete the activity. Then, allow them to check their answers with the **Show It AK**.
2. To extend your student's learning, have them pretend to be a meteorologist and present a weather forecast to their family. In their forecast, be sure they use key terms, such as *fronts* and *pressure*.

LESSON 86

Topic: Earth's Elements and Landforms

Learning Objectives

The activities in this lesson will help your student meet the following objectives:

- describe the weather elements of a type of storm
- define weather measurement tools

Materials

- art supplies
- drawing paper or poster board

Research Stormy Weather

Activate

1. Ask your student if they remember a time when they experienced a bad thunderstorm.
2. Then, ask them to describe what they heard, what they saw, and how they felt.
3. Tell them they will learn about thunderstorms.

Engage

1. After your student reads the content of the **Read It**, have them summarize the way in which lightning and thunder form during in a thunderstorm.
2. Next, have your student view the **Nature's Destructive Force - Watch It**.
3. After the video, have a discussion with your student about some of the destructive weather presented in the video.

Demonstrate

1. Next, have your student complete the activity in the **Show It**. Help them to search the Internet to find and organize information about their chosen type of severe storm before they begin their pamphlet.
2. Then, have your student compare their work to the example in the **Show It AK**.
3. To extend learning, the next time there is a thunderstorm, have your student count how many seconds there are between the sight of the lightning and the sound of the thunder. Explain to them that the number of seconds between the two is proportional to the number of miles the storm is from their location.

• • •

Weather Measurement Tools

Engage

1. As your student reads through the **Read It**, have them take notes about each type of weather tool.
2. Ask them which tools they have used.
3. Now, have your student move to the **Weather Tools - Watch It** and view the video.
4. Have your student follow the steps in the video to create an anemometer.

Demonstrate

1. Open the **Assess It** and have your student complete the activity. When they are finished, scan the document or take a photo of it and upload it to the Dropbox. For additional instructions on how to use the Dropbox, click on the paper clip icon in the upper-left corner of the **Assess It**.

LESSON 87

Topic: Earth's Elements and Landforms

Learning Objectives

The activities in this lesson will help your student meet the following objectives:

- explain the purpose of an anemometer
- build an anemometer

Materials

- five Styrofoam® cups
- pencil with eraser
- tape
- two straws
- colored marker
- pin

Purpose of an Anemometer

Activate

1. Ask your student to recall a time when they experienced a windy day. Have them describe what they felt. Ask them, "How did you know the wind was really fast?"
2. Tell your student they will learn about an instrument that measures the speed of the wind.

Engage

1. Have your student begin by reading the **Read It** content. Afterward, instruct them to compare and contrast a weather vane and an anemometer.
2. Now, have your student open the **Wind - Watch It** and ask them to make note of the username and password provided on the Discovery Education image. Be sure that they click the link for the video and enter the provided username and password to watch.

Demonstrate

1. Next, have your student complete the activity in the **Show It**. When they are finished, they can compare their paragraph to the sample in the **Show It AK**.
2. To provide an alternative to the **Show It**, have your student explain the benefits of an anemometer to you.
3. Then, have your student complete the **Reinforce It**.

• • •

Build an Anemometer

Engage

1. As your student reads the **Read It**, have a discussion with them about the ways in which anemometers can predict future weather.

Demonstrate

1. Next, gather all of the materials listed in the **Show It**. Then, help your student to follow the procedure and build an anemometer.
2. Then, have your student compare their paragraph to the sample in the **Show It AK**.
3. The next lesson is a **Mastery Assess It**. Encourage your student to review Lessons 55 through 87 in order to prepare for the assessment.

LESSON 88

SCIENCE 4 PARENT & TEACHER GUIDE

Topic | Earth's Elements and Landforms

Learning Objectives

The activities in this lesson will help your student meet the following objectives:

- not applicable

Materials

- none required

Mastery Assess It 5

1. **Mastery Assess It 5** will cover what your student has learned in Lessons 55 through 87.
2. Click on the **Mastery Assess It 5** icon to begin the online assessment.
3. Have your student read the instructions before they get started. Remind them to take their time and to do their best work.
4. When they are finished and ready for their assessment to be graded, have them click the **Submit** button.

SCIENCE 4 PARENT & TEACHER GUIDE

LESSON 89

Topic | Biological Sciences

Learning Objectives

The activities in this lesson will help your student meet the following objectives:

- explain how plants and animals can be grouped according to their observable features
- identify how plants can be grouped by their observable features
- group animals by their observable features

Materials

- magazine with animals

Observable Features

1. Give the following list of items to your student, and ask them to identify the room of their house in which each item belongs.

   - shower curtain
   - spatula
   - toilet paper
   - comforter
   - plate
   - mattress
   - fork
   - shampoo

2. Explain that these items can be separated based on the room in which they belong.
3. Tell your student that they will learn how animals are separated based on their features.

1. As your student reads through the **Read It**, have them create a bubble map graphic organizer like the one shown below. In the center circle, have them write the term *vertebrate*.
2. Then, in each outer circle, instruct your student write the name of each vertebrate discussed in the text. Have them write three pieces of information about that classification in the circle as well.

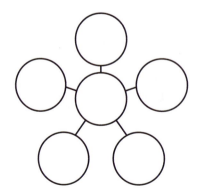

3. Now, have your student view the **Animal Classification - Watch It**.
4. Pause the video at 3:04 and discuss some similarities that your student has with their parents.

176   Copyright 2018 © Lincoln Learning Solutions. All rights reserved.

Demonstrate

1. Allow your student time to organize their thoughts by outlining information before completing the **Show It**. Also, be sure that they review the rubric before writing so that they know the expectations for the activity.
2. After completing the **Show It**, have your student reference the rubric again to make sure their work meets the criteria for evaluation. Then, have them compare their essay to the sample in the **Show It AK**.
3. To provide an alternative to the **Show It**, have your student look through an animal magazine and classify the animals into the five categories.

• • •

Plant Features

Activate

1. Have your student go outside and take pictures or draw some of the plants around their learning environment.
2. Then, have them verbally compare and contrast some features of the various plants.
3. Explain that they will learn about the classification of plants.

Engage

1. Now, have your student read the **Read It**. As they do so, discuss different examples of the classifications presented in the text.
2. Next, have your student move on to play the **Beakers Big Buzz-Plants - Play It** and the **Ecolibrium-Plants - Play It.**

Demonstrate

1. Then, have your student complete the **Show It** activity. Allow them time to compare their work to the examples in the **Show It AK**.
2. To provide an alternative to the **Show It**, have your student use the pictures or drawings from the Activate activity. Ask them to classify the plants into the classifications described in the **Read It**.

• • •

Animal Features

 **Engage**

1. While the student is reading the **Read It**, ask them to think of other examples of animals that use camouflage to stay safe from predators.
2. Now, have your student play the game in the **Beakers Big Buzz-Animals - Play It**.

 **Demonstrate**

1. Next, prompt your student to complete the **Show It** activity. When they are finished, encourage them to compare their work to the example provided in the **Show It AK**.
2. As an extension, consider taking your student to the nearest zoo or animal sanctuary. While visiting, have your student observe the various animals and their features. Ask them to identify which features they think may help that animal adapt to its environment.

LESSON 90

Topic: Biological Sciences

Learning Objectives

The activities in this lesson will help your student meet the following objectives:

- describe how plants and animals are classified based on shared characteristics
- explain that organisms grow and survive in particular habitats

Materials

- index cards

Organism Relatedness

Activate

1. Present your student with the following list of animal categories, and ask them to name an animal from each one. Then, have a discussion about the differences and similarities between the animals.
   - amphibians
   - birds
   - fish
   - mammals
   - reptiles
2. Tell your student that they will learn about classifying animals and plants based on their characteristics.

Engage

1. As your student reads the **Read It**, discuss the difference between vertebrates and invertebrates.
2. Then, have your student complete the **Frankenlab-Plants and Animals - Play It**.

Demonstrate

1. Then, direct your student to the **Show It** and have them follow the instructions to complete the activity.
2. Then, encourage them to compare their paragraph to the example in the **Show It AK**.
3. Alternatively, have your student create a brochure on the classification of vertebrate animals. Their brochure should include examples of vertebrates, a description of their characteristics, and images or drawings for each example.

• • •

Environmental Differences

**Activate**

1. Ask your student to describe why they would not see a polar bear in a tropical rain forest and why they would not see a tropical fern in the arctic.
2. Explain that they will learn more about plants and animal and the biomes in which they live.

**Engage**

1. As your student reads the content of the **Read It**, have them determine the biome in which they live.
2. Now, have your student move to the **Biomes of the World - Watch It**. Pause the video after each biome is presented, and have a discussion with your student about what makes each biome unique.
3. Next, have your student view the **From the Forest to the Plains - Watch It**.
4. Finally, allow your student time to play the game in the **Ecolibrium Habitats - Play It**.

**Demonstrate**

1. Next, have your student write the paragraph as directed in the **Show It**.
2. Then, allow them to compare their work to the example in the **Show It AK**.
3. As an alternative to the **Show It**, create a matching game for your student.
    a. Write the names of animals unique to each biome on index cards.
    b. Then, write the name of each biome on separate index cards.
    c. Have your student play a sorting game to sort the animals that belong within each biome.
4. As an extension to this lesson, challenge your student to pretend they are walking through a particular biome. Ask them to explain what they are seeing around them as you try to guess which biome they are describing. Have your student confirm if you guessed correctly.

LESSON 91

SCIENCE 4 PARENT & TEACHER GUIDE

Topic | Biological Science

Learning Objectives

The activities in this lesson will help your student meet the following objectives:

- brainstorm how the destruction of a habitat would affect the ability of its organisms to meet their four basic needs
- explain how a plant meets its basic needs
- describe how an animal meets its basic needs

Materials

- four bean seeds
- four cups
- soil
- water

Basic Needs

Activate

1. Have your student create a list of 10 things they think they could not live without.
2. Now, ask them to eliminate three things from their list. Then, have them eliminate three more.
3. Finally, have them identify the remaining items and discuss why they are the only items left on the list.
4. Tell your student they will learn about the basic needs of plants and animals.

Engage

1. Have your student begin by reading the **Read It** content. Ask them to brainstorm some answers to the questions in the section titled Basic Needs of Living Things. Once they have their answers, they can hover over the Answer Key within the text to check their work.
2. Now, have your student open and view the **Animal Habitats - Watch It**.

Demonstrate

1. Next, have your student complete the **Show It** activity. If they need help brainstorming ideas, allow them time to conduct some research on the consequences of rain forest destruction.
2. Then, have your student compare their ideas to the example answers in the **Show It AK**.
3. As an alternative to the **Show It**, have your student create a presentation about the destruction of a habitat and the steps people can take to help minimize the destruction of this habitat. Then, have them present their work to a family member.

• • •

Plant Needs

Engage

1. As your student is reading the **Read It**, have a discussion about the ways in which each of a plant's basic needs plays a role in its survival. For example, what would happen if a plant had sunlight, water, and air, but no soil? Could it survive?

Demonstrate

1. Instruct your student to complete the **Show It** and evaluate their work with the **Show It AK** example.
2. As an alternative to the **Show It**, have your student draw and label a picture of a plant within their habitat. Tell them to label all of the plant's basic needs and provide an explanation as to how each need is met and why it is important.
3. To extend learning, allow your student to observe a bean plant in several scenarios. In some, the plant's needs are met, and, in others, the plant's needs are not met. Have them follow the directions below to plant the bean seeds:
   a. Plant one seed in a cup of watered soil, and place the cup in a room **without** sunlight.
   b. Plant one seed in a cup of rocks with water, and place the cup in a room **with** sunlight.
   c. Plant one bean seed in a cup of soil with **no water**, and place the cup in a room **with** sunlight.
   d. Plant one seed in a cup of watered soil, and place the cup in a room **with** sunlight.
4. Have your student observe the bean seeds over one week and record their results. Then have them discuss their findings with you. How did the different scenarios affect the seed?

• • •

Animal Needs

Engage

1. Have your student to read the content of the **Read It**. Pause them after the Introduction section and have them answer the question posed. Ask them, "Besides a habitat, what else do they have in common with these animals?"
2. Then, have your student continue with the **Read It**. After they read the section about food, ask your student if they can think of any foods they probably **do not need** in order to survive.

Demonstrate

1. Next, direct your student complete the activity in the **Show It**. They can then compare their work to the example in the **Show It AK**.
2. As an alternative to the **Show It**, have your student observe an animal in the wild such as a squirrel or a bird. Instruct them record where this animal gets its food and makes its home.

SCIENCE 4 PARENT & TEACHER GUIDE

LESSON 92

Topic | Biological Sciences

Learning Objectives

The activities in this lesson will help your student meet the following objectives:

- explain that animals sometimes cause changes in their environments
- identify traits that animals have that help them to survive in their environments
- identify traits that plants have that help them survive in their environments

Materials

- camera
- food items with labels

Animal Effects

Activate

1. Prompt your student with the following scenario: A particular insect has damaged almost all of the corn crops in the midwestern United States.
2. Next, ask your student how this problem might impact them. They may respond by saying that there would be no corn to eat.
3. Then, have them view the ingredients of various food items. Many of these items may contain corn as an ingredient.
4. Explain that a shortage of corn caused by tiny insects would affect far more than just the corn on their dinner plate.

Engage

1. While your student reads the **Read It**, discuss the animals mentioned and the ways in which they can have a harmful or helpful effect on their ecosystems.
2. Then, ask your student to think of other animals that can harm or help their environment.

Demonstrate

1. Open the **Assess It** and have your student complete the activity. Help them to understand the expectations of the rubric before they begin writing. When they are finished, help them to review their work to make sure they have met the rubric expectations.
2. When they are finished, scan the document or take a photo of it and upload it to the Dropbox. For additional instructions on how to use the Dropbox, click on the paper clip icon in the upper-left corner of the **Assess It**.

Animal Survival

 Activate

1. Ask your student if they think they could survive outside on a cold winter's night without a tent, blanket, and warm clothes.
2. Then ask, "Why can other animals like deer, squirrels, and birds survive without these items?"
3. Tell them they will learn about the ways in which animals adapt to survive.

 Engage

1. Direct your student to read the content of the **Read It**. Afterward, have a discussion with them about other animals and their adaptations. Ask them to give you some additional examples. For instance, they could say a rabbit has eyes on the side of its head so that it can see predators coming from many angles. Also, the coloring of a toad helps it to blend in with its surroundings.
2. Now, have your student view the **Physical Adaptations of Animals - Watch It**.
3. Afterward, ask your student to describe four animal adaptations they learned about by watching the video.
4. Then, have your student view the **Behavioral Adaptations of Animals - Watch It**.
5. Ask your student if they can think of any behavioral adaptations of humans.

 Demonstrate

1. Next, instruct your student to complete the **Show It** and then compare their paragraph to the example in the **Show It AK**.
2. As an alternative to the **Show It**, play a back and forth naming game with your student.
    a. Begin by naming an adaptation.
    b. Ask your student to determine whether it is a physical or behavioral adaptation.
    c. Take turns playing each role.
3. To extend learning, encourage your student create a new animal. To represent the animal, they can draw it or create a three-dimensional replica.
    a. First, your student will need to determine the type of ecosystem in which their animal will live.
    b. Then, instruct them to create at least two physical adaptations and two behavioral adaptations for their animal to survive in this ecosystem.
    c. Finally, have your student present their new animal to family members. Make sure they explain how it lives and survives.

Plant Survival

Engage

1. Begin by having your student read the **Read It**. Afterward, have a discussion with them about the vegetation in their area and the adaptations these plants must make in order to survive. For example, deciduous trees lose their leaves in order to help them survive through the winter season.

Demonstrate

1. Next, direct your student to complete the **Show It** activity. Allow them to compare their work to the samples in the **Show It AK**.
2. As an extension, take your student on a hike through a wooded area. Have them take pictures of different plants they see along the way. When they return to their learning environment, have them conduct research on some of the plants to see how they have adapted to their ecosystem.

LESSON 93

Topic | Biological Sciences

Learning Objectives

The activities in this lesson will help your student meet the following objectives:

- explain how changes in an organism's habitat are sometimes beneficial
- explain how changes in an organism's habitat are sometimes harmful

Materials

- none required

Good Habitat Changes

 ### Activate

1. Ask your student if they have heard of a food chain. If they have not, take a moment to explain what is meant by this phrase. Then, ask them the following questions:
   a. What do you think is at the top of the food chain?
   b. What might happen if there is a break in the food chain?
2. Tell your student that they will learn how even small changes in habitats can have good and bad effects on the animals and plants living there.

 ### Engage

1. Direct your student to read the content of the **Read It**.
2. Once your student completes the reading, ask them to predict what might happen if a particular place that gets sufficient rainfall suddenly experienced a long drought.

 ### Demonstrate

1. Now, instruct your student to complete the **Show It** activity.
2. Then, have them compare their paragraph to the example in the **Show It AK**.
3. As an alternative to the **Show It**, have your student create a cause-effect table.
   a. Begin by asking your student to choose an ecosystem and write their choice in the center of a sheet of paper.
   b. Next, ask them to fold the paper in half vertically to create two columns.
   c. Have them to label the column on the left as *Cause: Change in Ecosystem*.
   d. Have them label the column on the right as *Effect of the Ecosystem Change*.
   e. Instruct them to list three causes, or changes to an ecosystem, and three effects the changes would have on the ecosystem.
4. As an extension, have your student write a story about an ecosystem where a good change has taken place. For example, your student may choose a local park as an ecosystem. In their story, the mayor of the town decides to create a man-made pond in the center of the park. Their story could describe how this change would have a positive effect on the animals and plants living in the park.

Bad Habitat Changes

Engage

1. Direct your student to read through the **Read It**. Have a conversation with them about other bad changes that can occur in an ecosystem. Ask them to think of a man-made change and a change that is naturally occurring.
2. Next, have your student view the **Deforestation - Watch It**.
3. After viewing the video, have your student discuss with you some ways they can help to reduce their impact on deforestation. For example, they can try to use less paper.

Demonstrate

1. Have your student complete the activity in the **Show It** and compare their response to the sample in the **Show It AK**.
2. As an extension, have your student conduct a research activity. Provide them with the following problem: The world's oceans are considered to be overfished, meaning people are removing fish from the ocean faster than the fish can reproduce. Why is ending overfishing important to the ocean ecosystem?

LESSON 94

SCIENCE 4 PARENT & TEACHER GUIDE

Topic: Biological Sciences

Learning Objectives

The activities in this lesson will help your student meet the following objectives:

- explain how different organisms have physical and behavioral characteristics that help them survive and reproduce
- describe ways in which organisms in one habitat are similar to those in another habitat

Materials

- none required

Species Survival

Activate

1. Ask your student if they recall seeing birds fly in the shape of a *V*. Then, ask them if they know where these birds are going and why.
2. Tell your student they will learn about ways that adaptations help species survive.

Engage

1. As your student reads through the **Read It**, ask them to think of additional examples for each type of adaptation discussed in the text. For example, there are insects that look like a twig to camouflage themselves.
2. Now, have your student open the **Forms of Animal Adaptation - Watch It**. Ask them to make note of the username and password provided on the Discovery Education image. Be sure that they click the link for the video and enter the provided username and password to watch.

Demonstrate

1. Now, instruct your student to complete the **Show It**. Allow them to conduct research on particular animals, if necessary.
2. Then, have your student evaluate their response by comparing it to the example in the **Show It AK**.

• • •

Differing Habitats

 Engage

1. Have your student create a two-column chart, with one column labeled *The Arctic* and the other labeled *The Forest*.
2. Then, have them read the content of the **Read It**.
3. While they read, ask your student to list at least five facts about the forest and arctic habitats and the animals that live there.
4. Next, direct your student to open and view the **Forests - Watch It**. Prompt them to add any new information to their column for *The Forest*.
5. Then, allow your student time to play the game in the **Wilda's Wild World Grasslands - Play It**.

Demonstrate

1. Then, direct your student to complete the chart in the **Show It**.
2. Finally, have them compare their answers to the example in the **Show It AK**.

SCIENCE 4 PARENT & TEACHER GUIDE

LESSON 95

Topic | Biological Sciences

Learning Objectives

The activities in this lesson will help your student meet the following objectives:

- identify characteristic differences between animals that give them advantages in survival and reproduction
- compare the changes that occur in humans during their life cycle, from birth to elder
- compare the changes that occur in plants during their life cycle

Materials

- a plant
- "Survival Advantages" activity page
- "Human Life Cycle Graphic Organizer" activity page

Survival Advantages

 ### Activate

1. Show your student images of the following types of birds:
   - American white ibis
   - hawk
   - hummingbird
   - owl
   - pelican
2. Once they see each image, have your student identify some similarities among the birds. For example, they all have beaks, two feet, two eyes, etc.
3. Now, have your student identify the differences. Ask them, "Why do you think these bird do not look the same?" Help to guide your student's thinking by asking them if the birds live in the same place and if they eat the same foods.

 ### Engage

1. Have your student begin by reading the **Read It**.
2. When they reach the section titled The Theory of Evolution, pause them and discuss the definition of *theory*.
3. Then, allow your student to finish reading the content.

 ### Demonstrate

1. Now, direct your student to complete the "Survival Advantages" activity page in the **Show It**.
2. Then, encourage your student to compare their answers to the samples in the **Show It AK**.
3. As an alternative to the **Show It**, present the following scenario to your student.
   a. A new predator has invaded the forest where animals A, B, and C live. Animal A has better eyesight than the other two. Animal B has more endurance, so it can run much longer and farther than the other animals. Animal C has more fur than animals A and B.
   b. Then, ask your student which animal would have a better chance of survival and why. How does their survival play into the concept of natural selection?

Human Life Cycle

Activate

1. Explain to your student the process by which baby sea turtles are born. The mother sea turtles comes to shore and lays her eggs in sand. She then returns to the sea, leaving her babies to hatch and get to the sea on their own. They must use their instincts to survive.
2. Then, ask your student if human babies would be able to use their instincts to survive on their own when they are first born. Why or why not?

Engage

1. Direct your student to read the content of the **Read It**. Pause them after each stage of the human life cycle and discuss some of the expectations of a human at each stage. For example, would a toddler be expected to do chores?
2. Next, have your student move to the **Infancy and Childhood - Watch It**. If possible, have a discussion with your student about when they reached some of the various developmental milestones presented in the video.
3. Then, have them view the **Teen to Adult - Watch It**. Discuss some of the activities your student may want to do, but is still not allowed to do. Explain that some actions and responsibilities are only allowed at certain stages in life.
4. Now, have your student view the video in the **Life - Watch It**.
5. Then, have your student play the game in the **Beakers Big Buzz-Human Body - Play It**.

Demonstrate

1. Next, direct your student to move to the **Show It** and complete the "Human Life Cycle Graphic Organizer" activity page.
2. Then, have them compare their completed activity page to the example provided in the **Show It AK**.

• • •

Plant Life Cycle

Activate

1. Provide your student with a plant or have them go outside and locate one. Ask them to try and identify the parts of the plant such as the stem, the roots, the leaves, etc.
2. Tell them they will learn about the life cycle of a plant.

Engage

1. Begin by having your student read the content of the **Read It** through the section that discusses the parts of a plant. Pause them, and have your student draw a plant with all of the parts discussed in the text. This activity will help them to remember the parts of a plant.
2. Then have them finish reading the **Read It**. Remind your student of the life cycle of a human and then ask them to compare it to the life cycle of a plant. What are the similarities?

Demonstrate

1. Now, direct your student to complete the **Show It** activity. Have them copy the chart on a sheet of paper and list two details about each stage of a plant's life cycle.
2. Once they complete their chart, help them to compare their answers to the sample response in the **Show It AK**. Allow your student to make any necessary corrections.
3. As an extension, take your student on a hike through a wooded area. Have them identify trees in the various stages of the life cycle: a seed, a sapling, a young adult tree, and a mature tree.

SCIENCE 4 PARENT & TEACHER GUIDE

LESSON 96

Topic | Biological Sciences

Learning Objectives

The activities in this lesson will help your student meet the following objectives:
- investigate how seeds change and grow into plants
- compare the changes that occur in animals during their life cycles

Materials
- seed
- small cup
- soil
- water

Plant a Seed

Activate

1. Ask your student if they have ever seen a bee buzzing around a flower. Then, ask, "What was the bee doing?" Explain to your student that this bee was actually helping the plant reproduce.
2. Tell your student they will learn about how seeds change and grow into plants.

Engage

1. Begin by having your student read through the content of the **Read It**.
2. Then, have them open and view the **How Plants Grow - Watch It**. Ask them to make note of the username and password provided on the Discovery Education image. Be sure that they click the link for the video and enter the provided username and password to watch.
3. Have your student document each stage of the plant life cycle that is presented in the video.

Demonstrate

1. Next, instruct your student to follow the procedure in the **Show It**.
2. Be sure that your student documents their observations over the two week time period. Once the experiment is complete, allow your student to compare their observations to the sample presented in the **Show It AK**.
3. As an extension, have your student plant a flower garden and observe the flowers as they grow from seeds.

• • •

Animal Life Cycle

Activate

1. Ask your student if they ever had a young animal as a pet, such as a kitten or puppy. If not, ask them to think about a friend or family member who has.
2. Ask them to think about and describe how the animal changed in the first few years of its life. Did the animal grow quickly? Did its personality change as it got older?

Engage

1. Now, direct your student to read the **Read It** content. Encourage them to pause to take time to view the images of the life cycle of different animals.
2. Then, have them compare the life cycle of animals to the life cycle of humans and plants.
3. Now, have your student view the video in the **Animal Life Cycles - Watch It**.
4. Next, have your student engage with **The Life Cycles - Practice It** to learn more about the life cycles of mammals, reptiles, birds, and amphibians.
5. Then, have them complete the activity in the **Animal Life Cycles - Practice It** by correctly ordering the stages of each animal's life cycle.

Demonstrate

1. Now, direct your student to complete the chart in the **Show It** and then compare their work to the sample in the **Show It AK**.
2. To extend the learning, consider taking your student to visit a farm or a local dog breeder. Find out if they can observe the incubation and hatching of chickens or watch newborn and young puppies interact with their environment.

SCIENCE 4 PARENT & TEACHER GUIDE

LESSON 97

Topic | Biological Sciences

Learning Objectives

The activities in this lesson will help your student meet the following objectives:

- compare the life cycles of different organisms
- explain the three identifiable stages in the life cycles of plants and animals

Materials

- colored pencils

Life Cycle Differences

Activate

1. Begin by having your student open and view the **Exploring Life Cycles - Watch It**. Ask them to make note of the username and password provided on the Discovery Education image. Be sure that they click the link for the video and enter the provided username and password to watch.
2. Inform your student that they will explore the differences between the life cycles of living things in this lesson.

Engage

1. As your student reads the **Read It**, begin a discussion about some similarities and differences between the life cycles of humans, animals, and plants. While they read, have them note the stages of each life cycle presented in the text.

Demonstrate

1. Open the **Assess It** and have your student complete the activity. Be sure that they review the expectations of the rubric before they begin. When they finish, help them to review the rubric again to make sure their work meets the expectations.
2. When they are finished, scan the document or take a photo of it and upload it to the Dropbox. For additional instructions on how to use the Dropbox, click on the paper clip icon in the upper-left corner of the **Assess It**.

• • •

Model Life Cycles

 **Engage**

1. Have your student read through the **Read It**.
2. Now, have your student open and view the **Plant Life Cycle - Watch It**.
3. Then, complete the **The Life Cycles - Practice It** and review key concepts introduced in the lesson.

 **Demonstrate**

1. Next, instruct your student to complete the graphic organizer as directed in the **Show It**. If your student has a difficult time drawing the images, you can help them by printing the images.
2. Then, have them compare their work to the example in the **Show It AK**.
3. As an extension, take your student to a pet store and have them identify the life stage of each animal.
4. The next lesson is a **Mastery Assess It**. Encourage your student to review Lessons 89 through 97 in order to prepare for the assessment.

LESSON 98

Topic: Biological Sciences

Learning Objectives

The activities in this lesson will help your student meet the following objectives:
- not applicable

Materials
- none required

Mastery Assess It 6

1. **Mastery Assess It 6** will cover what your student has learned in Lessons 89 through 97.
2. Click on the **Mastery Assess It 6** icon to begin the online assessment.
3. Have your student read the instructions before they get started. Remind them to take their time and to do their best work.
4. When they are finished and ready for their assessment to be graded, have them click the **Submit** button.

LESSON 99

Topic: Genetics

Learning Objectives

The activities in this lesson will help your student meet the following objectives:

- define the term *genetics*
- observe common physical features between adults and their offspring
- compare and contrast the characteristics of parents and their offspring

Materials

- dictionary or glossary
- index cards
- pictures of mother animals and their babies
- tape

Define *Genetics*

Activate

1. Ask your student if anyone has ever told them that they look like someone in their family.
2. Explain that they will learn how genetics plays a role in why people within the same family look similar.

Engage

1. Have your student read the Introduction in the **Read It** and answer the questions that are posed.
2. Then, have them continue reading. Ask your student to compare the mother and daughter, the two kittens, and the two ears of corn in the pictures shown.
3. Now, have your student open and view the **Planting Cells and DNA - Watch It**.

Demonstrate

1. Next, direct your student to complete the **Show It** activity, and then have them reference the **Show It AK** to evaluate their work.
2. As an alternative to the **Show It**, gather some family photos, if possible. Have your student compare the features of various family members. Then, have them explain how genetics play a role in the similarities they see. If family photos are not available, use the Internet to search for images of siblings, and allow your student to identify their similarities.

• • •

Compare Features

Engage

1. Start with the **Read It** and allow your student time to read the content and look at the images within the text. Discuss their answers to the questions at the end of the reading.
2. Next, have your student play the game in the **Ecolibrium-Heredity - Play It**.

Demonstrate

1. Then, have your student view the image in the **Show It** and follow the instructions. Allow your student to list additional similar traits if they can find more than three.
2. Then, move to the **Show It AK** and have your student compare their response to the samples provided.
3. As an extension, have your student answer the questions below. Then, ask them to determine from which parent they received each trait. If necessary, allow your student to interview a friend and their parents.
   - Are you tall or short?
   - What color is your hair?
   - Is your hair thick, thin, straight, or curly?
   - What color are your eyes?

• • •

Compare and Contrast

Engage

1. As your student reads through the **Read It**, have them look at the image of the parent and baby egret and identify similarities and differences.

Demonstrate

1. Next, direct your student to the **Show It** and have them complete the Venn diagram.
2. Then, they can compare their answers to samples in the **Show It AK**.
3. As an alternative to the **Show It**, create a matching game for your student.
   a. Search the Internet for images of five mother animals that are different from those pictured in the **Show It**. Print each image.
   b. Then, search for images of baby animals of the same species. Print each image.
   c. Tape each picture to an index card.
   d. Mix the cards and place them face down on a table.
   e. Have your student try to match the mother animal with its offspring. As they play, talk with them about the features that make each baby similar to its mother.

SCIENCE 4 PARENT & TEACHER GUIDE

LESSON 100

Topic | Genetics

Learning Objectives

The activities in this lesson will help your student meet the following objectives:

- describe physical characteristics that a human parent and child might have in common
- identify patterns in characteristics found in groups of animals

Materials

- none required

Common Features

Activate

1. Ask your student to tell you what they think the word *gene* means. Be sure they know you are not talking about the jeans they may be wearing.
2. Explain that they will learn about genes in this lesson.

Engage

1. As your student reads the **Read It**, have them view the pages of the flip-book and identify the similarities within the families shown.
2. Then, have your student move to the **Surveying Traits - Watch It**.
    a. Pause the video at 4:15, and have your student take a look at their hairline.
    b. Pause again at 4:31, and talk with your student about some of the traits listed.
    c. Finally, pause the video at 4:35, and have your student identify the hand they use for writing.

Demonstrate

1. Instruct your student to move to the **Show It** and complete the activity. Then, allow your student to compare their response to the sample in the **Show It AK**.
2. Finally, have your student complete the **Common Features - Extend It**.
3. To reinforce learning, help your student create their own genetics chart like the one discussed in the **Watch It**. The chart should include a few of your student's traits.

• • •

Observe Characteristics

1. Begin by having your student read the **Read It**. Discuss with them the similarities between the different cats shown in the images.
2. Ask your student to think of some other groups of animals that have similar characteristics such as dogs and wolves.

1. Then, have your student complete the **Show It** activity. Help them to compare their answers to the examples in the **Show It AK**.
2. As an alternative to the **Show It**, have your student search the Internet for images of different birds. Ask them to identify the similarities and differences between the birds they choose.
3. As an extension, have your student begin to take notice of the wildlife around their learning environment. Have them categorize the animals based on their characteristics.

LESSON 101

SCIENCE 4 PARENT & TEACHER GUIDE

Topic | Genetics

Learning Objectives

The activities in this lesson will help your student meet the following objectives:

- identify patterns in characteristics found in groups of animals
- list physical features that mature plants and the same type of young plants have in common
- identify common physical features of a mature plant and a young plant

Materials

- none required

Identify Patterns

1. Ask your student to pair the animals below based on similar traits.
   - rat
   - snake
   - lizard
   - deer
   - mouse
   - elk
2. Now, ask your student how they came to the conclusion of which animals to pair together. Your student should respond that their pairs have similar characteristics. For example, the rat and mouse are both small rodents with long tails and fur.

1. Next, instruct your student to read the **Read It**.
2. Then, ask them to share with you what they have learned about animals sharing traits and characteristics.

1. Direct your student to open and complete the **Show It**. Have them list as many characteristics as they can before evaluating their answers with the examples in the **Show It AK**.
2. As an alternative to the **Show It**, have your student conduct research on two animals that have similar characteristics such as alligator and crocodile. Then, have them create a Venn diagram to compare and contrast these animals.

Compare Plants

Engage

1. Direct your student to read through the **Read It**. Have them look at the similarities of the plants and discuss them with you. For example, they have roots, stems, etc.

Demonstrate

1. Next, instruct your student to complete the **Show It**, and allow them time to compare their answers to the examples in the **Show It AK**.
2. As an extension, take your student to a nursery and compare the various plants to see which ones have similarities.

•••

Identify Common Features

Engage

1. As your student reads the **Read It**, begin a discussion with them about some of the questions posed in the content.
2. Now, have your student open the **Common Features of a Plant - Watch It**. Ask them to make note of the username and password provided on the Discovery Education image. Be sure that they click the link for the video and enter the provided username and password to watch.
3. After the video, talk with your student about all the different ways a stem can look on a plant.

Demonstrate

1. Open the **Assess It** and have your student complete the activity. Ensure they review the expectations of the rubric before, during, and after they complete the activity.
2. When they are finished, scan the document or take a photo of it and upload it to the Dropbox. For additional instructions on how to use the Dropbox, click on the paper clip icon in the upper-left corner of the **Assess It**

SCIENCE 4 PARENT & TEACHER GUIDE

LESSON 102

Topic | Genetics

Learning Objectives

The activities in this lesson will help your student meet the following objectives:

- define the term *reproduction*
- explain how a single-celled organism reproduces

Materials

- dictionary or glossary
- scissors

Reproduction

 ### Activate

1. Ask your student to share what they know about what living things have in common. Your student may mention that they all have a beginning stage, they live, and they die.
2. If your student does not mention the term *reproduction* at first, ask them to explain what would happen to a species if *all* the animals lived and then died. Would the species continue? What else needs to happen?
3. Explain to your student that they will learn about reproduction.

 ### Engage

1. Have your student begin with the **Read It**. Talk with them about why it is important for a species to reproduce.

 ### Demonstrate

1. Next, have your student define the term *reproduction* in the **Show It** and compare their response to the definition in the **Show It AK**.
2. As an alternative to the **Show It**, follow the steps below to help your student represent the importance of reproduction.
   a. Begin by numbering five pieces of paper with the numbers 1 through 5. Then, give all five papers to your student.
   b. Next, have your student select the papers with the numbers 1 through 4. Ask them to cut these papers in half. After they cut the papers, have them write same number on the other half of the page.
   c. Explain to your student that the cutting represents reproduction of the organism.
   d. Next, have them crumple one half of each paper while leaving the other half alone. Also, have your student crumple the entire page with the number 5.
   e. Now, repeat this process and ask your student to cut pages 1 through 3 in half and crumple the original. Also, have them crumple page 4 since it was not cut in half.
   f. Continue this process with your student until you are left with only number one.
   g. Finally, ask your student what happened to the other organisms that quit reproducing in this activity.

• • •

204

Copyright 2018 © Lincoln Learning Solutions. All rights reserved.

Single-Celled Reproduction

Activate

1. Ask your student if they have ever seen a person take something printed on paper and make copies of it using a copier.
2. If so, ask your student if the copies look any different than the original.
3. Explain that they will learn how cells can reproduce by themselves and make exact copies.

Engage

1. Begin by having your student read the **Read It** content.
2. After reading, have your student explain the difference between a multicellular organism and a single-celled organism.
3. Now, have your student open the **Single-Celled vs. Multicellular Reproduction - Watch It**. Ask them to make note of the username and password provided on the Discovery Education image. Be sure that they click the link for the video and enter the provided username and password to watch.

Demonstrate

1. Next, have your student complete the drawing in the **Show It**.
2. Use the **Show It AK** to ensure your student's drawing accurately represents single-celled reproduction.
3. Extend your students learning by having them complete the following activity.
    a. Ask your student to draw something easy such as a butterfly or a tree.
    b. Next, have them color the object.
    c. Then, tell them to draw five more identical images.
    d. When they are finished, check to see that the drawings are identical. Explain that, sometimes, single-celled organisms make a mistake in the reproduction process, which causes some mutations.

LESSON 103

Topic | Genetics

Learning Objectives

The activities in this lesson will help your student meet the following objectives:

- illustrate how a single-celled organism reproduces
- illustrate how a plant reproduces
- explain the importance of reproduction for the continuation of life

Materials

- colored pencils or crayons

Asexual Reproduction

Activate

1. Ask your student if they look exactly like either of their parents. Then, ask them to explain why they are not a copy of one of their parents. Help them to understand that they are a mix of both parents.
2. Then, tell them they will learn how some organisms reproduce with only one parent, and those offspring *are* exact copies of their parents.

Engage

1. Next, have your student read the **Read It** and discuss with them the image showing the process of asexual reproduction.
2. Now, have your student open the **Asexual Reproduction - Watch It** and ask them to make note of the username and password provided on the Discovery Education image. Be sure that they click the link for the video and enter the provided username and password to watch.
3. Pause the video at 0:50, and explain the word *microscopic*. Tell your student that this image is magnified many times in order for them to see the organisms reproducing.

Demonstrate

1. Next, have your student complete the **Show It** activity as a review of representing the asexual reproduction process.
2. Then, direct your student to the **Show It AK**. Have them use the description to evaluate their drawing.
3. Allow your student to complete the **Extend It** to learn more about binary fission and budding, specific types of asexual reproduction.

Plant Reproduction

 ## Engage

1. Have your student begin by reading the content of the **Read It**. Once they are finished, ask them to explain the differences and similarities between flowering and nonflowering plant reproduction.
2. Next, have them view the **Plant Reproduction - Watch It**.

Demonstrate

1. Now, have your student move to the **Show It** and complete the activity. Encourage them to compare their drawing to the description in the **Show It AK**.
2. As an extension, take your student on a hike and have them identify various plants.
    a. Before you go, ask them to copy the chart below in a notebook.
    b. Have them place the names of each plant in the chart and mark whether they are flowering or nonflowering and which type of reproduction they use. They can also draw a picture of each plant in the chart if they choose.

Type of Plant	Flowering	Nonflowering	Sexual Reproduction	Asexual Reproduction

Continuation

 ## Engage

1. As your student begins to read the **Read It**, discuss the meaning of the term *extinct* with them.
2. Then, ask your student if they can think of a species that became extinct. If your student has time, have them conduct some informal research on this animal to see how it became extinct.

Demonstrate

1. Now, have your student complete the **Show It** by writing a paragraph about the importance of reproduction.
2. Then, have them compare their paragraph to the example in the **Show It AK**.
3. As an alternative to the **Show It**, have your student pretend they are a senior scientist who must deliver a speech to explain to the world why bees are important to the survival of many plant species. Have them discuss the following topics in their speech.
    a. how plants reproduce
    b. how bees help plants to reproduce
    c. how to keep bees from going extinct

LESSON 104

SCIENCE 4 PARENT & TEACHER GUIDE

Topic | Genetics

Learning Objectives

The activities in this lesson will help your student meet the following objectives:

- identify characteristic patterns found in plants
- display patterns in the characteristics of living things

Materials

- glue
- magazine source with plant and animal images
- scissors
- three live flowers

Identify Plant Patterns

Activate

1. Ask your student to discuss with you why they think roses come in more than one color.
2. Next, ask them to identify what all roses *do* have in common, even though they are not the same color.
3. Then, explain that they will learn that all plants are different, but they have similar characteristics.

Engage

1. Begin by having your student read the content of the **Read It**. Be sure that they view the pages of the flip-book to look at the variations of plants.

Demonstrate

1. Next, help your student to gather the flowering plants needed for the **Show It**, and instruct them to complete the activity.
2. When they are finished, they can evaluate their response using the samples in the **Show It AK**.
3. As an extension, take your student to a nursery where there are many plants with various colors. Have your student observe the number of variations of each type of flowering plant.

• • •

Create Displays

Engage

1. Have your student view the similarities in the organisms that are shown in the images in the **Read It**.
2. Discuss with them another group of animals and plants that share characteristics. Examples include mice and rats or snakes and lizards.

Demonstrate

1. Open the **Assess It** and have your student complete the activity. Help them to understand the expectations of the rubric before they begin. When they are finished, help them to review their work to make sure they have met the rubric expectations.
2. When they are finished, scan the document or take a photo of it and upload it to the Dropbox. For additional instructions on how to use the Dropbox, click on the paper clip icon in the upper-left corner of the **Assess It**.
3. The next lesson is a **Mastery Assess It**. Encourage your student to review Lessons 99 through 104 in order to prepare for the assessment.

LESSON 105

Topic: Genetics

Learning Objectives

The activities in this lesson will help your student meet the following objectives:

- not applicable

Materials

- none required

Mastery Assess It 7

1. **Mastery Assess It 7** will cover what your student has learned in Lessons 99 through 104.
2. Click on the **Mastery Assess It 7** icon to begin the online assessment.
3. Have your student read the instructions before they get started. Remind them to take their time and to do their best work.
4. When they are finished and ready for their assessment to be graded, have them click the **Submit** button.

LESSON 106

| Topic | Evolution |

Learning Objectives

The activities in this lesson will help your student meet the following objectives:

- identify predators and prey
- identify examples of animal camouflage
- describe how camouflage helps animals survive in their habitats

Materials

- dry erase board and marker
- paint
- six rocks

Predator-Prey Relationships

Activate

1. Write the following animals on the dry erase board, and have your student determine which is at the top of the food chain.
   - snake
   - frog
   - eagle
   - grasshopper
2. Then, ask your student to explain the animal relationships within the order of the food chain. Which animals are predators and which are prey?

Engage

1. Next, have your student read through the content of the **Read It**.
2. Pause and ask them to offer an example of when an animal could be the predator or the prey. For example, a snake that is hunting a mouse is a predator, but high above, an eagle is about to prey on the snake.

Demonstrate

1. Next, have your student complete the **Show It** by identifying the predator and prey in each of the animal pairs.
2. Then, have them evaluate their answers using the **Show It AK**.
3. As an extension, have your student view an animated movie and ask them to point out the predator and prey relationships throughout.

Animal Camouflage

Activate

1. Begin by asking your student why they think a hunter needs to wear camouflage when they go hunting.
2. Inform your student that they will learn how animals naturally camouflage themselves for protection.

Engage

1. While your student reads the content of the **Read It**, ask them to think of other animals that belong in each of the categories of camouflage.
2. When your student is finished reading, have them research an animal to find out more about its camouflaging techniques.

Demonstrate

1. Now, have your student view the images in the **Show It** and complete the activity. Allow them to refer to the **Read It** if they need a reminder of the types of camouflage.
2. As an alternative to the **Show It**, help your student to create a camouflage activity by following these steps:
   a. Have your student paint six rocks, and make each one a different color. Suggested colors are red, blue, yellow, brown, green, and black.
   b. Then, instruct them to take the rocks outside and try to hide them so they are camouflaged. Most likely, the brighter colors will be found more easily.
   c. Search for your student's rocks. After all the rocks have been found, talk with your student about why you were able to find some more easily than others.

• • •

Camouflage Aids Survival

Engage

1. While your student reads through the **Read It**, discuss with them what would happen to an animal if it were relocated into a new environment. Would it have the means to survive? For example, if a polar bear were placed into a deciduous forest in the summer, it would likely have a difficult time surviving. Its white fur would make it difficult for the bear to hunt and hide from its prey.
2. Next, have your student view the **Surviving the Elements - Watch It**.
3. Pause the video at 0:55 and discuss with your student what is meant in the video when the speaker states that "evolution has done a fine job helping animals to survive."

Demonstrate

1. Now have your student move on to the **Show It** and complete the activity. Then, allow them to compare their paragraph to the example in the **Show It AK**.
2. As an alternative to the **Show It**, help your student to create the following activity.
   a. Begin by giving your student five different colors of construction paper.
   b. Have them cut each piece of construction paper into 10 squares. When finished, they should have a total of 50 squares.
   c. Then, have your student sit in another room while you hide the squares around their learning environment.
   d. Then, tell your student to pretend they are a predator looking for prey. Give them one minute to find as many squares as possible.
   e. After the one minute, have your student count how many squares of each color they found. Discuss with them how this activity is very similar to the ways in which animals camouflage themselves to survive.

SCIENCE 4 PARENT & TEACHER GUIDE

LESSON 107

Topic | Evolution

Learning Objectives

The activities in this lesson will help your student meet the following objectives:

- describe how camouflage is important to animal survival
- identify ways in which cacti have protection from predators

Materials

- colored pencils or crayons

Camouflage

Activate

1. Prior to the lesson, search the Internet to find a few images of camouflaged animals.
2. Then, share the pictures with your student and ask them to explain how the camouflage helps each animal. Remind your student that an animal can be both predator and prey.

Engage

1. Next, have your student read the **Read It**, and discuss with them the importance of camouflage for species survival.
2. Instruct your student to list the types of camouflaging they learned about in previous lessons, and ask them to determine which of the camouflaging techniques the animals in the images are using.

Demonstrate

1. Next, have your student complete the **Show It** activity and compare their work to the example in the **Show It AK**.
2. As an alternative to the **Show It**, play a game of Hide and Seek with your student. Have them use any type of camouflage in order to hide themselves. For example, they could cover themselves with clothes if they are in a closet.
3. As an extension, the next time you are outside with your student and see different animals, have them observe and discuss whether or not they think the animals are camouflaged.

•••

Cacti Protection

Activate

1. Ask your student, "What is the first thing that comes to your mind when you hear the word *cactus*?" Most likely, they will say something about the spines.
2. Explain that they will learn about how a cactus can protect itself for survival.

Engage

1. Before your student begins reading the **Read It**, have them take a piece of paper and fold it into three even sections.
2. Then, have them begin reading the content. Each time they come across a new way a cactus protects itself, have them write it in one of the columns. At the end of the reading, they should have something written in each space.
3. Now, have your student open the **Marvelous Plant Adaptations - Watch It** and ask them to make note of the username and password provided on the Discovery Education image. Be sure that they click the link for the video and enter the provided username and password to watch.

Demonstrate

1. Next, direct your student to complete the **Show It** activity. Allow them to use the information they gathered from the **Read It**.
2. Then, have them evaluate their answers with the examples in the **Show It AK**.
3. To extend learning, take your student on a hike and help them to search for other ways that plants protect themselves from predators. Have them sketch the plants they discover and create a booklet. Be sure that they identify the plant's method of protection.

SCIENCE 4 PARENT & TEACHER GUIDE

LESSON 108

Topic Evolution

Learning Objectives

The activities in this lesson will help your student meet the following objectives:

- describe how a cactus's physical characteristics protect it from its predators
- explain the relationship between endangered animals and their gestation periods
- come up with an imaginary animal and give it specific characteristics that would help it to survive and reproduce

Materials

- art supplies
- presentation software

Physical Traits of Cacti

Activate

1. Remind your student about the discussion of a cactus from Lesson 107. Ask them to share ways that a cactus can protect itself.
2. Then, have your student think of things they use to help protect themselves. For example, helmets, padding, a house, etc.

Engage

1. Now, have your student read the **Read It** and discuss the term *adaptation* with them. Have your student use the terms *natural selection* and *evolution* to discuss how a species' offspring can change over time to develop characteristics that help the species to survive in its environment.

Demonstrate

1. Next, prompt your student complete the **Show It** activity, and encourage them to check their response with the examples in the **Show It AK**. If they need to make any adjustments, allow them to do so.
2. As an extension, have your student create a pretend informative web page that discusses a cactus and how it survives. They can do this on paper or by using presentation software. If needed, assist your student with researching more information or printing pictures.

● ● ●

Endangered Animals

Activate

1. Ask your student to determine what they think the following animals have in common.
   - orangutan
   - Cross River gorilla
   - fin whale
   - green turtle
   - Indian elephant
   - Galapagos penguin
2. Explain that all of these animals are endangered species, and they will learn about how animals become extinct.

Engage

1. While your student reads the **Read It**, have them discuss with you the issues surrounding endangered animals and who or what they think may be causing them to be endangered. Your student may name humans as a possible reason that animals are endangered.
2. Ask your student what may happen if endangered animals are not protected.
3. Next, direct your student to the **Practice It** where they will learn the difference between threatened, endangered, and extinct species and read about examples of each.

Demonstrate

1. Now, instruct your student to read the information provided in the **Show It** and complete the activity.
2. Once they have finished, have them check their response by comparing it to the example in the **Show It AK**.
3. Then, direct your student to complete the **Reinforce It**.
4. To extend learning, have your student choose an endangered species, conduct research about the animals, and create a plan of action to possibly help bring them off the endangered species list.

Characteristics for Survival

**Engage**

1. While your student is reading the **Read It**, pause and ask them to discuss the characteristics humans have that help them to survive. Your student may have many ideas.
2. Tell your student to think about an animal that lives near their home and state two characteristics that help it to survive. For example, a squirrel blends in to its surroundings, and it also collects food, which it stores for the winter.

**Demonstrate**

1. Have your student brainstorm three ideas before beginning the activity in the **Show It**.
    a. Provide them with the graphic organizer below to help them gather their thoughts.
    b. Direct your student to add the name of their imagined animal, or a sketch of it, inside each box and list its characteristics on the lines below.

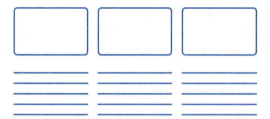

2. If your student is struggling to find an idea for an imaginary animal, allow them to view the example in the **Show It AK** to spark their creativity.

LESSON 109

SCIENCE 4 PARENT & TEACHER GUIDE

Topic | **Evolution**

Learning Objectives

The activities in this lesson will help your student meet the following objectives:

- discuss how plants and animals can be affected by water pollution
- explain how humans can cause environmental changes that result in the extinction of plants and animals

Materials

- art supplies
- poster board

Impacts of Polluted Water

Activate

1. Search the Internet for an image of animals in an oil spill. Ask your student to describe what they observe in the image.
2. Then, ask them to think about where the oil came from and how it might affect the animals that rely on the water as their home.

Engage

1. Next, have your student read the **Read It**. Discuss their thoughts on the fact presented in the Introduction.
2. Now, have your student view the **Chesapeake Bay - Watch It**.
3. After the video, have a discussion with your student about the different ways that humans are causing negative impacts on the environment surrounding the Chesapeake Bay.

Demonstrate

1. Now, have your student answer the questions found in the **Show It**. Allow them to reference the **Read It** if needed.
2. Then, have your student check their answers using the **Show It AK**. Allow them to mark any incorrect answers, and encourage them to make corrections.
3. As an extension, have your student create a list of ways they, along with their family, can help to prevent water pollution. Encourage them to create a poster to inform their family members of various methods of pollution prevention.

• • •

Human-Caused Extinction

 Activate

1. Ask your student what they think of when they hear the word *extinct*.
2. Next, ask your student why they think the dinosaurs went extinct. Remind them that humans were not around when dinosaurs were roaming the earth. Tell your student that dinosaur extinction had to do with natural causes.
3. Then, ask your student to think about any possible human causes that would impact animals today.

 Engage

1. Begin by having your student read the **Read It** to learn about human causes of extinction, discussing with them how humans can have an indirect impact on the animals in the environment.
2. Challenge your student to talk with a neighbor or relative who has lived in the area for many years. Direct your student to ask this person about what the landscape looked like 50 years ago. Your student will likely hear that more buildings and homes have been constructed over the years. If your student is unable to speak with someone directly, have them do a quick online search for pictures of their area from 50 years ago.
3. Now, have your student view the **Threats to Organisms - Watch It**.
4. Pause the video at 0:33 and discuss with your student the reasons why eliminating one necessity of a species (water, food, or habitat) can have a huge impact on those animals.

 Demonstrate

1. Open the **Assess It** and have your student complete the activity. Be sure that they review the expectations of the rubric before and after writing.
2. When they are finished, scan the document or take a photo of it and upload it to the Dropbox. For additional instructions on how to use the Dropbox, click on the paper clip icon in the upper-left corner of the **Assess It**.
3. As an extension, the next time you visit the zoo with your student, help them to recognize all of the animals that are listed as endangered.

SCIENCE 4 PARENT & TEACHER GUIDE

LESSON 110

Topic | **Evolution**

Learning Objectives

The activities in this lesson will help your student meet the following objectives:

- define the word *adaptation*
- explain the physical components of a cactus that are important to its survival
- match animals to adaptations that are important to their survival

Materials

- bowl
- dictionary or glossary
- popcorn
- salad tongs
- straw
- tweezers

Adaptation

Activate

1. Ask your student to name some things they do to stay warm when the weather turns cold. Some answers may include putting on a coat, staying inside, or wearing boots.
2. Now, ask them if the wild animals outside are able to do similar things to stay warm during the winter. Your student should say no, wild animals cannot go into a warm house or put on a coat when the weather turns cold.
3. Inform your student that they will explore how animals adapt to their environment so they can survive all types of weather conditions.

Engage

1. While your student begins to read the **Read It**, have them think of another animal, besides a rabbit, that has adapted to its environment.
2. Next, have your student view the **Changing Traits for Adaptation - Watch It**.
3. Have a discussion with your student about some of the animals mentioned in the video. Ask your student why they think these animals might have a difficult time surviving in a different environment.

Demonstrate

1. Instruct your student to complete the **Show It** and compare their sentence to the example in the **Show It AK**.
2. As an extension, have your student investigate how birds' beaks have adapted to their environment and food source.
   a. Begin by popping some popcorn and placing it in a bowl.
   b. Provide your student with a pair of tweezers, salad tongs, and a straw.
   c. Ask them to try and pick up the popcorn with each utensil and explain which one is better suited for picking up the popcorn. (Answer: The salad tongs would be best for picking up this food source.)
   d. Then, ask them to explain which utensil would be best for picking up the food sources listed below.
      i. sunflower seeds (Answer: tweezers)
      ii. rice (Answer: straw)

Cactus

Engage

1. Begin by having your student read the **Read It**. Ask them if they think the cactus could live in other environments. Have them explain why or why not.

Demonstrate

1. Next, have your student complete the **Show It** activity and compare their response to the sample in the **Show It AK**.
2. As an alternative to the **Show It**, have your student complete the following activity.
   a. Give your student a piece of paper and ask them to fold the top and bottom ends inward so that there is an opening in the middle.
   b. Have them rotate the paper so that the flaps open to the left and right.
   c. Next, have them close both flaps and draw a cactus on the front.
   d. On the inside of the left flap, have your student write the environmental issue that the cactus has adapted to overcome.
   e. On the inside of the right flap, ask your student to write the way in which the cactus has adapted to survive in its environment.

• • •

Animal Adaptations

Engage

1. Begin by having your student read the Introduction section in the **Read It** and answer the question.
2. Then, have your student continue reading. When they are finished, have a discussion with them about the animal adaptations presented in the reading.
3. Now, have your student open and view the **Desert, Forest, Polar Habitat - Watch It**.

Demonstrate

1. Now, instruct your student to move on to the **Show It** and complete the matching activity.
2. Then, have your student evaluate their answers in the **Show It AK**.
3. To help your student better understand animal adaptations, have them complete the **Extend It**.
4. As an added extension, provide your student with the names of animals and tell them you are putting each animal into a new environment. For example, you are moving the penguins to the desert. What would the penguins have to do to adapt to their new surroundings?

LESSON 111

Topic: Evolution

Learning Objectives

The activities in this lesson will help your student meet the following objectives:

- match plants to adaptations that are important to their survival
- identify fossils as either plant or animal fossils

Materials

- none required

Plant Adaptations

Activate

1. Ask your student to share their thoughts on why, in some environments, trees lose their leaves in the fall, but pine trees keep their needles all year long. If your student does not live in an area where trees lose their leaves, search the Internet to find images of trees during the fall and winter months where this process occurs.
2. Explain to your student that this is an adaptation that some trees undergo to survive in winter conditions. They will learn about some other plant adaptations.

Engage

1. Have your student read through the **Read It**.
2. Then, ask your student to explain the purpose of adaptation in plants. They should mention that plants adapt to survive in the conditions of their ecosystem.
3. Next, have your student move to view the **Amazing Plant Adaptations - Watch It**.
4. While watching, have your student list the various plant adaptations they learn about. For example, they may list that plants in the tundra tend to be darker in color and grow in clumps. Cacti engorge with water in a desert climate, and some seeds have hook-like features that allow them to be easily picked up and transported.

Demonstrate

1. Have your student examine the images and match them with the descriptions in the **Show It**. Encourage your student to look closely at each image.
2. Then, have your student check their answers in the **Show It AK**.
3. To provide an alternative to the **Show It**, take your student on a walk outside to closely examine various plants. Ask them to identify different adaptations they observe.

• • •

Fossils

 Activate

1. Ask your student to think about life when dinosaurs roamed Earth and then draw what they are imagining.
2. Then, have your student explain how they knew what to draw since no humans were alive to take pictures or record how Earth looked when dinosaurs were alive.
3. Explain that fossils are one way that scientists learn about Earth's past. Tell them they will learn more about fossils

 Engage

1. As they read through the **Read It**, have a discussion with your student about the types of information scientists might learn about animals through their fossils, aside from what they looked like.

 Demonstrate

1. Have your student complete the **Show It** activity and then compare their work to the sample in the **Show It AK**.
2. As an extension, take your student to a natural history museum and point out all of the fossils that have been found. If a trip to a museum is not possible, have your student go on a virtual tour through a natural history museum.

LESSON 112

| Topic | Evolution |

Learning Objectives

The activities in this lesson will help your student meet the following objectives:

- compare and contrast the anatomical similarities and differences of plant fossils and living plants
- compare and contrast the anatomical similarities and differences of animal fossils and living animals

Materials

- leaves
- modeling clay

Plants

Activate

1. Ask your student, "What would have to happen in order for a leaf to turn into a fossil?" Your student may mention the word *preserve* in their answer. For example, they may say that the leaf is preserved in the layers of soil or a plant was preserved in some tree sap.
2. Then, explain that they will learn about plant fossils.

Engage

1. Have your student read the entire **Read It**, and then have a discussion with them about the reasons why a plant may not stay preserved completely. Be sure that they mention the environmental effects that would interrupt the fossilization process.

Demonstrate

1. Instruct your student create a Venn diagram and complete the **Show It** activity.
2. Next, use the **Show It AK** and work with your student to review the example answers.
3. As an alternative to the **Show It**, have your student make their own plant fossils using modeling clay and the leaves from different plants and trees. Allow them to go outside, gather a few leaves, and press them into the clay.

• • •

Animal Fossils

## Engage

1. After your student reads through the **Read It**, ask them to imagine whether or not there could be more animals that existed millions of years ago that scientists will never know about because they were not fossilized.
2. Now, have your student open the **Fossils: How They Formed - Watch It** and ask them to make note of the username and password provided on the Discovery Education image. Be sure that they click the link for the video and enter the provided username and password to watch.
3. Discuss the process of fossilization with your student, and be sure to mention the parts of an animal that are not preserved.

## Demonstrate

1. Open the **Assess It** and have your student complete the activity. Be sure that they review the expectations of the rubric before, during, and after they complete the activity.
2. When they are finished, scan the document or take a photo of it and upload it to the Dropbox. For additional instructions on how to use the Dropbox, click on the paper clip icon in the upper-left corner of the **Assess It**.

LESSON 113

SCIENCE 4 PARENT & TEACHER GUIDE

Topic | Evolution

Learning Objectives

The activities in this lesson will help your student meet the following objectives:
- define the term *fossil*
- identify and study a fossil

Materials
- dictionary or glossary
- flour
- modeling clay
- various toys with feet
- wind-up toy with feet

What are Fossils

Activate

1. Ask your student to create a list of all the things they can learn about an animal based on its fossil.
2. Explain that they will learn more about fossils and their importance to piecing together the past.

Engage

1. Have your student begin reading the **Read It**. Explain that the reading only discusses one way a fossil can form. There are other types of fossils that aren't necessarily formed in mud and water. A frozen woolly mammoth is a good example.

Demonstrate

1. Next, have your student move to the **Show It** and complete the activity.
2. Then, have your student take time to compare their sentence with the example in the **Show It AK**. Help your student make any changes that might be necessary.
3. To extend learning, help your student to experience working with fossils by completing the activities below.
   a. First, gather some modeling clay and a few of your student's toys that have feet.
   b. Next, without your student seeing, place the toy's feet in the clay.
   c. Then, ask your student to determine which fossil belongs with which toy.
   d. Next, take some flour and place it on a flat surface. Without your student watching, position a wind-up toy to walk through the flour
   e. Then, have your student observe the tracks made by the wind-up toy. Ask them to explain what they imagine the toy was doing and where it went.

• • •

Types of Fossils

Engage

1. Direct your student to read the **Read It**, paying close attention to the process of fossilization shown in the images. Have them identify the part of the animal that was left, and ask your student why they think this part was left behind.
2. Discuss with your student the importance of the environmental conditions necessary for an organism to fossilize.

Demonstrate

1. Next, direct your student to complete the activity in the **Show It**. Help them to compare their paragraph to the example in the **Show It AK**.
2. As an alternative to the **Show It**, have your student create a comic strip of an animal as it fossilizes. Be sure they include all the steps involved in the process. Each step should be a new frame in the comic strip.
3. To extend your student's learning, have them conduct research on paleontologists and what they must do in order to find fossils.
4. The next lesson is a **Mastery Assess It**. Encourage your student to review Lessons 106 through 113 in order to prepare for the assessment.

LESSON 114

Topic: Evolution

Learning Objectives

The activities in this lesson will help your student meet the following objectives:

- not applicable

Materials

- none required

Mastery Assess It 8

1. **Mastery Assess It 8** will cover what your student has learned in Lessons 106 through 113.
2. Click on the **Mastery Assess It 8** icon to begin the online assessment.
3. Have your student read the instructions before they get started. Remind them to take their time and to do their best work.
4. When they are finished and ready for their assessment to be graded, have them click the **Submit** button.

SCIENCE 4 PARENT & TEACHER GUIDE

LESSON 115

Topic | Ecology

Learning Objectives

The activities in this lesson will help your student meet the following objectives:

- define the terms *living* and *nonliving*
- identify living and nonliving things that humans depend on for survival
- identify living and nonliving things that animals depend on for survival

Materials

- colored pencils
- dictionary or glossary

Living and Nonliving

Activate

1. Have your student open the **Am I Alive? - Watch It** to view the video.
2. Prompt them to look out the window and identify living and nonliving things.

Engage

1. After your student reads the content of the **Read It**, ask them to explain the difference between living and nonliving things. Distinguishing the meanings will help them to focus on the definition of the terms.
2. Then, guide them to complete the activity in the **Practice It**.

Demonstrate

1. Now, instruct your student to move on to the **Show It** to complete the activity.
2. Then, work with them to check their definitions using the example in the **Show It AK**. Guide them to make any necessary changes to their definitions. By making alterations, your student corrects any misconceptions about the scientific terms.
3. As an alternative to the **Show It**, allow your student to create a poster that illustrates living and nonliving things. Encourage them to group and title the items on their poster. In addition, have your student include a definition for each category.

Daily Basic Needs

Activate

1. Direct your student to open the **Farmers: Feeding the World - Watch It** to view the video.
2. Then, ask them to explain how farmers help humans to meet their basic needs.

Engage

1. While your student reads the **Read It**, ask them, "Which of the items presented in the text are living and which are nonliving?" Confirm that all five basic needs are nonliving. However, before fruits and vegetables are harvested, they *are* living.
2. Then, pose the following question to your student.
   - "If a human's basic needs were not met, what would happen to that person?" (Answer: They would become ill and eventually die.)

Demonstrate

1. Now, have your student complete the activity in the **Show It**. Encourage them to elaborate on their list and explain why the items are needed for human survival.
2. Then, assist your student in evaluating their responses using the **Show It AK**.
3. As an alternative to the **Show It**, instruct your student to pretend that they are a news reporter who must give a briefing on the daily basic needs of humans. Direct them to classify the needs into the categories of living and nonliving.
4. To extend your student's learning, have them explain how their basic needs are being met while they eat lunch.

Animal Survival Needs

Engage

1. As your student reads the text of the **Read It**, have them compare an animal's basic needs to the basic needs of humans that they have already learned.

Demonstrate

1. Now, have your student complete the activity in the **Show It**. When they are finished, they can compare their work to the sample in the **Show It AK**.
2. To provide an alternative to the **Show It**, instruct your student to create a comic strip that shows an animal in search of its basic needs.
3. To extend learning, ask your student to think about their pet, if they have one. Then, ask them to share how their pet's basic needs are met. If they do not have a pet, encourage them to imagine how a pet's needs are met.

SCIENCE 4 PARENT & TEACHER GUIDE

LESSON 116

Topic | Ecology

Learning Objectives

The activities in this lesson will help your student meet the following objectives:

- identify living and nonliving things that plants depend on for survival
- describe basic needs that humans, animals, and plants have in common

Materials

- clothesline or crafting cord
- gravel or sand
- hammer and nail (or drill)
- plants
- scissors
- soil
- tape or sealant
- two-liter plastic bottle
- water

Plant Survival Needs

Activate

1. Direct your student to open the **Plant Growth - Watch It** to view the video.
2. Then, prompt them to explain what plants need to grow.

Engage

1. As your student reads the **Read It**, encourage them to draw a diagram that shows a plant obtaining its basic needs from the environment. Direct them to label the elements depicted in their diagram.

Demonstrate

1. Now, have your student move on to the **Show It** to make a TerrAqua Column. Be sure that they complete the list as directed below the TerrAqua Column instructions.
2. Then, direct your student to the **Show It AK** to check their work.
3. To extend learning, instruct your student to mark the level of the water with a permanent marker once they complete the assembly of the TerrAqua Column.
   a. Then, direct them to make an additional mark to show where the water line drops each day.
   b. Tell your student to create a table and record the space between the lines each day for a week.

• • •

Common Needs

1. While your student reads the **Read It**, ask them to explain how plants, animals, and humans are connected. Plants, animals, and humans are connected because they are living things that have basic needs such as water, air, food, and sunlight.

1. Now, instruct your student to complete the activity in the **Show It** and evaluate their work using the sample in the **Show It AK**.
2. As an alternative to the **Show It**, guide them to draw and label a scientific drawing of plants, animals, and humans getting at least three basic needs.

SCIENCE 4 PARENT & TEACHER GUIDE

LESSON 117

Topic | Ecology

Learning Objectives

The activities in this lesson will help your student meet the following objectives:

- formulate a hypothesis about the effects of removing a food source from an animal's habitat
- draw a food web
- compare and contrast single-celled and multicellular organisms

Materials

- colored pencils or crayons
- dry erase board and marker
- "Cellular Organisms Venn Diagram" activity page

Food Chains

Activate

1. Ask your student to identify some of their favorite foods.
2. Ask them to explain where those food items come from and to tell you what would happen if those sources disappeared. They may mention a grocery store as a source for their food and that, if it closed one day, they may need to find a farm or another store to get their food.
3. Let your student know they will learn about how animals sometimes need to move elsewhere to find food.

Engage

1. While your student reads the content of the **Read It**, discuss how some animals already have patterns of moving out of their habitat in search of food during the winter. This is called migration. However, not all animals have the ability to migrate regularly.

Demonstrate

1. Now, have your student complete the activity in the **Show It**. Then, work with them to evaluate their response using the sample paragraph in the **Show It AK**.
2. As an alternative to the **Show It**, allow your student to search the Internet for information about a specific animal and its food sources. Guide them to create a photo essay using the images they find. Their essay should show the effects of removing the animal's food sources.

• • •

Food Webs

Activate

1. Have your student open the **From Food Chains to Food Webs - Watch It** to view the video.
2. Prompt them to explain the difference between a food chain and a food web. A food chain focuses on a lineage of a top predator to a bottom producer. On the other hand, a food web shows the connections of all the plants and animals in a food chain with other plants and animals. In other words, a food web is a combination of multiple food chains.

Engage

1. As your student reads the **Read It**, have them use their finger to trace the path of at least three organisms in the image. Encourage them to explain where the energy begins in the chain.

Demonstrate

1. Now, guide your student to complete the activity in the **Show It**.
2. Finally, help them to evaluate their web using the information provided in the **Show It AK**.
3. To extend learning, allow your student to add more parts to the web they created in the **Show It**. Encourage them to connect at least five more plants or animals. Then, have them explain all the paths and connections.

Cellular Organisms

Activate

1. Begin by asking your student to tell you what they know about cells. They may mention that cells make up organisms such as plants and animals.
2. Then, write the words *single* and *multi* on the dry erase board. Have your student draw a quick picture under each word to show what each term means.
3. Tell your student that they will learn the difference between single-celled and multicellular organisms.

Engage

1. After your student reads the **Read It**, have them verbally explain the difference between single-celled and multicellular organisms.

Demonstrate

1. Open the **Assess It** and have your student complete the activity. Be sure that they review the expectations of the rubric before and after writing.
2. When they are finished, scan the document or take a photo of it and upload it to the Dropbox. For additional instructions on how to use the Dropbox, click on the paper clip icon in the upper-left corner of the **Assess It**.

SCIENCE 4 PARENT & TEACHER GUIDE

LESSON 118

Topic | **Ecology**

Learning Objectives

The activities in this lesson will help your student meet the following objectives:

- define the terms *consumer*, *decomposer*, *producer*, and *scavenger*
- illustrate how matter moves through an ecosystem
- discuss how death cycles matter through an ecosystem

Materials

- colored pencils
- dictionary
- grass or leaves
- scissors
- stuffed animals or plastic animal figurines
- "Cycle Diagram" activity page

Ecosystem Cycles

Activate

1. Have your student open the **Creating a Water Ecosystem - Watch It** to view the video.
2. Prompt them to draw and label a diagram of a water ecosystem.

Engage

1. As your student reads the **Read It**, have them explain the cycle of organisms. Ask them, "How are consumers, decomposers, producers, and scavengers connected?"
2. Then, direct your student to view the video in the **Relationships in an Ecosystem - Watch It**.
3. Next, allow them time to complete the activity in the **Practice It**.
4. Last, guide them to play the game in the **Ecolibrium-Food Chain - Play It**.

Demonstrate

1. Now, have your student move on to the **Show It** to complete the activity. Then, direct them to the **Show It AK** to check their definitions. Be sure that they make any necessary corrections.
2. As an alternative to the **Show It**, instruct your student to make a flip-the-flap book with four sections. Guide them to complete the following steps:
   a. Have them fold a piece of paper in half lengthwise and then divide one side into the four sections.
   b. Tell them to cut along the lines to the fold. There should be four flaps that open up like doors. An image has been provided below for your reference.

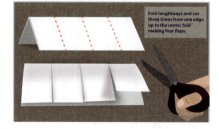

3. Direct your student to title each flap with one of the terms (*consumers*, *decomposers*, *producers*, and *scavengers*) and write a definition underneath the flap. Encourage them to draw an image as an example for each term.

236   Copyright 2018 © Lincoln Learning Solutions. All rights reserved.

Cycling Matter

Engage

1. While your student reads the **Read It**, ask them to explain what gets passed through the food chain from one organism to the next. Matter and energy get passed from one organism to another as each organism is consumed by another.

Demonstrate

1. Now, instruct your student to complete the "Cycle Diagram" activity page in the **Show It**.
2. Then, help your student to check their responses with the **Show It AK**.
3. To provide an alternative to the **Show It**, guide them to create a cycle of organisms with their stuffed animals or plastic figurines and some grass or leaves.

• • •

Carbon Cycle

Activate

1. Instruct your student to open the **The Carbon and Oxygen Cycle - Watch It** to view the video.
2. Prompt them to explain the importance of the carbon and oxygen cycle by asking them, "How are humans part of the carbon cycle?" Humans are part of the carbon cycle because they eat foods that contain carbon and exhale it through the respiration cycle.

Engage

1. After your student reads the content of the **Read It**, ask them to explain other ways that humans affect the carbon cycle. Humans also burn wood, coal, and fossil fuels that add carbon dioxide into the air.

Demonstrate

1. Now, have your student complete the activity in the **Show It**, and work with them to check their response with the **Show It AK**.
2. As an alternative to the **Show It**, instruct your student to draw and label a diagram of the carbon cycle. Allow them to reference the **Read It**, if necessary. When they are finished, have them verbally explain the process.

SCIENCE 4 PARENT & TEACHER GUIDE

LESSON 119

Topic | Ecology

Learning Objectives

The activities in this lesson will help your student meet the following objectives:

- explain how growth cycles matter through an ecosystem
- draw the process of photosynthesis

Materials

- colored pencils

Nitrogen Cycle

 ### Activate

1. Instruct your student to open the **Watch It** titled **The Nitrogen Cycle** to view the video.
2. Ask them to name three parts of the nitrogen cycle. For example, nitrogen is found in the air. Bacteria and fungi in soil modify it into a usable form. Plants absorb the nitrogen from the soil, and it helps them grow.

 ### Engage

1. As your student reads the **Read It**, discuss with them how nitrogen helps the growth cycle. Nitrogen is important for plants to grow to their necessary height.
2. Then, have them open the **Ecolibrium-Nitrogen Cycle - Play It** to play the game.

 ### Demonstrate

1. Now, direct your student to the **Show It** to complete the activity. Then, allow your student to compare their response to the sample in the **Show It AK**.
2. As an alternative to the **Show It**, have your student make a poster of the nitrogen cycle and then verbally explain the process. Allow them to search the Internet for a nitrogen cycle chart to reference.

Photosynthesis

Activate

1. Tell your student to open the **Examining Photosynthesis - Watch It** to view the video.
2. Pause at 0:56 for them to repeat the root meanings of the word *photosynthesis*.
3. Then, ask them to verbally summarize the process of photosynthesis.

Engage

1. While your student reads the content of the **Read It**, have them explain the process of photosynthesis while looking at the diagram.
2. Then, direct them to open the **Ecolibrium-Plants - Play It** and play the game.

Demonstrate

1. Now, instruct your student to create the diagram in the **Show It**. Allow them to reference the diagram in the **Read It**, if necessary.
2. Finally, encourage them to check their work using the sample provided in the **Show It AK**.
3. To extend learning, encourage your student to explain the steps of the photosynthesis process by writing a sentence for each part of the diagram.

SCIENCE 4 PARENT & TEACHER GUIDE

LESSON 120

Topic | Ecology

Learning Objectives

The activities in this lesson will help your student meet the following objectives:

- define the terms *sun*, *solar energy*, *renewable*, and *fossil fuel*
- list the advantages and disadvantages of solar energy
- define the terms *thermal*, *photon*, and *photovoltaic*

Materials

- bamboo sticks
- black paper
- foil
- glue
- plastic wrap
- potato
- scissors
- shoe box with lid
- shredded cheese
- tortilla

Renewable Energy

Activate

1. Give your student a potato and ask them, "How long do you think it takes to grow a potato?"
2. Tell them that it takes only three months to grow a potato. This timeframe is considered to be relatively fast, making the potato a renewable food source because it can be reproduced often.

Engage

1. As your student reads the text of the **Read It**, discuss with them the definition of *nonrenewable resources* such as fossil fuels. Nonrenewable resources take a very long time to reproduce.
2. Then, ask your student if they can think of other examples of renewable energy sources such as wind power.

Demonstrate

1. Now, direct your student to complete the activity in the **Show It**.
2. Then, assist them to check their definitions with the **Show It AK**. Encourage your student to add any missing details to their definitions.
3. As an alternative to the **Show It**, have them verbally use the terms *sun*, *solar energy*, *renewable*, and *fossil fuel* in a sentence.

• • •

Solar Energy

Engage

1. While your student reads the **Read It**, ask them to share a time that the sun helped them to be warm. Then, have them share a time that the sun was too hot and gave them a sunburn.

Demonstrate

1. Now, guide your student to complete the activity in the **Show It**.
2. Finally, work with them to check their responses with the **Show It AK**.

• • •

Solar Power

Activate

1. Instruct your student to open the **Solar and Thermal Energy - Watch It**.
2. Pause the video at 1:55 and ask them to explain conduction, convection, and radiation.
   - Conduction is when heat is transferring to another object through direct contact.
   - Convection is when heat is transferred through the circulation of a gas or liquid.
   - Radiation is the emission of heat through waves.

Engage

1. After your student reads the **Read It**, prompt them to explain how the terms *thermal*, *photon*, and *photovoltaic* are related to the sun.
2. Once they have shared their answers, confirm that thermal energy can be captured from the sun. Photons are light particles from the sun. Photovoltaic entails converting light to electricity such as through solar power.

Demonstrate

1. Now have your student move on to the **Show It** to write definitions for the terms.
2. Then, assist them to evaluate their definitions with the **Show It AK**. Encourage them to make any necessary changes.
3. As an alternative to the **Show It**, have them follow the steps below to make a solar oven.
   a. Cover the outside of the box with black paper.
   b. Cover the inside of the box with foil, including the lid.
   c. Place a tortilla at the bottom of the box and top it with a layer of shredded cheese.
   d. With the lid open, place a piece of plastic wrap over the opening of the box.
   e. Prop up the lid with bamboo sticks to keep it open.
   f. Set the box in the sun and record the time.
   g. Have your student determine how long it takes for the cheese to melt. Check the tortilla every five minutes to note its progress. The cheese should be melted in about 30 minutes, depending on the outside temperature.

LESSON 121

Topic: Ecology

Learning Objectives

The activities in this lesson will help your student meet the following objectives:

- explain how solar energy is collected
- define the terms *environment*, *adaptation*, and *evolution*

Materials

- dictionary

Collecting Energy

Activate

1. Have your student open the **Solar Energy - Watch It** and ask them to make note of the username and password provided on the Discovery Education image. Be sure that they click the link for the video and enter the provided username and password to watch.
2. Prompt them to explain how the ideas presented in the video support the ways in which solar energy is collected. The video explains how heat from the sun can get trapped, which is a method of collecting energy from the sun.

Engage

1. After your student reads the **Read It**, ask them if they could collect energy from their family's car on a hot summer day. Talk with them about how the car gets very hot during the summer. Have them think about opening the door of a hot car and the way in which a gust of hot air releases. When this happens, they most likely have to step back to allow it to escape.
2. Then, assist your student in searching the Internet for images of photovoltaic systems and thermal panels.

Demonstrate

1. Now, have your student complete the activity in the **Show It**.
2. Then, work with them to check their responses using the examples in the **Show It AK**.
3. As an alternative to the **Show It**, instruct your student to make a brochure about the various ways to collect solar energy. Encourage them to add images for each description.
4. To extend learning, assist your student in setting up an interview with someone who has solar panels at their home. Help your student to brainstorm three key questions to ask the interviewee to learn about how the solar panels are beneficial to their livelihood.

Adaptations

Activate

1. Direct your student to open the **Exploring Adaptations - Watch It** to view the video.
2. Discuss possible answers to the question presented at the end of the video. Hawks beaks are curved to kill and cut their prey. Pelicans have long, pouch-like beaks to scoop up fish.

1. As your student reads the **Read It**, begin a conversation about how humans have adapted. Ask them, "How do you think humans have adapted to their environment?" Answers may include the following:
   - Humans have adapted to run long distances.
   - The human body sweats to cool down when it is hot.
   - Since humans stand on two legs, they have two arms to use in other ways such as to throw with accuracy.

Demonstrate

1. Now, have your student move on to the **Show It** to complete the activity. When they are finished, allow them to compare their response to the sample in the **Show It AK**.
2. As an alternative to the **Show It**, instruct your student to choose an animal adaptation presented in the **Watch It**. Then, tell them to describe this adaption using the terms *environment*, *adaptation*, and *evolution*.

SCIENCE 4 PARENT & TEACHER GUIDE

LESSON 122

Topic | Ecology

Learning Objectives

The activities in this lesson will help your student meet the following objectives:

- explain the differences among physical, behavioral, and technological adaptations
- explain how humans have borrowed adaptations from other organisms
- identify ways in which human activities have affected an ecosystem

Materials

- scissors

Human Adaptations

Activate

1. Ask your student, "How do you think your body adapts as the seasons change?" They may mention that on cold winter days, their body may shiver to warm itself up more quickly. On hot summer days, their body may sweat to cool down quickly.

1. While your student reads the **Read It**, talk with them about the ways in which they use technology daily. Explain how some of the technological devices they use were not available when you were a child. Share what you used instead.

1. Now, instruct them to complete the activity in the **Show It**.
2. Then, assist your student to evaluate their responses with the **Show It AK**.
3. As an alternative to the **Show It**, have them make a paper doll cut out. Search the Internet to find instructions on how to make it.
   a. Have them create a chain with three paper dolls.
   b. Then, tell them to write examples of the three main types of human adaptations on each portion of the paper doll chain.

• • •

244

Borrowed Adaptations

1. As your student reads the **Read It**, ask them, "If you were to borrow any adaptation from another animal, what would you choose?" Follow up by asking, "How would this adaptation help you to survive better in your environment?"

Demonstrate

1. Open the **Assess It** and have your student complete the activity. Be sure that they read the expectations of the rubric before and after writing.
2. When they are finished, scan the document or take a photo of it and upload it to the Dropbox. For additional instructions on how to use the Dropbox, click on the paper clip icon in the upper-left corner of the **Assess It**.

Human Effects

Activate

1. Direct your student to open the **Endangered and Extinct - Watch It** to view the video.
2. Then, have your student list how humans have caused animals to become endangered or extinct. Habitat destruction, poaching or hunting, and pollution are all examples of animal endangerment and extinction caused by humans.

1. After your student reads the **Read It**, have them complete the following sentence stem:
   - I really want to find out about....

Demonstrate

1. Now, guide your student to complete the activity in the **Show It**. Encourage them to use the Internet to search for specific examples of ecosystem destruction caused by humans.
2. Finally, help your student to evaluate their responses using the **Show It AK**.
3. To provide an alternative to the **Show It**, instruct your student to create a problem and solution chart for human effects on ecosystems. For each problem they list, have them devise a solution or search for solutions on the Internet.

SCIENCE 4 PARENT & TEACHER GUIDE

LESSON 123

| Topic | Ecology |

Learning Objectives

The activities in this lesson will help your student meet the following objectives:

- identify ways in which natural or human influences have affected an ecosystem
- explain how agriculture can negatively impact an ecosystem

Materials

- plastic container
- soil
- toy trees or small branches
- water

Natural Effects

Activate

1. Direct your student to place some soil on one side of a container and set toy trees or small branches in the soil to represent a natural landscape.
2. Prompt them to shake the container like an earthquake and have them observe the effects.
3. Then, have them pour water up to the base of the trees in the container to simulate a flood. Discuss the effects a flood can have on an ecosystem.

Engage

1. As your student reads the content of the **Read It**, discuss any natural disasters that have occurred recently. You may want to look up articles in an online newspaper. Discuss the natural effects of the disaster with your student.
2. Then, instruct them to open the **Beaker's Big Buzz-Ecosystem - Play It** to play the game. Tell them to look up information on the Internet for any unknown answers.

Demonstrate

1. Now, direct your student to complete the activity in the **Show It**.
2. Then, use the **Show It AK** to help them check their responses.
3. To provide an alternative to the **Show It**, have your student create a comic strip that shows the human and natural effects on the environment.
4. To extend learning, take your student on a hike. While you walk, ask them to focus on the way in which the development of the trail affects the ecosystem by causing erosion or animal habitat destruction.

● ● ●

Farming Effects

Engage

1. Have your student identify the positive and negative effects of farming by creating a T-chart.
    a. Direct them to label the left side of the chart *Positive Effects of Farming* and the right side *Negative Effects of Farming*.
    b. Then, direct your student to read through the content of the **Read It**. As they read, ask them to complete the T-chart by listing the positive and negative effects of farming on the ecosystem.

Demonstrate

1. Now, have your student move on to the **Show It** to complete the activity, and encourage them to use the **Show It AK** to evaluate their response.
2. As an alternative to the **Show It**, help your student to locate historical images of a local farming area. Then, search the Internet for current pictures of the same area. Consider using a tool such as Google Earth. Instruct your student to describe the changes to the environment.
3. The next lesson is a **Mastery Assess It**. Encourage your student to review Lessons 115 through 123 in order to prepare for the assessment.

LESSON 124

Topic: Ecology

Learning Objectives

The activities in this lesson will help your student meet the following objectives:

- not applicable

Materials

- none required

Mastery Assess It 9

1. **Mastery Assess It 9** will cover what your student has learned in Lessons 115 through 123.
2. Click on the **Mastery Assess It 9** icon to begin the online assessment.
3. Have your student read the instructions before they get started. Remind them to take their time and to do their best work.
4. When they are finished and ready for their assessment to be graded, have them click the **Submit** button.

SCIENCE 4 PARENT & TEACHER GUIDE

LESSON 125

Topic: Watershed and Wetlands

Learning Objectives

The activities in this lesson will help your student meet the following objectives:

- explain the physical characteristics of a watershed
- identify what determines the boundaries of a watershed
- identify water systems and their components as either lotic or lentic and either biotic or abiotic

Materials

- baking sheet
- colored pencils or markers
- dictionary or glossary
- local geographical map
- play dough or modeling clay
- soil
- water

Watershed Defined

Activate

1. Have your student open the **Watershed - Watch It** to view the video.
2. If time permits, allow them to complete the watershed activity from the video and make observations about the flow of water.

Engage

1. After your student reads the **Read It**, have them draw a diagram of a watershed. Encourage them to color it and label its main parts: *source* or *headwaters*, *mouth*, and *tributaries*.

Demonstrate

1. Now, instruct your student to complete the activity in the **Show It**. Then, help them to compare their work to the sample in the **Show It AK**.
2. As an alternative to the **Show It**, have your student create a watershed model with play dough or modeling clay. Be sure they include the source or headwaters, mouth, and tributaries.

• • •

Watershed Boundaries

Engage

1. As your student reads the **Read It**, have them explain the term *watershed boundaries* in their own words. Help them to identify their local watershed boundaries (the highest areas).

Demonstrate

1. Now, have your student complete the activity in the **Show It**.
2. Then, work with them to evaluate their diagram using the example in the **Show It AK**.

• • •

Water Systems

Engage

1. While your student reads the **Read It**, discuss any local rivers, lakes, or streams they have visited. Ask them to use the terms from the content to describe the flow of the water and any organisms they noticed.

Demonstrate

1. Now, guide your student to complete the T-chart activities in the **Show It**.
2. Finally, assist them to check their responses by referring to the **Show It AK**.
3. To extend learning, help your student identify local water systems on a map. Have them look for rivers, lakes, and creeks.

SCIENCE 4 PARENT & TEACHER GUIDE

LESSON 126

Topic | Watersheds and Wetlands

Learning Objectives

The activities in this lesson will help your student meet the following objectives:

- describe the different kinds of wetlands
- explain the life cycles of freshwater organisms

Materials

- colored pencils
- paper plates

Wetland Types

 ### Activate

1. Have your student open the **Wetlands in the U.S. - Watch It** to learn about wetlands.
2. Then, ask them to describe the examples of wetlands presented in the video.

 ### Engage

1. Next, have your student read the content of the **Read It**. Then, have them draw an image of each wetland type. Instruct them to make sure that their drawings include the details that classify each wetland.

 ### Demonstrate

1. Open the **Assess It** and have your student complete the activity. When they are finished, scan the document or take a photo of it and upload it to the Dropbox. For additional instructions on how to use the Dropbox, click on the paper clip icon in the upper-left corner of the **Assess It**.

Life Cycles

Activate

1. Ask your student to describe the major growth stages of humans from baby to adult. They may mention that humans start as babies, then become children. Next, they develop into teenagers, and, finally, they become adults.

Engage

1. While your student reads the **Read It**, discuss the similarities between the frog and fish life cycles. For example, they both begin as eggs that hatch.
2. Next, direct your student to read the information in the **Practice It**.

Demonstrate

1. Now, have them move on to the activity in the **Show It**. They may need to look up information on the life cycle of ducks to complete the activity.
2. Then, allow your student to compare their response to the sample provided in the **Show It AK**.
3. As an alternative to the **Show It**, instruct your student to draw and label the life cycles of the duck and frog on a paper plate.
4. To extend learning, visit a pet store to see animals in the various stages of their life cycles.

SCIENCE 4 PARENT & TEACHER GUIDE

LESSON 127

Topic | **Natural Resources**

Learning Objectives

The activities in this lesson will help your student meet the following objectives:

- identify resources used to provide humans with energy, food, employment, housing, and water
- identify how humans depend on natural resources for survival
- identify the geographic origins of natural resources

Materials

- colored pencils
- index cards

Human and Natural Resources

Activate

1. Have your student open the **Farmers: Feeding the World - Watch It** to view the video.
2. Then, ask them, "Where do you think your food comes from?" Guide them to think beyond the grocery store.

Engage

1. As your student reads the content of the **Read It**, have them explain the term *natural resources*. (Answer: Natural resources are resources found in nature that can be used for other products.)
2. Then, ask them, "How do humans depend on natural resources?" (Answer: Humans rely on natural resources to make everything ranging from food, to lumber, to technology.)
3. Next, tell them to open the **Ecolibrium-Natural Resources - Play It** to play the game.

Demonstrate

1. Now, instruct your student to complete the activity in the **Show It**. Then, encourage them to compare their response to the sample in the **Show It AK**.
2. To provide an alternative to the **Show It**, have your student create a natural resource web. They can use the image below to get started.
    a. Instruct your student to write the name of a natural resource in the center circle.
    b. Then, have them write one way that humans use the resource in each of the outer circles.
    c. Allow them to draw images in the outer circles as well.
    d. Repeat these steps for various natural resources.

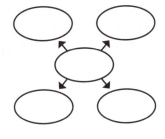

253

Human Survival

Engage

1. While your student reads the content of the **Read It**, discuss the natural resources they have used for survival throughout the day. Help them to distinguish the difference between what is needed for survival and what is used for leisure.

Demonstrate

1. Open the **Assess It** and have your student complete the activity. Be sure they review the expectations of the rubric before they begin to write.
2. When they are finished, scan the document or take a photo of it and upload it to the Dropbox. For additional instructions on how to use the Dropbox, click on the paper clip icon in the upper-left corner of the **Assess It**.

• • •

Resource Origins

Engage

1. Instruct your student to open the **Types of Natural Resources - Watch It** to view the video.
2. Then, ask them, "What are the advantages and disadvantages of renewable and nonrenewable resources?"
   - The advantage of renewable resources is that they can be replenished, but the disadvantage is that they require a lot of work to continue to renew.
   - The advantage of nonrenewable resources is that they are already created, but the disadvantage is that they cannot be replenished.
3. Then, direct your student to read the **Read It**. Discuss the local natural resources in your student's region. You may need to help them look up their state's natural resources if they are not familiar with this information.

Demonstrate

1. Now, tell your student to move on to the **Show It** to complete the matching activity.
2. Finally, assist them to check their responses with the **Show It AK**.
3. To extend learning, have your student make a matching game with index cards.
   a. Instruct them to draw images of the natural resources on index cards.
   b. Then, have them draw each resource's corresponding geographical location on additional cards.
   c. Finally, mix the cards, and allow your student to match the natural resource to its geographical region of origin.

LESSON 128

Topic: Humans' Effect on Earth

Learning Objectives

The activities in this lesson will help your student meet the following objectives:

- define the term *fuel*
- match natural resources to the correct forms of energy they produce
- identify the negative impacts to the environment of using fossil fuels

Materials

- chocolate chip cookie
- crayons or markers
- dictionary
- plate
- poster board
- toothpicks

Fuels

Activate

1. Set a chocolate chip cookie on a plate, and give your student two toothpicks. Tell them that the cookie represents the Earth, and the chocolate chips represent coal. Explain that they are to mine for the chocolate chips using only the toothpicks. Encourage them to make two piles, one for the chocolate chips and another for the remains.
2. When they finished, ask them, "What did you discover about mining for chocolate chip coal?" They should responded by saying that it requires a lot of work, and it is difficult to separate the chocolate chips without losing a lot of the cookie.
3. Then, ask them, "Will the Earth (cookie) ever return to the way it was?" (Answer: No, once the Earth is broken apart for coal, it will not return to its original form.)

Engage

1. While your student reads the **Read It**, discuss the types of fuels used in their home. For example, talk with them about the type of energy their stove or furnace uses?

Demonstrate

1. Now, have them move on to the **Show It** to complete the activity.
2. Then, help your student to check their definition with the **Show It AK**.
3. As an alternative to the **Show It**, instruct your student to create a diagram that shows types of fuels and describes how they are used.

Energy Sources

 **Activate**

1. Instruct your student to open the **Power to the People - Watch It** to view the video.
2. After the video, have them explain a risk of mining for fossil fuels. (Answer: There can be oil spills that destroy ecosystems.)

 **Engage**

1. As your student reads the **Read It**, ask them, "What alternative would you suggest for fossil fuels? Why would you make this suggestion?"
2. Then, direct your student to complete the activity in the **Extend It**.

 **Demonstrate**

1. Now, have your student complete the matching activity in the **Show It**.
2. Finally, help them to use the **Show It AK** to check their answers.

• • •

Fuel to Energy

 **Engage**

1. Guide your student to open the **Naturally Resourceful - Watch It** to view the video.
2. Then, have them read the content of the **Read It** and explain the negative effects of extracting fossil fuels.

 **Demonstrate**

1. Now, have your student create a poster as explained in the **Show It**.
2. Finally, assist them to evaluate their poster with the **Show It AK**.
3. To extend learning, encourage your student to present their poster to a small audience of peers or family members.

LESSON 129

SCIENCE 4 PARENT & TEACHER GUIDE

Topic: Humans' Effect on Earth

Learning Objectives

The activities in this lesson will help your student meet the following objectives:

- describe ways in which fuels derived from natural resources affect the environment
- define the term *local*

Materials

- colored pencils
- dead leaves or grass
- dictionary
- dirt
- eye dropper
- plastic cup
- sand
- small sponge
- water

List Effects

Activate

1. Ask your student, "How are fossil fuels formed underground?"
2. Then, have them complete the following steps to simulate fossil fuel formation.
   a. Cut the sponge to fit it inside the bottom of the cup.
   b. Add a layer of dead leaves or grass on top of the sponge. Explain that, millions of years ago, plants and animals died.
   c. Add a layer of dirt. Explain to your student that layers of dirt covered the plants and animals that died.
   d. Add a layer of sand on top of the dirt. Then, explain that more layers of sand compacted the dead plants and animals. Tell them that the plants and animals did not decay immediately, but the Earth slowly heated them.
   e. Pour water over the layers.
   f. Use the eyedropper to simulate drilling to the sponge. Extract the simulated oil from the bottom. Explain to your student that oil is found in pockets of the earth where the plants and animals were changed due to Earth's pressure and heat.

Engage

1. While your student reads the **Read It**, ask them to devise a plan to reduce their use of fossil fuels.
2. Discuss the challenges of reducing fossil fuel usage by helping them to understand human dependency on them.

Demonstrate

1. Now, have your student complete the **Show It** activity.
2. Then, work with your student to compare their response with the example in the **Show It AK**.
3. As an alternative to the **Show It**, instruct your student to create a diagram depicting the formation of fossil fuels. If they have trouble getting started, help them to recall the Activate activity.

Copyright 2018 © Lincoln Learning Solutions. All rights reserved.

Define *Local*

 **Activate**

1. Ask your student, "Before there were grocery stores, how did people get food?" Have a discussion with them about farming and the ways in which many farmers traded goods with each other.

 **Engage**

1. As your student reads the **Read It**, share with them any items that you purchase from local sources such as a farmers' market.

 **Demonstrate**

1. Now, direct your student to complete the activity in the **Show It**.
2. Then, help your student compare their response to the sample in the **Show It AK**.
3. Alternatively, search the Internet for local farmers' markets to determine their location. Also, look for the day and time of the market. Then, take your student to a farmers' market and help them to identify the origins of local items.

SCIENCE 4 PARENT & TEACHER GUIDE

LESSON 130

Topic: Humans' Effect on Earth

Learning Objectives

The activities in this lesson will help your student meet the following objectives:

- show how an agricultural commodity progresses from production to transportation to local consumption
- define the term *global*
- show how an agricultural commodity progresses from production to transportation to retailing to consumption

Materials

- ball
- colored pencils
- permanent marker
- produce with sticker labels
- world map

Local Production

Activate

1. Have your student open the **Fresh and Local or Not? - Watch It** and ask them to make note of the username and password provided on the Discovery Education image. Be sure that they click the link for the video and enter the provided username and password to watch.
2. Ask them, "How do you get the most nutrition from a fruit or vegetable?" Your student may respond by saying that eating foods that are grown locally will be more nutritious because they are harvested when the fruits and vegetables are ripe and contain the most vitamins.

Engage

1. While your student reads the **Read It**, discuss any experiences they have had on a farm. If they have never been on a farm, search the Internet to find a virtual farm tour.

Demonstrate

1. Now, have your student move on to the **Show It** to complete the activity.
2. Then, work with your student to check their responses with the **Show It AK**.
3. To provide an alternative to the **Show It**, instruct your student to draw and label a diagram of the steps to buy food from a farmers' market.

259

Define *Global*

Engage

1. As your student reads the **Read It**, have them explain what they think of when they hear the word *global*. They may think of a globe, which is spherical representation of Earth.

Demonstrate

1. Now, instruct them to complete the activity in the **Show It**. Then, help your student to evaluate their definition with the **Show It AK**.
2. Alternatively, direct your student to draw an outline of the continents on a ball. Allow them to reference a world map, if necessary.

• • •

Global Production

Engage

1. Direct your student to read the content of the **Read It**. Then, help them to examine the sticker labels on a few pieces of produce. Assist your student in identifying from where the produce originated.

Demonstrate

1. Now, guide your student to complete the activity in the **Show It**.
2. Assist them to check their response with the **Show It AK**.
3. Alternatively, have them draw and label the diagram of rice production from the **Show It**.
4. To extend learning, invite your student to go on a scavenger hunt to look for the origins of produce when they are at the grocery store.

SCIENCE 4 PARENT & TEACHER GUIDE

LESSON 131

Topic: Humans' Effect on Earth

Learning Objectives

The activities in this lesson will help your student meet the following objectives:

- compare and contrast the journey of local agricultural commodities to the journey of global agricultural commodities
- match the terms *agriculture*, *processing*, *transportation*, and *retailing* to their correct definition

Materials

- boxes of various sizes
- world map

Global Versus Local

Activate

1. Have your student choose a country on the world map. Then, using an online distance calculator, help them determine the distance from the country they chose to their home city.
2. Repeat these steps to determine the distance for three other countries. Discuss the ways in which food must be transported from these far away places. Goods would have to travel on boats, trucks, or planes for many days to arrive in your student's city.

Engage

1. While your student reads the **Read It**, discuss the benefits of local and global food. Local food is fresher, but global food allows humans to eat all types of foods all year long.

Demonstrate

1. Open the **Assess It** and have your student complete the activity. Direct them to read the expectations of the rubric before they begin writing.
2. When they are finished, scan the document or take a photo of it and upload it to the Dropbox. For additional instructions on how to use the Dropbox, click on the paper clip icon in the upper-left corner of the **Assess It**.

Distinguish Terms

Engage

1. As your student reads the **Read It**, invite them to explain the terms *agriculture*, *processing*, *transportation*, and *retailing* in their own words.
2. Then, ask them to identify the differences between the terms.

Demonstrate

1. Now, instruct your student to complete the activity in the **Show It**.
2. When they are finished, have them check their responses with the **Show It AK**.
3. Alternatively, assist them to create a crossword puzzle using the terms from the **Show It**.
4. To extend learning, guide your student to create a model of the process by which food travels from farm to plate. Tell them to use boxes of various sizes to represent the steps of this process.

SCIENCE 4 PARENT & TEACHER GUIDE

LESSON 132

Topic: Humans' Effect on Earth

Learning Objectives

The activities in this lesson will help your student meet the following objectives:
- describe how humans rely on the food and fiber system
- identify important agricultural products in their state

Materials
- colored pencils or markers
- poster board
- recipe

Food and Fiber System

Activate

1. Have your student open the **Food - Watch It** and ask them to make note of the username and password provided on the Discovery Education image. Be sure that they click the link for the video and enter the provided username and password to watch.
2. Then, prompt them to describe the steps it takes to make the bread found in the grocery store.

Engage

1. While your student reads the **Read It**, help them to determine what their shirt is made from by reading the tag. Discuss how these materials have to be produced from natural resources.

Demonstrate

1. Now, have your student move on to the **Show It** to complete the activity.
2. Then, help them to compare their response to the sample provided in the **Show It AK**.
3. As an alternative to the **Show It**, instruct your student to identify how each ingredient in a recipe is produced. Then, ask them to explain how these ingredients are part of the food and fiber system.

• • •

State Agricultural Products

1. As your student reads the **Read It**, discuss any local agricultural industries near their city. Ask them if they know of any factories in the area. If so, what agricultural products do they rely on?

1. Now, direct your student to complete the **Show It** activity to create a poster. Encourage them to include images with labels.
2. Finally, help them to evaluate their poster. Be sure that they included all of the top crops of their state and provided images and labels for each one.
3. To extend learning, arrange a factory tour for you and your student so that they can get a first-hand look at the process by which food is packaged.

SCIENCE 4 PARENT & TEACHER GUIDE

LESSON 133

Topic: Humans' Effect on Earth

Learning Objectives

The activities in this lesson will help your student meet the following objectives:

- describe the importance of one of the main agricultural products in your state
- predict the effects that soil type will have on seed growth

Materials

- colored pencils
- three planting pots
- three seeds
- three soil samples
- "Soil Types Investigation" activity page

Describe State Products

Activate

1. Invite your student to look for products in their learning environment that are produced in their state. Help them look for and read the distribution labels.
2. If they cannot find any products from their state, ask them, "From which state did most of the items originate?"

Engage

1. While your student reads the **Read It**, ask them which of the products presented in the text is their favorite.

Demonstrate

1. Now, have your student move on to the **Show It** to complete the activity.
2. Then, work with your student to evaluate their response. They can reference the **Show It AK** for an example paragraph.
3. As an alternative to the **Show It**, allow your student to choose a neighboring state to study its top agricultural products. Instruct them to draw the outline of their chosen state and label it. Then, have them list and draw the top five commodities of that state.
4. To extend learning, take your student for a drive into the countryside to look at some crop fields. Help them to determine the types of crops they see.

• • •

Copyright 2018 © Lincoln Learning Solutions. All rights reserved.

Soil Types

1. Have your student open the **Soils - Watch It** to view the video.
2. Then, ask them which soil type is the best for growing plants? (Answer: Loam soil is the best because it has a balanced mixture of the three main types of soils and humus.)

1. After your student reads the **Read It**, have them go on a scavenger hunt outside for the three main types of soil. They may not find them all.

1. Now, guide your student to predict the outcome of the experiment in the **Show It**. Encourage them to complete only the Hypotheses section of the activity page. The remainder of the activity page will be completed in Lesson 134.
2. Finally, check your student's hypothesis. You may want to reference the **Show It AK** for an example, but their prediction can be anything related to the results of the plant growth based on the varying types of soil.
3. To extend learning, have your student identify the soil at the base of different plants growing outdoors.

LESSON 134

Topic: Humans' Effect on Earth

Learning Objectives

The activities in this lesson will help your student meet the following objectives:

- list the materials used to perform a soil experiment
- list the steps taken to perform a soil experiment in order
- perform an experiment to observe the differences in composition of various soils

Materials

- clay
- cups or planting containers
- recipe
- sand
- silt
- three of the same type of seed
- "Soil Types Investigation" activity page

List Materials

Activate

1. Have your student read the list of ingredients in a recipe.
2. Then, ask them, "How is a recipe similar to an experiment?" They may mention that recipes and experiments both list materials and the steps and procedures that need to be taken to use those materials.

Engage

1. While your student reads the **Read It**, ask them, "What would happen if you misread one of the ingredients from the recipe?" Your student may respond by saying that the food being prepared would not taste very good.
2. Have a discussion with your student about the importance of gathering all the ingredients for a recipe, or materials for an experiment, before beginning. Explain that they should also double check the list of ingredients or materials to make sure they did not miss anything.

Demonstrate

1. Now, instruct your student to complete the materials list section of the activity page in the **Show It**. Explain that they will complete the remaining portions later in Lessons 134 and 135.
2. Then, direct them to reference the **Show It AK** to check the list of materials.
3. To provide an alternative to the **Show It**, have your student collect all the materials for the experiment and set them aside for later use.

Experiment Steps

 Engage

1. As your student reads the content of the **Read It**, ask them what would happen if you forget to complete a step in a recipe? (Answer: The food might not turn out correctly.)
2. Discuss the importance of reading or writing all the steps of an experiment before beginning. Explain to your student that doing so will help them to understand the entire process.
3. Then, explain to your student that, after reading all the steps to an experiment, they should reread them one-by-one as they complete the experiment.

 Demonstrate

1. Now, guide your student to complete the experiment steps of the activity page in the **Show It**.
2. Finally, help them to check their steps with the **Show It AK**.

• • •

Soil Experiment

 Engage

1. Direct your student to read the content of the **Read It**.
2. Then, have them review the purpose of and procedure for the soil experiment. The purpose is to see in which soil sample the seeds grow best. First, they will plant the seeds in three different soil samples. Then, your student will water the seeds regularly for six weeks to see which plant grows best.

 Demonstrate

1. Now, have your student move on to conducting the experiment in the **Show It**.
2. Since this experiment will take six weeks to complete, encourage them to record their observations and return to the questions when the experiment is complete.
3. You can reference the **Show It AK** so you know what to look for in the final results of the experiment.

LESSON 135

SCIENCE 4 PARENT & TEACHER GUIDE

Topic: Humans' Effect on Earth

Learning Objectives

The activities in this lesson will help your student meet the following objectives:

- illustrate the daily observations of a soil experiment
- summarize the daily observations of a soil experiment

Materials

- camera or smartphone
- colored pencils or crayons
- daily observations from soil experiment
- house plant or leaf
- "Soil Types Investigation" activity page

Draw Pictures

Activate

1. Set a house plant or leaf in front of your student and ask them to describe what they see. Guide them to focus on the lines of the stems, leaf edges, and branches.
2. Then, tell them to draw the plant or leaf and pay close attention to all the details. Explain that it is important to notice details when drawing observations.

Engage

1. Prompt your student to read the **Read It**.
2. Then, ask them to explain the importance of drawing pictures when conducting experiments. Your student should mention that, by drawing pictures, change over time can be communicated to others. The pictures also provide a record of learning.

Demonstrate

1. Now, have your student move to the **Show It**, where they will begin the illustrations of the experiment.
   a. Direct them to the Draw Pictures section of the activity page, which is found on the second page.
   b. Explain that they will draw their observations once a week for five weeks.
2. Once all of their illustrations are complete, help your student to check that they have drawn and labeled each plant for each week of growth.
3. To provide an alternative to the **Show It**, allow your student to take digital pictures of the plants each week. Help them compile these images in a document and record the sample number and date.

• • •

Observations

Engage

1. Next, have your student read the content of the **Read It**.
2. Then, ask them to explain why it is important to make observations. They should mention that making observations allows for the collection of information. For example, when observing plant growth, drawing and recording measurements are ways to collect data.

Demonstrate

1. Now, guide your student to the **Show It**. Since the experiment may not be complete yet, discuss how they can summarize the first few steps they have completed. When the experiment is finished, they can add more details about the process.
2. Finally, review the **Show It AK** with your student so that they know what to look for as the experiment continues.
3. To extend learning, allow your student to choose an outdoor plant, possibly one in their backyard, and draw it weekly. Encourage them to describe the differences they notice, especially during the spring, as plants begin to flourish.

LESSON 136

Topic: Humans' Effect on Earth

Learning Objectives

The activities in this lesson will help your student meet the following objectives:

- conclude an experiment involving testing three different types of soil
- compare an original hypothesis with the actual results of an experiment
- explain the differences between the compositions of three different types of soil and their ability to grow seedlings

Materials

- plants or seeds
- results of the soil experiment
- three types of soil
- "Soil Types Investigation" activity page

Conclude Results

Activate

1. Have your student verbally describe their activities from the previous day. Explain that they do not need to give an opinion, but only focus on what actually happened. Encourage them to use the transition words *first*, *then*, *next*, and *last*.

1. While your student reads the **Read It**, emphasize that the conclusion focuses only on the actual results. Explain that the following sentence stem is a good way to start a conclusion of results.
   - During the experiment, I observed…
2. Then, direct your student to open the **Ecolibrium-Soil - Play It** to play the game.

Demonstrate

1. Now, have your student move on to complete the Results section on the "Soil Types Investigation" activity page as directed in the **Show It**. If your student has not yet completed the previous sections of the activity page, have them do so before writing their results paragraph.
2. Then, allow your student to compare their results paragraph with the example provided in the **Show It AK**.

• • •

Compare Hypothesis

Engage

1. As your student reads the **Read It**, share the following sentence stem with them to use when they compare their hypothesis with the results.
   - My hypothesis was supported/rejected by the results because…

Demonstrate

1. Now, instruct your student to complete the activity in the **Show It**.
   a. Have them reread their hypothesis. If the experiment is not complete yet, allow them to verbally explain whether or not their hypothesis is supported so far.
   b. Then, guide them to complete the Compare Hypothesis section of the activity page when the experiment is finished.
2. Finally, work with your student to check that they compared their hypothesis with the results. There isn't a correct answer since the comparison is based on each individual's prediction and the test results.

• • •

Draw Conclusions about Soil

Engage

1. After your student reads the **Read It**, ask them to complete the following sentence stem to draw conclusions about soil experiment.
   - At the end of this experiment, I learned…

Demonstrate

1. Now, have your student move on to the **Show It** to complete the activity page. If they have not finished the experiment yet, then have them complete this section when they are done.
2. Finally, review the sample response in the **Show It AK** with your student. It will allow them to see an example of a concluding statement for an experiment.
3. To extend learning, allow your student to grow more seeds in pots or in the area outside where the best soil samples were collected.

LESSON 137

SCIENCE 4 PARENT & TEACHER GUIDE

Topic | Humans' Effect on Earth

Learning Objectives

The activities in this lesson will help your student meet the following objectives:
- define a hunter-gatherer society
- define the term *domesticated*

Materials
- dictionary
- markers
- poster board

Hunter-Gatherer

Activate

1. Have your student open the **Hunter-Gatherer Communities - Watch It** and ask them to make note of the username and password provided on the Discovery Education image. Be sure that they click the link for the video and enter the provided username and password to watch.
2. Ask them, "How can you verbally describe a hunter-gatherer society?" A possible response may be, "A hunter-gatherer society moves from place to place in search of food."

Engage

1. As your student reads the **Read It**, ask them if they have ever gone camping. Discuss all the work it takes to go camping, such as packing everything they will need including a tent, bedding, clothes, food, and water. Emphasize the amount of work it takes to pack up and move many times.

Demonstrate

1. Now, direct your student to complete the activity in the **Show It**. Then guide them to compare their response to the sample in the **Show It AK**.
2. As an alternative to the **Show It**, ask your student to draw a scene showing a hunter-gatherer society. Tell them to include a caption under the drawing that explains the scene.

• • •

Define *Domesticated*

Engage

1. While your student reads the **Read It**, ask them if they have any domesticated animals as pets.
2. Extend the conversation by discussing how wild animals, such as lions, bears, and alligators, are not good for domestication.

Demonstrate

1. Now, instruct your student to complete the activity in the **Show It** by defining the word *domesticated*.
2. Next, assist your student to check their work using the sample definition provided in the **Show It AK**.
3. As an alternative to the **Show It**, guide your student to make a poster of domesticated animals and wild animals. Allow them to search the Internet for additional examples of domesticated and wild animals.

LESSON 138

| Topic | Humans' Effect on Earth |

Learning Objectives

The activities in this lesson will help your student meet the following objectives:

- explain how domesticated animals affected agricultural production
- identify famous inventors and their inventions
- describe how an invention affected agricultural production

Materials

- colored pencils

Domestication Effects

Activate

1. Sing the song "Old MacDonald Had a Farm" with your student. Ask them to identify which animals used in the song are domesticated. For example, cows, chickens, and pigs are all domesticated animals.

Engage

1. As your student reads the **Read It**, discuss how they depend on domesticated animals to meet one of their basic needs: food. Domesticated animals provide humans with foods such as meat, milk, and cheese.

Demonstrate

1. Now, have your student move on to the **Show It** to complete the activity.
2. Then, allow them to compare their response to the sample in the **Show It AK**.
3. To provide an alternative to the **Show It**, allow your student to create a comic strip that shows the effect of domesticated animals on agriculture.

• • •

Inventions

 Activate

1. Have your student open the **Farm Tech - Watch It** to view the video.
2. Ask them, "How are machines connected to agricultural production?" (Answer: Machines have helped agricultural production to become more efficient. With the help of machines, farms can now produce more food using less time and space.)

 Engage

1. While your student reads the **Read It**, prompt them to verbally explain the purpose of each invention and name its inventor.
2. Then, tell them to open the **Nueva's Cross Country Chase-Amazing Inventors - Play It** to learn about inventors. Discuss which of the inventions pertain to agriculture.

 Demonstrate

1. Now, direct your student to complete the activity in the **Show It**. Allow them to reference the **Read It**, if necessary.
2. Then, have them check their answers with the **Show It AK**.
3. As an alternative to the **Show It**, instruct your student to design an invention what would help agricultural production. Have them draw a diagram of their invention and describe its function and purpose.

• • •

Invention Effects

 Engage

1. As your student reads the **Read It**, discuss the idea that even though these machines were helpful, they took job opportunities away from people.

 Demonstrate

1. Now, guide your student to complete the **Show It** activity and compare their response to example in the **Show It AK**.
2. To provide an alternative to the **Show It**, instruct your student to create a newspaper ad for an agricultural invention. Tell them to include details about how the invention is helpful and how it increases production.

LESSON 139

SCIENCE 4 PARENT & TEACHER GUIDE

Topic: Humans' Effect on Earth

Learning Objectives

The activities in this lesson will help your student meet the following objectives:

- distinguish between the terms *sustainable resource* and *nonsustainable resource*
- identify resources as either sustainable or nonsustainable

Materials

- crayons, markers, or colored pencils
- dictionary

Sustainability

Activate

1. Have your student open the **Sustainability - Watch It** and ask them to make note of the username and password provided on the Discovery Education image. Be sure that they click the link for the video and enter the provided username and password to watch.
2. Pause at 0:30, and allow your student to answer the question in the video.

Engage

1. As your student reads the **Read It**, ask them, "How would you explain the difference between the terms *sustainable* and *nonsustainable*?"
2. Then, tie in the terms *renewable* and *nonrenewable* from Lesson 120. Prompt them to think about how the terms *sustainable* and *renewable* are alike. *Sustainable* and *renewable* are terms that both describe something that can be replenished.
3. Next, ask them how the terms *nonsustainable* and *nonrenewable* are alike. *Nonsustainable* and *nonrenewable* are terms that describe something that is not replenishable.

Demonstrate

1. Now, direct your student to complete the Venn diagram in the **Show It**.
2. Finally, have them evaluate their response with the **Show It AK**.

• • •

Identify Resources

## Activate

1. Instruct your student to open the **Paths to Sustainability - Watch It** to view the video.
2. Pause the video at 0:37, and allow them to answer the question.
3. Then, discuss the ways in which they live sustainably.

## Engage

1. While your student reads the **Read It**, emphasize that even though some plastic is recyclable, it is made from petroleum oil, which is not a sustainable resource.

## Demonstrate

1. Now, have your student complete the T-chart as directed in the **Show It**.
2. Finally, allow them to use the **Show It AK** to check their answers.
3. To extend learning, invite your student to design a new toy that uses only sustainable resources. Instruct them to create an advertisement that depicts the new toy and describes the materials used to create it.

LESSON 140

SCIENCE 4 PARENT & TEACHER GUIDE

Topic: Humans' Effect on Earth

Learning Objectives

The activities in this lesson will help your student meet the following objectives:

- describe a natural resource
- define the term *pest* as it relates to organisms
- explain the reasons why a boll weevil is considered a pest to cotton farmers

Materials

- dictionary

Natural Resources

Activate

1. Invite your student to look around their learning environment and identify the natural resources used to make five items. For example, a wooden chair is made from trees.

1. As your student reads the **Read It**, help them to brainstorm a list of additional natural resources beyond those presented in the text. Use the following list as a guide:
   - minerals
   - soil
   - plants
   - animals
   - copper
   - iron

Demonstrate

1. Open the **Assess It** and have your student complete the activity. Make sure they review the expectations of the rubric before and after they complete the activity.
2. When they are finished, scan the document or take a photo of it and upload it to the Dropbox. For additional instructions on how to use the Dropbox, click on the paper clip icon in the upper-left corner of the **Assess It**.

Pests

Activate

1. Have your student open the **Controlling Pests - Watch It** to view the video.
2. Ask them to explain the difference between beneficial insects and pests. Beneficial insects help plants, such as the bees that pollinate flowers. On the other hand, pests, such as grasshoppers, can eat an entire crop.

Engage

1. While your student reads the **Read It**, ask them if they can remember a time that an insect was bothering them. Many people are bothered by mosquitoes or flies.

Demonstrate

1. Now, have your student move on to the activity in the **Show It**. Then, reference the **Show It AK** to help them check their definition.
2. As an alternative to the **Show It**, allow your student to examine some plants and search for any pests that may be eating those plants. Encourage them to determine the damage that the pest is causing to the plant. Roses usually have aphids attacking them.

Boll Weevil

Engage

1. As your student reads the **Read It**, have them explain why cotton is an important crop. They may mention that it is important because humans use cotton to make fabrics for clothing and other household items.

Demonstrate

1. Now, direct your student to complete the task in the **Show It**. Then, work with them to evaluate their response with the **Show It AK**.
2. As an alternative to the **Show It**, help your student search the Internet for the lyrics to the song "The Boll Weevil" by Brook Benton. Explain that this song was originally written in the 1920s when the boll weevil destroyed many American cotton farms. Ask them to identify the lines of the song that explain why a boll weevil is a pest.
   - The following lines explain how an entire family of boll weevils moves in and takes over. A female boll weevil can lay 200 eggs in about 12 days.

     Say yep, my whole darn family's here
     We gotta have a home

   - These following lines explain that once the boll weevils lay their eggs in the cotton, then the cotton is ruined and the crop is destroyed. The farmer will not be able to sell it and will become so poor that he cannot buy gasoline.

     'Cause when I'm through with your cotton
     Heh, you can't even buy gasoline
     I'm gonna take me a home

SCIENCE 4 PARENT & TEACHER GUIDE

LESSON 141

Topic | Humans' Effect on Earth

Learning Objectives

The activities in this lesson will help your student meet the following objectives:

- explain the measures that farmers take to eradicate pests and the possible consequences of these actions
- list ways in which human activities might negatively affect the environment

Materials

- crayons, markers, or colored pencils

Pesticides

 ### Activate

1. Have your student open the **Environmental Impact - Watch It** to view the video.
2. Pause at 2:58 for them to explain the meaning of organic food and why it is helpful to the environment. They may mention that organic food is grown without the use of pesticides, which helps to keep harmful chemicals out of the natural environment.

1. After your student reads the **Read It**, ask them, "Which of the following solutions would you choose to fix a snail problem in your garden?" Ask them to explain their reasoning for their choice.
   - Use a snail pesticide, which is not good for the environment.
   - Spray plants with cold coffee or scatter coffee grounds at their base, which does not harm the earth.

 ### Demonstrate

1. Now, have your student move on to the **Show It** to complete the activity.
2. Then, work with them to evaluate their response by comparing it to the sample in the **Show It AK**.
3. To provide an alternative to the **Show It**, help your student create a skit about an insect pest that eats a plant. Have them include a solution to the problem in their skit. Instruct them to explain the possible consequences of the solution to the pest problem.

• • •

282   Copyright 2018 © Lincoln Learning Solutions. All rights reserved.

Human Activity

 Engage

1. Prompt your student to read the content of the **Read It**. When they are finished, ask them to share some ideas for solving some of the environmental problems caused by humans that were presented in the text.

 Demonstrate

1. Now direct your student to compile a list as directed in the **Show It**. A sample list is provided in the **Show It AK**.
2. Alternatively, instruct your student to create a booklet that illustrates and describes the ways in which human activity can harm the planet.

LESSON 142

Topic: Humans' Effect on Earth

Learning Objectives

The activities in this lesson will help your student meet the following objectives:

- explain the negative effects of plastic on the environment
- explain the positive effects of plastic in everyday life
- list ways in which the use of automobiles affects people's lives and the environment

Materials

- various plastic objects

Plastics

 Activate

1. Place the various plastic objects in front of your student for them to make observations.
   a. Direct them to look for the recycling symbol on each object and identify the number.
   b. Explain to your student that the number they see refers to the type of plastic from which the object is made.
2. Finally, explain that even though there is a chasing arrow symbol, it does not mean that all types of plastic are recyclable.

 Engage

1. While your student reads the **Read It**, discuss some ways in which they can reduce the amount of plastic they use. For example, do they have a reusable water bottle? Instead of disposable plastic bags, can they place food in reusable containers for storage?

 Demonstrate

1. Now, have your student move on to the **Show It**. Then, instruct them to check their response with the **Show It AK**.
2. As an alternative to the **Show It**, invite your student to research a type(s) of plastic they observed in the Activate activity.
   a. Have them focus on learning about the process used to make each type of plastic and determine whether or not it is recyclable.
   b. Then, tell them to create and label a diagram of the steps it takes to make the plastic material.

Positives of Plastics

Engage

1. As your student reads the **Read It**, have them explain the term *biodegradable* in their own words.
2. Then, ask them to look for three plastic objects in their learning environment that help them with their daily tasks.

Demonstrate

1. Now, guide your student to complete the activity in the **Show It**. Next, assist them to evaluate their response by comparing it to the sample in the **Show It AK**.
2. As an alternative to the **Show It**, instruct your student to research the plastic recycling process on the Internet. Have them create and label a diagram that shows the steps used to recycle plastic.

• • •

Automobiles

Activate

1. Have your student open the **Automobiles: Pros and Cons - Watch It** and ask them to make note of the username and password provided on the Discovery Education image. Be sure that they click the link for the video and enter the provided username and password to watch.
2. Then, help them to determine an estimate of how many times a day they travel in an automobile. Do they go somewhere every day?

Engage

1. After your student reads the **Read It**, ask them if they think the automobile is a good or bad invention? Encourage them to give reasons to support their response.

Demonstrate

1. Now, prompt your student to complete the T-chart as directed in the **Show It**. Then, allow them to compare their response to the sample in the **Show It AK**.
2. To extend learning, allow your student to search the Internet for images of automobiles from the 1930s, the 1950s, and today. Then, tell them to draw or print the images to create a brochure to show how automobiles have changed over time.

SCIENCE 4 PARENT & TEACHER GUIDE

LESSON 143

Topic: Humans' Effect on Earth

Learning Objectives

The activities in this lesson will help your student meet the following objectives:

- explain how agriculture can have a negative impact on water systems
- illustrate ways to improve the use of natural resources

Materials

- art supplies
- poster board
- rectangular storage container
- sand
- soil
- water

Agriculture and Water

Activate

1. Begin by placing the sand in the storage container. Then, have your student create two hillsides with a valley in between them.
2. Next, ask them to designate an area inside the container for a farm by adding a layer of soil to a small section.
3. Next, ask your student, "What do you think will happen when you pour water over the farm area?" Guide them to think about the runoff from the farm that will go into the valley area.
4. Last, tell them to pour water over the farm and observe what happens. Prompt them to share what they observe. They should notice that the soil moves towards the valley, which could also be considered a river bed area.

Engage

1. As your student reads the **Read It**, discuss the origins of the water they drink. For example, do they drink water directly from the tap? Do they drink filtered water or bottled water?
2. Then, tell them to open the **Ecolibrium-Agriculture - Play It** to play the game.

Demonstrate

1. Now, direct your student to complete the activity in the **Show It**. Then, direct them to the **Show It AK** to evaluate their response.
2. As an alternative to the **Show It**, prompt your student to pretend they are a lawmaker in the government.
   a. Tell them that it is their job to create a new law that prohibits the contamination of water from agricultural practices.
   b. The law must focus on specific causes of contamination such as pesticides, fertilizers, and animal waste runoff.
   c. Encourage your student to determine the punishment for breaking the law.

Improve the Use of Resources

Engage

1. While your student reads the **Read It**, ask them to share how they use natural resources in their day-to-day activities.

Demonstrate

1. Now, have your student complete the poster as directed in the **Show It**.
2. Then, use the **Show It AK** to make sure your student's poster meets the expectations for the activity. They should have identified a natural resource and three ways to improve its use.
3. To extend learning, allow your student to search their learning environment to find three items that are recycled, or can be recycled for a secondary use instead of being thrown away. For example, a canned food container can be used to hold pencils.

SCIENCE 4 PARENT & TEACHER GUIDE

LESSON 144

Topic Humans' Effect on Earth

Learning Objectives

The activities in this lesson will help your student meet the following objectives:

- define the term *pollution*
- describe how air pollution can negatively affect a person's well-being
- list diseases that can be transmitted through unclean water

Materials

- dictionary or glossary
- colored pencils
- index cards

Define *Pollution*

 Activate

1. Have your student open the **Pollution and You - Watch It** to view the video.
2. Pause at 1:15, and ask them to explain the term *pollutant*. A pollutant is something that is harmful to the environment such as some chemicals.

 Engage

1. While your student reads the **Read It**, guide them to identify the types of pollution in the images. Encourage them to share any experiences they have with seeing these types of pollution.

 Demonstrate

1. Now, instruct your student to complete the activity in the **Show It**. Then, work with them to check their definition with the **Show It AK**. Allow them to make revisions to their response, if necessary.
2. As an alternative to the **Show It**, allow your student to draw images of pollution and verbally explain the term using the images as a visual aid.

• • •

Air Pollution

Engage

1. As your student reads the **Read It**, discuss how contaminated air causes many cases of asthma. People who live in large agricultural communities or cities often have issues with asthma.
2. Then, have them open the **Ecolibrium-Pollution - Play It** to play the game.

Demonstrate

1. Now, direct your student to complete the activity in the **Show It**. Then help them compare their response to the sample in the **Show It AK**.
2. As an alternative to the **Show It**, instruct your student to make three air pollution trading cards.
   a. Help them to search the Internet for types of air pollution, and ask them to choose three on which to focus.
   b. Then, tell them to label and describe the type of air pollution on one side of an index card.
   c. Next, have them draw an image for each type of air pollution on the opposite side of each card.

Water Pollution

Engage

1. After your student reads the **Read It**, ask them what they wonder about water pollution.
2. Then, tell them to open and view the video in the **Types of Pollution - Watch It**.
3. Next, guide them to read the information and answer the questions in the **Extend It**.

Demonstrate

1. Now, have your student complete the activity in the **Show It**.
2. Finally, use the **Show It AK** to help them check their work.
3. To extend learning, encourage your student to make a booklet that describes the diseases that can be transmitted through unclean water.

LESSON 145

Topic: Humans' Effect on Earth

Learning Objectives

The activities in this lesson will help your student meet the following objectives:

- illustrate ways in which pollution can negatively affect human health
- define the term *waste stream*

Materials

- art supplies
- colored pencils
- crayons, markers, or paint
- poster board

Pollution and Health

Activate

1. Have your student open the **Pollution - Watch It** and ask them to make note of the username and password provided on the Discovery Education image. Be sure that they click the link for the video and enter the provided username and password to watch.
2. Pause the video at 0:29, and allow them to answer the question. Encourage your student to give a reason to support their response.

Engage

1. As your student reads the **Read It**, have them take note of the illnesses caused by each type of pollution. They can use these notes while completing the **Assess It**.
2. Then, tell them to open the **Ecolibrium-Pollution - Play It** to play the game.

Demonstrate

1. Open the **Assess It** and have your student complete the activity. Be sure that they review the expectations in the rubric before they begin.
2. When they are finished, scan the document or take a photo of it and upload it to the Dropbox. For additional instructions on how to use the Dropbox, click on the paper clip icon in the upper-left corner of the **Assess It**.

Waste Streams

Engage

1. As your student reads the **Read It**, ask them to identify the day of the week that garbage is picked up from their home.
2. Then, ask your student if they know where their trash is taken to be disposed of. If they don't know, help them determine the location of their local landfill by looking at a map or describing landmarks near it.

Demonstrate

1. Now, instruct your student to complete the activity in the **Show It**. Then, help them to evaluate their definition with the **Show It AK**.
2. As an alternative to the **Show It**, allow your student to draw and label a diagram that shows various waste streams coming from their home such as garbage, liquid, and recycling.

SCIENCE 4 PARENT & TEACHER GUIDE

LESSON 146

Topic | Humans' Effect on Earth

Learning Objectives

The activities in this lesson will help your student meet the following objectives:

- list ways in which your household adds to the waste stream
- describe the impact that strip mining can have on the land and environment
- identify items that can be recycled and those that cannot

Materials

- colored pencils
- trash can

Waste

Activate

1. Tell your student to look at the items in the trash can, without touching it, and list five items that they see.
2. Then, ask them, "Could any of the items be reused, recycled or composted?" Containers can be reused or recycled and food scraps can be composted.

Engage

1. After your student reads the **Read It**, allow them to collect the mail and sort the envelopes into two piles. Ask them to make one pile for important documents and another for junk mail.
2. Then, ask them, "Which pile has more waste?"

Demonstrate

1. Now, direct your student to complete the activity in the **Show It**.
2. Then, use the **Show It AK** and work with them to check their response.
3. To extend learning, allow your student to start a compost bin to decompose food scraps.
   a. Help them to research types of homemade compost bins on the Internet.
   b. Also, it is important that they know what types of food scraps are good for composting. Help them to research a list of food that can be composted.

• • •

Strip Mining

Engage

1. As your student reads the **Read It**, encourage them to describe the images of strip mining from the text.
2. Then, ask them, "How would you change the way the mineral deposits are removed from the earth? Can you think of ways that aren't so destructive to the environment?"

Demonstrate

1. Now, instruct your student to complete the activity in the **Show It**. Then, have them reference the **Show It AK** to evaluate their response with the sample answer.
2. To provide an alternative to the **Show It**, allow your student to draw a before and after picture of a natural setting that has been strip mined. If necessary, have them reference images on the Internet.

Recycling

Activate

1. Tell your student to open the **Reused and Recycled - Watch It** to view the video.
2. Then, have them explain the terms *reuse*, *reduce*, and *recycle*.

Engage

1. While your student reads the **Read It**, ask them to name some items that they recycle on a regular basis, if possible. Some cities do not offer recycling pick-up, so you may want to discuss where your student could take items to be recycled.

Demonstrate

1. Now, direct your student to complete the activity in the **Show It**. When they are finished, work with them to compare their lists to the samples provided in the **Show It AK**.
2. As an alternative to the **Show It**, instruct your student to point out five recyclable and nonrecyclable items in their learning environment.

SCIENCE 4 PARENT & TEACHER GUIDE

LESSON 147

Topic | Humans' Effect on Earth

Learning Objectives

The activities in this lesson will help your student meet the following objectives:

- describe how to reduce the effect of everyday activities on natural resources
- list catastrophic natural events that have major impacts on humans

Materials

- colored pencils

Persuade to Conserve

Activate

1. Ask your student, "If you wanted to go to the movies with a friend, how would you convince your parent or guardian to take you?"
2. Tell your student to give three details to support their reasoning.

Engage

1. While your student reads the **Read It**, have them note the methods of conserving natural resources presented in the text. Then, have a discussion with them about some pros and cons of these methods.

Demonstrate

1. Now, instruct your student to complete the persuasive letter in the **Show It**. Help them to brainstorm ideas about a topic before they begin to write.
2. Finally, work with your student to evaluate their letter and check that they included the following criteria:
    - They named one natural resource.
    - They described how the natural resource is affected by human daily use.
    - They provided steps to reduce the use of the natural resource.
3. To provide an alternative to the **Show It**, guide your student to design and teach a class about the ways in which a specific natural resource is used. Be sure that they also teach their class ways to reduce the use of this resource.

• • •

Natural Processes

Activate

1. Have your student open the **Natural Disasters - Watch It** to view the video.
2. Encourage them to create the tectonic plates with their hands as demonstrated in the video.
3. Once the video ends, prompt your student to explain the ways in which natural disasters affect humans.

Engage

1. As your student reads the **Read It**, have a discussion with them about where each type of natural process usually occurs in the United States. For example, earthquakes commonly occur along the Pacific coast. Tornadoes often occur in Florida and the south-central region of the United States.
2. Then, allow your student time to engage with the games in the **Play Its** titled **Ecolibrium-Disasters**, **Disaster Strikes-Tornado**, and **Disaster Strikes-Natural Disasters**.

Demonstrate

1. Now, direct your student to complete the activity in the **Show It**.
2. Then, allow them to evaluate their work by comparing their response to the sample in the **Show It AK**.
3. To extend learning, instruct your student to make a map of the United States that indicates the major natural disasters that occur in specific regions.
   a. Allow them to reference information on the Internet to create their map.
   b. Instruct them to use symbols to represent the natural disasters and create a key that labels the symbols.

SCIENCE 4 PARENT & TEACHER GUIDE

LESSON 148

Topic | Humans' Effect on Earth

Learning Objectives

The activities in this lesson will help your student meet the following objectives:

- compare and contrast solutions for reducing the impact of a catastrophic natural Earth process on humans
- list noncatastrophic natural Earth processes
- describe possible solutions for reducing the impacts of a noncatastrophic natural Earth process on humans

Materials

- card stock or drawing paper
- colored pencils, crayons, or markers
- index cards

Reducing Impact

Activate

1. Help your student identify the volcano closest to where they live by searching the Internet.
2. Then, discuss whether or not it is a concern for them if it were to erupt.

Engage

1. As your student reads the **Read It**, ask them if they have any ideas of other ways to reduce the impact of natural processes.

Demonstrate

1. Now, instruct your student to complete the brochure activity in the **Show It**.
2. Finally, reference the **Show It AK** to evaluate your student's brochure, and help them to identify areas where they can make improvements.

• • •

Minor Processes

Engage

1. After your student reads the **Read It**, ask them, "How would you compare the effects of minor and major natural processes on humans?" Major natural processes cause significant damage to an area in a short amount of time, whereas minor natural processes are slower and cause smaller amounts of damage over a longer period of time.
2. Then, direct your student to open the **Disaster Strikes-Flood - Play It** and allow them time to play the game.

Demonstrate

1. Now, instruct your student to complete the **Show It** activity.
2. Finally, use the **Show It AK** to assist your student in checking their response.
3. To extend learning, take your student for a walk in a natural setting. Ask them to observe signs of erosion, landslides, weathering, or drought.

• • •

Solutions for Processes

Engage

1. While your student reads the **Read It**, ask them, "What evidence from the text can you find that describes solutions for minor natural processes?"

Demonstrate

1. Now, direct your student to complete the **Show It** activity. Then, help them to evaluate their paragraph with the sample in the **Show It AK**. Allow them to make any necessary revisions.
2. As an alternative to the **Show It**, have your student make puzzle pieces that match natural process problems with their solutions.
   a. Instruct your student to use an index card as a two-piece puzzle by drawing a curved line that looks like a puzzle piece.
   b. On one side of the index card, name the natural process. On the other side, describe the solution.
   c. Cut out the puzzle pieces, mix them up, and have your student complete the puzzle.
3. The next lesson is a **Mastery Assess It**. Encourage your student to review Lessons 128 through 148 in order to prepare for the assessment.

LESSON 149

Topic: Humans' Effect on Earth

Learning Objectives

The activities in this lesson will help your student meet the following objectives:

- not applicable

Materials

- none required

Mastery Assess It 10

1. **Mastery Assess It 10** will cover what your student has learned in Lessons 128 through 148.
2. Click on the **Mastery Assess It 10** icon to begin the online assessment.
3. Have your student read the instructions before they get started. Remind them to take their time and to do their best work.
4. When they are finished and ready for their assessment to be graded, have them click the **Submit** button.

LESSON 150

SCIENCE 4 PARENT & TEACHER GUIDE

Topic Technology and Engineering

Learning Objectives

The activities in this lesson will help your student meet the following objectives:

- identify the materials and skills needed to accomplish design tasks
- identify materials and tools needed to construct a prototype
- explain the appropriate materials and tools needed to safely construct a prototype

Materials

- tool box or an image of tools in a tool box

Material Matching

Activate

1. Invite your student to look through a tool box. If a tool box is not available, have them look at an image of tools in a tool box.
2. Next, instruct your student to name some of the tools and explain their use.

Engage

1. As your student reads the **Read It**, have them share a time that they made something and needed to gather the materials first. Prompt them to verbally list the materials and steps they used for the project.

Demonstrate

1. Now, direct your student to complete the matching activity in the **Show It**.
2. Then, direct them to the **Show It AK** to check their answers.
3. To extend learning, show your student where the jack and spare tire are located in a car.

Prototype Materials

Engage

1. Before your student reads the **Read It**, ask them to describe how they would build a birdhouse. What materials would they need?
2. Then, have them compare their method with the process described in the **Read It**.

Demonstrate

1. Now, instruct your student to complete the activity in the **Show It**. Allow them to draw their table design before they list their materials.
2. Finally, allow your student to compare their materials list to the sample in the **Show It AK**. Encourage them to give explanations for any items that are different than those provided the answer key.

• • •

Materials Paragraph

Engage

1. While your student reads the **Read It**, ask them if they would use different materials, tools, or steps to construct a ladder or sew a pair of pants.

Demonstrate

1. Now, direct your student to complete the activity in the **Show It**.
2. Then, help them to use the **Show It AK** to evaluate their paragraph, and invite them to make any necessary revisions.
3. To provide an alternative to the **Show It**, allow your student to create their own design prototype for a pair of pants by drawing a diagram. Then, tell them to list the materials, tools, and steps needed to create their design.

SCIENCE 4 PARENT & TEACHER GUIDE

LESSON 151

Topic: Technology and Engineering

Learning Objectives

The activities in this lesson will help your student meet the following objectives:

- build a prototype out of wooden sticks and glue
- summarize skills needed to construct a prototype
- explain how simple tools can be replaced with complex tools or machines when creating a prototype

Materials

- glue
- wooden sticks

Table Skills

Activate

1. Guide your student to examine a table in their learning environment.
2. Prompt them to describe how they think the table was made. Ask them, "What materials, tools, and steps did the builder have to take in order to make the table?"

Engage

1. After your student reads the **Read It**, ask them what steps they would take to make a table from wooden sticks.

Demonstrate

1. Now, instruct your student to complete the activity in the **Show It**. Encourage them to make a design plan before they begin to construct their table.
2. Finally, check that their table stands alone and has a table top. Ask them what worked well with their design and what parts could be improved.

• • •

Table Skills Reporting

Engage

1. As your student reads the **Read It**, prompt them to explain the skills needed for each step of constructing a table.

Demonstrate

1. Open the **Assess It** and have your student complete the activity. Be sure that they review the expectations of the rubric before they begin to write.
2. When they are finished, scan the document or take a photo of it and upload it to the Dropbox. For additional instructions on how to use the Dropbox, click on the paper clip icon in the upper-left corner of the **Assess It**.

System of Tools Paragraph

Engage

1. While your student reads the **Read It**, ask them if they have ever used any of the simple tools described in the text. Have they seen any of the complex tools? Then, prompt them to share how the tools were used.

Demonstrate

1. Now, instruct your student to complete the task in the **Show It**. Then, help them to evaluate their paragraph by comparing it to the sample in the **Show It AK**.
2. As an alternative to the **Show It**, allow your student to create a puppet show where a character is building something with a simple tool, which is taking a very long time. Have them use another character to help the first character solve the problem by replacing the simple tool with a complex tool.

LESSON 152

SCIENCE 4 PARENT & TEACHER GUIDE

Topic: Technology and Engineering

Learning Objectives

The activities in this lesson will help your student meet the following objectives:

- identify differences between simple and complex machines
- explain differences between simple and complex machines
- identify tools, machines, and electronic devices used to do a job

Materials

- can opener
- electric beater
- four eggs
- one cup heavy whipping cream
- one can of canned food
- piece of wood
- screw
- screw driver
- wire whisk

Simple Vs. Complex Machines

Activate

1. Give your student a can of canned food, and ask them to open the can. They should realize that they need a tool such as a can opener.
2. Then, give them a can opener, and have them open the can. Ask them if they can think of an easier way to open the can.

Engage

1. After your student reads the **Read It**, instruct them to use the screwdriver to drive the screw into the wood.
2. Then ask them, "What did you discover about using a screwdriver?" They should have realized how tiresome it can be to use a screwdriver to drive a screw into a piece of wood.
3. Next, tell them to open the **Ecolibrium-Simple Machines - Play It** to play the game.

Demonstrate

1. Now, have your student move on to the task in the **Show It**. Then, use the sample answer in the **Show It AK** to help your student evaluate their work.
2. As an alternative to the **Show It**, invite your student to create a photo essay of simple and complex machines using images from the Internet.

Machine Persuasive Paragraph

Activate

1. Have your student open the **Types of Simple Machines - Watch It** to view the video.
2. Pause the video at 0:35 to allow your student time to brainstorm an answer to the question. They may not think of an answer, but allow them to sit with the question for a minute or two.
3. After watching the video, prompt your student to share a few of the simple machines that were discussed.

Engage

1. While your student reads the **Read It**, instruct them to draw and label the examples of simple machines.
2. Then, direct them to open the **Compound Machines - Watch It**. Pause the video at 2:13, and prompt your student to explain how simple machines are related to compound machines.
3. Next, direct your student to open the **Brick's Simple Machines - Play It** to play the game.

Demonstrate

1. Now, have your student complete the activity in the **Show It**. Then, help them to evaluate their paragraph with the **Show It AK**.
2. As an alternative to the **Show It**, allow your student to experiment with a simple machine and a complex machine.
    a. Instruct them to whip two eggs and a half cup of heavy whipping cream with a wire whisk. Time them to see how long it takes to mix the ingredients.
    b. Then, have them whip the same ingredients with an electric beater and time the process.
    c. Encourage your student to share what they discover about the difference between using a hand mixer and an electric beater.

• • •

Technology Professional Tools

Engage

1. After your student reads the **Read It**, prompt them to name any electronic devices that they have in their kitchen such as a refrigerator, dishwasher, or toaster.

Demonstrate

1. Now, instruct your student to complete the activity in the **Show It**. Then, allow them to compare their list with the example in the **Show It AK**.
2. As an alternative to the **Show It**, allow your student to design their ideal kitchen with as many electronic devices as they see fit. Encourage them to draw out their kitchen plan on a piece of paper and label the devices.

LESSON 153

SCIENCE 4 PARENT & TEACHER GUIDE

Topic: Technology and Engineering

Learning Objectives

The activities in this lesson will help your student meet the following objectives:

- explain how technology is used by professionals to perform their jobs
- show the importance of a professional's use of technology in performing daily tasks
- identify technologies used by humans to get from one place to another

Materials

- glue
- markers or colored pencils
- old magazines
- poster board

Technology Professionals Paragraph

Activate

1. Ask your student to open the **Producing Produce - Watch It** to view the video.
2. After they have finished watching the video, have them share a type of technology used to harvest produce.

Engage

1. While your student reads the **Read It**, ask them if they can think of any other ways that technology is used for jobs. Computers are a big part of many jobs today.
2. Then, tell your student to open the **Technology to Space - Watch It** to view the video about technology advancements in space travel.

Demonstrate

1. Now, direct your student to complete the activity in the **Show It**. Then, help them to evaluate their paragraph with the **Show It AK**.
2. As an alternative to the **Show It**, allow your student to interview an adult in the community and ask them how technology is part of their job.

• • •

Technology Professionals Poster

1. As your student reads the **Read It**, prompt them to share their experiences with any of the devices presented in the text.

1. Now, have your student move on to the poster activity in the **Show It**.
2. Finally, work with them to evaluate their poster with the **Show It AK**.

• • •

Transportation Technology

1. As your student reads the **Read It**, discuss the transportation technology they use each day such as a car or bus.
2. Then, direct them to learn about changes in technology in the **Practice It**.

1. Now, guide your student to complete the activity in the **Show It**. Then, help them to compare their list with the sample provided in the **Show It AK**.
2. As an alternative to the **Show It**, direct them to explore a vehicle and name any types of technology they observe inside such as a stereo, heater, or air conditioning.

SCIENCE 4 PARENT & TEACHER GUIDE

LESSON 154

Topic Technology and Engineering

Learning Objectives

The activities in this lesson will help your student meet the following objectives:

- compare and contrast forms of transportation
- describe how technology could affect the way humans get from one place to another in the future
- identify ways humans can eliminate the use of technology and help the environment

Materials

- none required

Transportation Venn Diagram

Activate

1. Begin a conversation with your student about how their life would be different if they had to walk everywhere they go. Discuss how it would take more time to travel from one place to another.

1. After your student reads the **Read It**, discuss with them how the mechanics of a skateboard and motorcycle are similar and different.

Demonstrate

1. Open the **Assess It** and have your student complete the activity. Be sure that they review the rubric before they begin so that they understand the expectations of the activity.
2. When they are finished, scan the document or take a photo of it and upload it to the Dropbox. For additional instructions on how to use the Dropbox, click on the paper clip icon in the upper-left corner of the **Assess It**.

• • •

Transportation Narrative

1. While your student reads the **Read It**, ask them if they have seen any futuristic vehicles on television shows or in movies. Prompt them to describe which features make them futuristic.

1. Now, direct your student to complete the activity in the **Show It**. Then, work with them to evaluate their narrative using the example provided the **Show It AK**.
2. As an alternative to the **Show It**, allow your student to create a skit that includes a futuristic transportation system. Encourage them to use details to describe the futuristic vehicle(s) in their skit.

• • •

Humans, Tech, and Environment

1. As your student reads the **Read It**, help them determine the distance from their home to the grocery store. Is it realistic for them to ride a bike or walk to the store?

1. Now, guide your student to complete the activity in the **Show It**. Then, help them to evaluate their response with the **Show It AK**.
2. To provide an alternative to the **Show It**, allow your student to teach a lesson to peers or family members about how to hang clothes to dry instead of using a dryer in order to reduce the use of technology that uses electricity.

SCIENCE 4 PARENT & TEACHER GUIDE

LESSON 155

| Topic | Technology and Engineering |

Learning Objectives

The activities in this lesson will help your student meet the following objectives:

- identify ways humans use technology that helps the environment
- compare and contrast how different forms of transportation affect the environment
- identify technologies that humans use to communicate

Materials

- colored pencils
- computer
- phone

Environmental Technology

Activate

1. Have your student open the **Investigate: Reuse, Reduce, Recycle - Watch It** and ask them to make note of the username and password provided on the Discovery Education image. Be sure that they click the link for the video and enter the provided username and password to watch.
2. Pause the video at 1:01, and prompt your student to respond to the question. Help them to brainstorm ideas for ways to reuse the bag.

Engage

1. After your student reads the **Read It**, have them name a few ways that technology is used to help the environment.

Demonstrate

1. Now, direct your student to move on to the **Show It** to complete the activity. Then, work with them to check their response with the **Show It AK**.
2. To provide an alternative to the **Show It**, allow your student to illustrate the design for a structure that uses technology to help the environment. A house that uses skylights instead of lamps is one example.

Transportation and Environment

1. While your student reads the **Read It**, tell them that many cars are designed to be fuel efficient. Explain how fuel efficiency works by calculating the average miles per gallon a car gets.

1. Now, guide your student to complete the Venn diagram in the **Show It**.
2. Finally, help them evaluate their response using the examples provided in the **Show It AK**.

• • •

Communication Technology

1. As your student reads the **Read It**, discuss which types of communication technology they have in their home.
2. Then, have them open the **Ecolibrium-Technology - Play It** to play the game.

1. Now, guide your student to complete the activity as directed in the **Show It**. Then, have them compare their response to the sample in the **Show It AK**.
2. As an alternative to the **Show It**, allow your student to choose two different types of communication technology, such as the phone and a computer, and allow them to correspond with someone. Then, ask them to explain which technology they prefer and why.

LESSON 156

Topic: Technology and Engineering

Learning Objectives

The activities in this lesson will help your student meet the following objectives:

- compare and contrast forms of communication
- identify ways new or improved technologies help to solve problems
- explain how new and improved technologies solve problems

Materials

- presentation software

Communication Venn Diagram

Activate

1. Instruct your student to look around their learning environment and search for devices that are used to communicate.
2. Ask them, "Which form of communication do you think is used most often?" They may mention that a cell phone is the most commonly used form of communication because people can call, text, and email using the same device.

Engage

1. As your student reads the **Read It**, ask them why they think cell phones were developed.
2. Help them to search the Internet to find the answer.

Demonstrate

1. Now, have your student complete the Venn diagram as directed in the **Show It**.
2. Then, use the **Show It AK** and work with them to check their response.

• • •

Technology T-Chart

1. While your student reads the **Read It**, ask them to imagine a technological device they would design to solve a specific problem.
2. Then, have them open the **Beaker's Big Buzz-Technology - Play It** to play the game.
3. Next, allow your student to review the information in the **Practice It**.

Demonstrate

1. Now, guide your student to complete the T-chart in the **Show It**.
2. Then, assist them in comparing their work to the example in the **Show It AK**.
3. To extend learning, visit a thrift store with your student and look at old phones. Ask them if they have any questions about how the old phones work.

• • •

New Technology Paragraph

1. After your student reads the **Read It**, ask them to identify several ways in which technology makes their life easier.

Demonstrate

1. Now, instruct your student to complete the activity in the **Show It**. Work with them to evaluate their response with the sample paragraph in the **Show It AK**.
2. To provide an alternative to the **Show It**, have them create a digital presentation comparing two technological devices. Be sure that their presentation explains how these devices have improved over time and how they solve a specific problem.

SCIENCE 4 PARENT & TEACHER GUIDE

LESSON 157

| Topic | Technology and Engineering |

Learning Objectives

The activities in this lesson will help your student meet the following objectives:

- explain how new and improved technologies make performing certain tasks easier
- identify effects of technological developments in transportation
- identify technologies developed during the sixteenth and seventeenth centuries

Materials

- colored pencils

Technology Paragraph

Activate

1. Have your student open and view the **Living/Working with Technology - Watch It**.
2. Pause the video at 1:27, and prompt your student to share some technological advances presented in the video.

Engage

1. As your student reads the **Read It**, instruct them to identify information in the text that explains how each type of technology makes the tasks easier.

Demonstrate

1. Now, direct your student to complete the activity in the **Show It**. Then, help them to evaluate their writing with the **Show It AK**.
2. As an alternative to the **Show It**, allow your student to draw the steps to hand wash dishes Then, have the draw the steps for using a dishwasher. Ask them to explain which method is easier.

• • •

Technological Developments

Engage

1. While your student reads the **Read It**, discuss some of the pros and cons of each type of transportation presented in the text. Airplanes produce a lot of pollution, so even though flying is more convenient, it has negative effects on the environment.

Demonstrate

1. Now, direct your student to complete the **Show It** activity. Then, allow them to check their response with the **Show It AK**.
2. As an alternative to the **Show It**, allow your student to draw and label a diagram showing the results of technological developments in transportation. For example, they may draw a boat with cargo at a port.

• • •

16th & 17th Century Developments

Engage

1. As your student reads the content of the **Read It**, discuss what their life would be like without the devices presented in the text.

Demonstrate

1. Now, instruct your student to complete the activity in the **Show It**. Then, work with them to check that they wrote about five technologies and included a fact for each one.
2. As an alternative to the **Show It**, allow your student to create a timeline with images of five technologies. The timeline should depict when each technology was invented, and it should include a fact about each technological development.

LESSON 158

SCIENCE 4 PARENT & TEACHER GUIDE

Topic | Technology and Engineering

Learning Objectives

The activities in this lesson will help your student meet the following objectives:

- explain how the invention of the hot-air balloon helped to expand civilization in the eighteenth century
- compare and contrast the technologies used to navigate eighteenth- and nineteenth-century hot-air balloons
- describe the expansion of civilization as a result of aviation technological developments from the eighteenth to twentieth centuries

Materials

- balloon
- colored pencils
- empty bottles of varying sizes
- empty plastic water bottle
- hot and cold water
- two bowls

Hot-Air Balloons

Activate

1. Pour hot water in one bowl and cold water in the other bowl. Have your student place the opening of the balloon over the mouth of the plastic water bottle so that it is sealed.
2. Then, tell them to set the bottom of the water bottle inside the bowl of hot water so that it is standing up.
3. Next, ask them what did they discovered. They should have discovered that the balloon inflates.
    - Ask your student why they think the balloon inflates. (Answer: The hot water heats up the air inside the bottle, which creates more pressure on the balloon and, therefore, inflates the balloon.)
4. Last, have them place the bottle in the cold water and ask them what they discover. They should observe that the balloon deflates.
    - Ask them why they think the balloon deflates. (Answer: The air in both the bottle and the balloon lose heat, which causes reduced pressure on the balloon; therefore, the balloon deflates.)

Engage

1. While your student reads the **Read It**, have them explain how the hot-air balloon helped expand civilization. They should respond by saying that the hot-air balloon provided the first means of transportation for both cargo and people across long distances.

Demonstrate

1. Now, guide your student to complete the activity in the **Show It**. Then, work with them to compare their response to the sample in the **Show It AK**.
2. To provide an alternative to the **Show It**, allow them to create a skit that depicts the effect of hot-air balloons on civilization.

Hot-Air Balloon Venn Diagram

1. After your student reads the **Read It**, ask them to explain how the eighteenth century hot-air balloon differed from the nineteenth century model. The nineteenth century models had a rip panel and a drag rope.

1. Now, instruct your student to complete the Venn diagram as directed in the **Show It**.
2. Then, help them to compare their diagram to the example provided in the **Show It AK**.

Civilization Paragraph

1. As your student reads the **Read It**, ask them how hot-air balloons, airships, and airplanes are connected to changes in civilization? Each technological advancement made traveling long distances easier.

1. Now, guide your student to complete the activity in the **Show It**. Then, assist them with evaluating their writing by comparing their response to the sample in the **Show It AK**.
2. As an alternative to the **Show It**, allow your student to create a miniature museum exhibit that displays the three main types of aircrafts (hot-air balloons, airships, and airplanes). They can draw images of each aircraft or make miniature models using bottles or other materials.

LESSON 159

SCIENCE 4 PARENT & TEACHER GUIDE

Topic: Technology and Engineering

Learning Objectives

The activities in this lesson will help your student meet the following objectives:

- identify a design problem
- show how a design problem can be represented in different ways
- list the steps in the engineering design process

Materials

- metal coat hanger
- scissors
- thick piece of cardboard

Design Problem

Activate

1. Set a metal coat hanger in front of your student, and ask them to think of at least three things they can do with it besides hanging clothes. For example, it can be used to create a hanging mobile craft or to hook something that is stuck. It could also be stretched out to make a marshmallow roaster.

Engage

1. After your student reads the **Read It**, prompt them explain the problems with the different designs of cargo pants.

Demonstrate

1. Now, have your student move on to the **Show It** activity. Then, use the **Show It AK** to help them check their response.
2. As an alternative to the **Show It**, instruct your student to carefully cut a thick piece of cardboard with scissors. The cardboard should be difficult to cut. Ask them, "What is the design problem in this scenario?" They should recognize that the scissors need to be sharper and stronger.

• • •

Represent Design Problems

Engage

1. While your student reads the **Read It**, ask them to explain how the Wright brothers worked to solve their design problems. (Answer: They made observations of the flaws in their aircraft and altered the design to make the aircraft better.)

Demonstrate

1. Now, guide your student to complete the activity in the **Show It**. Then, use the **Show It AK** and help them to evaluate their response.
2. As an alternative to the **Show It**, tell your student that they need to make a booklet that they will use to write a story.
   a. Have them develop three different designs for making a booklet.
   b. Allow them to create each design, if possible.

• • •

EDP Steps

Engage

1. Have your student open and view **The Design Problem - Watch It**.
2. Then, instruct them to read the content of the **Read It**. Encourage them to take note of the steps in the engineering design process for future reference.

Demonstrate

1. Now, direct your student to complete the activity in the **Show It**. Once they are finished, help them to test their airplane design.
2. Finally, use the **Show It AK** to check that they have included all the steps of the engineering design process in their response.

SCIENCE 4 PARENT & TEACHER GUIDE

LESSON 160

Topic: Technology and Engineering

Learning Objectives

The activities in this lesson will help your student meet the following objectives:

- describe how the engineering design process can be applied
- identify relevant design features for building a prototype
- outline a possible solution to a design problem

Materials

- art supplies
- board game for children
- circular objects or wheels
- glue
- small box
- straws
- tape
- wooden skewers

EDP Steps Example

Activate

1. Set a board game for children in front of your student, and ask them to describe how they think it was designed. For example, the designer of a board game likely began their design by laying out the route a player would travel across the board. Then, they chose a set of cards, dice, or a spinner to direct the players along the path.

Engage

1. As your student reads the **Read It**, invite them to verbally explain how they would complete each step of the design process.

Demonstrate

1. Now, instruct your student to complete the task in the **Show It**. Then, work with them to evaluate their steps with the **Show It AK**.
2. To provide an alternative to the **Show It**, have your student use the design process to create a board game. Then, encourage them to follow the steps of the design process to make the game. Finally, have them test their game with peers.

• • •

Prototype Design Features

Engage

1. After your student reads the **Read It**, ask them, "What makes a good designer?" A good designer identifies all the aspects that need to be fixed before they redesign a new prototype.

Demonstrate

1. Now, direct your student to move on to the activity in the **Show It**. Then, help them to evaluate their response with the **Show It AK**.
2. As an alternative to the **Show It**, allow them to design and build a car with household materials such as straws, wooden skewers, tape, a small box, circular objects or wheels, and glue. Encourage them to follow the steps of the design process to complete the activity.

• • •

Design Problem Solutions

Engage

1. While your student reads the **Read It**, encourage them to share any other possible solutions to the design problem presented in the text.

Demonstrate

1. Now, guide your student to complete the activity in the **Show It**.
2. Then, assist them to compare their responses to the sample in the **Show It AK**. Encourage your student to analyze which solutions would provide a better outcome.
3. Alternatively, allow your student to illustrate their solution to each design problem presented in the **Show It**.

SCIENCE 4 PARENT & TEACHER GUIDE

LESSON 161

Topic | Technology and Engineering

Learning Objectives

The activities in this lesson will help your student meet the following objectives:

- explain how the design process can help to construct a possible solution to a design problem
- compare a natural system with a mechanical system
- identify types of bridges

Materials

- colored pencils

Design Process Solution

Activate

1. Prompt your student to list the steps of the engineering design process. Their list should include the following steps.
   - Define a problem or need.
   - Do background research.
   - Specify requirements.
   - Brainstorm results.
   - Choose the best solution.
   - Build a prototype.
   - Test and redesign if needed.

Engage

1. As your student reads the **Read It**, have them look around their learning environment to find a problem that can be solved. For example, a door slams shut every time it is opened. A possible solution to this problem is a door hydraulic system that slows the door down so that is shuts softly.

Demonstrate

1. Open the **Assess It** and have your student complete the activity. Be sure that they review the expectations presented in the rubric before they begin.
2. When they are finished, scan the document or take a photo of it and upload it to the Dropbox. For additional instructions on how to use the Dropbox, click on the paper clip icon in the upper-left corner of the **Assess It**.

Natural versus Mechanical Systems

Engage

1. Have your student open the **Physics of Flight - Watch It** and ask them to make note of the username and password provided on the Discovery Education image. Be sure that they click the link for the video and enter the provided username and password to watch.
2. Pause the video at 1:41, and have your student explain how an airplane gets lift. The difference in flow above and below the wings results in a difference in air pressure, causing an upward force.
3. As your student reads the **Read It**, have them compare the flight of a bird to an airplane. They both have wings that help them fly.

Demonstrate

1. Now, instruct your student to complete the Venn diagram in the **Show It**. Then, use the **Show It AK** and work with them to evaluate their response.
2. To provide an alternative to the **Show It**, allow your student to observe birds in flight. Take them to a park or lake where there are many birds. Ask them, "What did you observe that you can compare to the flight of an airplane?"

• • •

Types of Bridges

Engage

1. Invite your student to open the **Understanding Bridges - Watch It** to learn about bridges. Consider starting the video at 2:10 and stopping at 6:21.
2. At 6:21, pause the video and ask your student to explain the three main types of bridges: beam, arch, and suspension.
3. While they read the **Read It**, have them focus on the additional types of bridges presented in the text. Then, have them compare the various types of bridges.

Demonstrate

1. Now, direct your student to complete the activity in the **Show It**. Then, help them to check their responses with the **Show It AK**.
2. As an alternative to the **Show It**, allow your student make a booklet the includes an illustration, title, and description of each type of bridge.

LESSON 162

SCIENCE 4 PARENT & TEACHER GUIDE

Topic: Technology and Engineering

Learning Objectives

The activities in this lesson will help your student meet the following objectives:

- compare and contrast styles of bridges
- draw a prototype of a bridge
- construct a prototype of a bridge

Materials

- blueprint plan of a bridge prototype
- glue
- 100 craft sticks
- pennies
- small weights or objects totaling 2 lbs.
- strip of paper
- wax or parchment paper

Compare and Contrast Bridges

Activate

1. Begin by asking your student how many pennies they think the strip of paper can hold.
2. Next, hold the strip of paper between both hands so that it is taut. Then, instruct your student to place pennies on the paper, one at a time, to see how many the paper can hold.
3. When the paper breaks or the pennies topple over, ask them to describe what they discovered.

Engage

1. As your student reads the **Read It**, instruct them to pay special attention to the origin of each bridge design. In other words, what inspired the bridge's designer? For example, some bridge types were inspired by a natural form, while some were inspired by another bridge structure.

Demonstrate

1. Now, guide your student to complete the T-chart as directed in the **Show It**.
2. Then, work with them to compare their responses with the example in **Show It AK**. Since your student's responses will be different than the answer key, use the sample as a teaching opportunity for your student to learn about more similarities and differences between the various bridge designs.

Create a Bridge

1. While your student reads the **Read It**, prompt them to identify the bridge designs in the images of the bridges built with craft sticks.
2. Then ask them, "Which design would be the easiest to make?"

1. Now, instruct your student to complete the bridge design activity in the **Show It**, and refer to the **Show It AK** to ensure their work meets the criteria.
2. To reinforce learning, encourage your student to verbally explain the steps they will need to take to build the bridge.

• • •

Construct a Bridge

1. As your student reads the **Read It**, ask them if they would change any elements of the bridge models in the text. Encourage them to explain their thinking and determine why they think these changes would make their bridge stronger.

1. Now, direct your student to complete the bridge building activity in the **Show It**.
2. Then, work with them to test their bridge by placing two pounds of weight on it. If the bridge breaks, have a discussion with your student about ways they could redesign the bridge to make it stronger.

SCIENCE 4 PARENT & TEACHER GUIDE

LESSON 163

Topic: Technology and Engineering

Learning Objectives

The activities in this lesson will help your student meet the following objectives:

- test a prototype of a bridge
- redesign a prototype of a bridge
- identify measurement systems, symbols, and icons

Materials

- craft stick bridge prototype
- glue
- 8 or more 4 oz. weights (or objects equal to that weight)
- 100 craft sticks
- varying types of containers with measurement labels
- wax or parchment paper

Test a Bridge

Activate

1. Prompt your student to draw a bridge designed to cross a river. Ask them, "What are the best materials to build your bridge?"

Engage

1. As your student reads the **Read It**, discuss why it is important to test bridges before they are used.

Demonstrate

1. Now, instruct your student to complete the bridge test activity in the **Show It**. Then, check that they recorded the amount of weight their bridge could sustain.
2. Alternatively, if your student already tested their bridge in Lesson 162, allow them to create a new bridge design to test.

• • •

Redesign a Bridge

**Engage**

1. While your student reads the **Read It**, invite them to look around their learning environment and identify objects that can be redesigned. For example, a chair that is too rigid could be redesigned to have cushions.

**Demonstrate**

1. Now, direct your student to complete the activity in the **Show It**. Then, work with them to evaluate their bridge redesign.
2. As an alternative to the **Show It**, allow your student to build the redesigned bridge and test its weight capacity.

•••

Measurement Systems

**Activate**

1. Have your student open the **Standards of Measurement - Watch It** and ask them to make note of the username and password provided on the Discovery Education image. Be sure that they click the link for the video and enter the provided username and password to watch.
2. After they have watched the video, ask them which measurement systems they are familiar with using.

**Engage**

1. After your student reads the **Read It**, prompt them to identify the measurement labels on various types of containers.

**Demonstrate**

1. Now, direct your student to complete the activity in the **Show It**. Then, help them check their answers with the **Show It AK**.
2. To extend learning, encourage your student to read measurement labels while at the grocery store.

SCIENCE 4 PARENT & TEACHER GUIDE

LESSON 164

Topic: Technology and Engineering

Learning Objectives

The activities in this lesson will help your student meet the following objectives:
- use a scale to weigh objects
- record weights of objects
- identify how technology affects daily life

Materials
- apple
- colored pencils
- five small items to be weighed
- graph paper
- orange
- ruler
- triple beam balance scale

Measuring Weights

 ### Activate

1. Have your student hold an apple in one hand and an orange in the other. Then, ask them, "Which fruit is heavier?"
2. Discuss how guessing which fruit is heavier is not very accurate. Prompt them to identify what they might use to determine the weight of each fruit. (Answer: A scale is tool used to measure weight.)

 ### Engage

1. As your student reads the **Read It**, allow them to manipulate the triple beam balance scale to get familiar with it.

 ### Demonstrate

1. Now, have your student move on to the weighing activity in the **Show It**.
2. Finally, review the weight of their objects and help them determine if the weight is reasonable. Allow them to make any necessary revisions.

• • •

Recording Weights

Engage

1. Instruct your student to read the steps for building a line graph presented in the **Read It**. Have them draw the sample graph while they read.

Demonstrate

1. Now, direct your student to complete the graph as directed in the **Show It**.
2. Finally, use the **Show It AK** to help your student evaluate their work.

• • •

Technology in Daily Life

Activate

1. Tell your student to open the **Technology: Good or Bad? - Watch It** to view the video.
2. Afterward, prompt them to share some positive and negative aspects of technologies.

Engage

1. As your student reads the **Read It**, ask them to share if and how they use some of the technologies presented in the text.
2. Then, invite them to open the **Ecolibrium-Technology - Play It** to play the game.

Demonstrate

1. Now, direct your student to complete the activity in the **Show It**. Encourage them to explain the positive and negative aspects of the technologies they use each day.
2. Then, allow them to compare their list to the sample in the **Show It AK**.
3. To provide an alternative to the **Show It**, instruct your student to create a comic strip where the main character encounters a positive and negative aspect of a piece of technology.

LESSON 165

Topic | Technology and Engineering

Learning Objectives

The activities in this lesson will help your student meet the following objectives:

- explain how families use television
- describe how television improves community communication
- describe how television affects the environment

Materials

- television

Television and Family Life

Activate

1. Ask your student, "When was the last time you watched something on television?" Discuss how often they watch TV and whether or not they have any restrictions such as time limits for viewing programs.

Engage

1. As your student reads the **Read It**, discuss how their family uses the television on a daily basis.

Demonstrate

1. Now, direct your student to complete the activity in the **Show It**. Then, work them to evaluate their response with the **Show It AK**.
2. As an alternative to the **Show It**, allow your student to record their family's daily use of the television for a week.
   a. Instruct them to create a running log on a piece of paper. Be sure they include the following information on their log.
      - name of family member
      - date
      - type of use
   b. At the end of the week, ask your student what they discovered.

• • •

Community Communications

1. While your student reads the **Read It**, have them determine how they receive channels or access to programs on their television. Do they have cable, an antenna, or Internet streaming?

1. Now, instruct your student to complete the activity in the **Show It**.
2. Then, use the examples in the **Show It AK** to help your student evaluate their response.
3. As an alternative to the **Show It**, have your student search through the community channels to identify the types of programming that are available. Particularly, help them find the news channels where they can get information about important issues.

Television and the Environment

1. After your student reads the **Read It**, ask them, "What is the problem with televisions?" Televisions require a lot of materials to be made and create waste when they are no longer working.

1. Now, instruct your student to complete the list as directed in the **Show It**. Then, allow them to compare their work to example in the **Show It AK**.
2. As an alternative to the **Show It**, help your student to research the main components of a television. Then, instruct them to draw and label a diagram of a television.

LESSON 166

Topic: Technology and Engineering

Learning Objectives

The activities in this lesson will help your student meet the following objectives:

- identify tools used by doctors to assess a person's health
- explain tools designed to be used at home to help a person live a healthful lifestyle
- describe tools that are helpful for living a healthful lifestyle

Materials

- pedometer or step-tracking device
- thermometer

Health Professional Tools

Activate

1. Have your student open the **Community Health Professionals - Watch It** to view the video.
2. Discuss the location of the hospital nearest to their home.

Engage

1. Have your student read the content of the **Read It**. Then, ask them to share whether or not any of the medical tools presented in the text have been used on them while they visited the doctor.

Demonstrate

1. Now, direct your student to complete the activity in the **Show It**. Then, help them check their answers with the **Show It AK**.
2. As an alternative to the **Show It**, instruct your student to check and record their temperature for three days.
   a. Have them check their temperature in both the morning and evening.
   b. After three days, ask them what they discovered about their body temperature. For example, was their temperature colder in the morning than in the evening?

• • •

Home Health Tools

Engage

1. As your student reads the **Read It**, discuss any tools they use to monitor their health. If they do not use any of the tools mentioned in the text, ask them which tools family members might use.

Demonstrate

1. Open the **Assess It** and have your student complete the activity. Help them to review the expectations provided in the rubric before they begin writing.
2. When they are finished, scan the document or take a photo of it and upload it to the Dropbox. For additional instructions on how to use the Dropbox, click on the paper clip icon in the upper-left corner of the **Assess It**.

• • •

Living a Healthful Lifestyle

Engage

1. After your student reads the **Read It**, have them count the number of steps it takes to walk from one side of their learning environment to the other.
2. Then, have them estimate how many times a day they walk back and forth. Help them determine the approximate number of steps they take each day while moving around in their learning environment.

Demonstrate

1. Now, direct your student to complete the activity in the **Show It**. Then, use the sample in the **Show It AK** to help your student evaluate their work.
2. As an alternative to the **Show It**, take a walk with your student and allow them to wear a pedometer or step-tracking device. Then, discuss their results, and ask them if they were surprised by the number of steps they took.

LESSON 167

Topic: Technology and Engineering

Learning Objectives

The activities in this lesson will help your student meet the following objectives:

- define the term *biotechnology*
- identify ways biotechnology has changed how plants are grown
- describe how GPS has changed agriculture

Materials

- colored pencils
- dictionary

Biotechnology

Activate

1. Ask your student to name their favorite fruit. Then, discuss when it is in season. For example, strawberries are in season in the United States during the spring. However, they can be found in grocery stores year-round because they are imported.
2. Next, pose the following scenario to your student.
    - What if the strawberry plant could be changed so that it grows in the United States year-round?
3. Explain that scientists change the makeup of plants to help them grow better.

Engage

1. As your student reads the **Read It**, have them explain the term *biotechnology* in their own words.

Demonstrate

1. Now, direct your student to complete the definition activity in the **Show It**. Then, help them compare their definition to the sample provided in the **Show It AK**.
2. As an alternative to the **Show It**, instruct your student to make a web graphic organizer that illustrates the term *biotechnology*.
    a. Have them begin by drawing a circle in the center of a sheet of paper.
    b. Next, have them write the term biotechnology inside the circle.
    c. Then, have them draw lines coming off the center circle. At the end of each line, direct them to draw additional circles.
    d. Inside the empty circles, have your student draw images to show how biotechnology is used.

Growing Plants Biotechnology

Engage

1. While your student reads the **Read It**, discuss how biotechnology helps farmers. Biotechnology helps farmers by improving the seeds or plants so that they can produce better crops.

Demonstrate

1. Now, guide your student to complete the activity in the **Show It**. Then, use the **Show It AK** to help them evaluate their response.
2. As an alternative to the **Show It**, have your student create a new type of produce that combines the traits of two different fruits or vegetables. Instruct them to draw their new type of produce and write a description of its traits.

• • •

GPS and Agriculture

Engage

1. As your student reads the **Read It**, ask them if they have ever used a GPS device to navigate to a destination.
2. Explain that people often use a navigation app on their phone that uses GPS. The app allows them to enter the address of a destination, and it will give them turn-by-turn directions for reaching the address.

Demonstrate

1. Now, instruct your student to complete the activity in the **Show It**. Then, help them to evaluate their response using the example in the **Show It AK**.
2. As an alternative to the **Show It**, invite your student to draw a map of an imaginary farm. Direct them to include three different crop areas, an irrigation system, roads, and any natural formations such as boulders or streams.

LESSON 168

SCIENCE 4 PARENT & TEACHER GUIDE

Topic: Technology and Engineering

Learning Objectives

The activities in this lesson will help your student meet the following objectives:

- describe how robots have changed agriculture
- describe how RFID has changed agriculture
- describe how phone-controlled sprinklers have changed agriculture

Materials

- colored pencils

Robots and Agriculture

Activate

1. Ask your student, "If you could have a robot do one of your chores, which chore would you choose?" They might mention that they would want a robot to make their bed every day.

Engage

1. As your student reads the **Read It**, ask them how robots help farmers. (Answer: Robots help farmers by doing some of the tasks associated with maintaining a farm.)

Demonstrate

1. Then, prompt your student to complete the activity in the **Show It**.
2. Now, have your student refer to the **Show It AK** to see an example paragraph.
3. As an alternative to the **Show It**, instruct your student to design a robot that would help farmers with their crops or livestock. If your student needs ideas, encourage them to do a quick Internet search for farm robots.

• • •

Radio Frequency Agriculture

Engage

1. While your student reads the **Read It**, have them explain RFID in their own words.
2. Next, ask your student what questions they have about RFID.

Demonstrate

1. Move on to the **Show It** and have your student complete the activity.
2. Now, go to the **Show It AK** so your student can check their response.
3. As an alternative to the **Show It**, encourage your student to brainstorm ways that RFID could be useful in their daily routine. For example, a chip could be placed in their backpack so they would be able to find their backpack easily if they lose it.

• • •

Phone-Controlled Sprinklers

Engage

1. After your student reads the **Read It**, discuss how phone-controlled sprinklers save time for farmers. (Answer: Farmers do not have to run out to check their crops or turn the sprinklers on by hand.)

Demonstrate

1. Now, have your student complete the paragraph in the **Show It**.
2. Next, instruct your student to compare their response to the example in the **Show It AK**.
3. As an alternative to the **Show It**, prompt your student to research remote-controlled devices, such as a home alarm system, for daily use. Then, tell them to illustrate an advertisement for a remote-controlled device and include details about its convenience.

LESSON 169

SCIENCE 4 PARENT & TEACHER GUIDE

Topic: Technology and Engineering

Learning Objectives

The activities in this lesson will help your student meet the following objectives:

- define the terms *mechanical energy, sound energy, chemical energy, light energy, electrical energy, heat energy,* and *nuclear energy*
- identify different types of energy
- identify how energy conservation helps the planet

Materials

- colored pencils or markers
- dictionary
- glue
- poster board
- scissors
- "Different Types of Energy" activity page

Energy Terms

Activate

1. Have your student open the **Different Types of Energy - Watch It** to view the video.
2. Then, ask your student to discuss some of the types of energy presented in the video.

Engage

1. While your student reads the **Read It**, have them share which types of energy they come in contact with every day. They should recognize that they encounter sound, chemical, light, electrical, and heat energy each day.
2. Now, instruct your student to open the **Beaker's Big Buzz-Energy - Play It** to play the game. Allow them to look up any unknown answers on the Internet.

Demonstrate

1. Next, prompt your student to complete the definition activity in the **Show It**.
2. Afterward, have your student check their definitions in the **Show It AK**.
3. To provide an alternative to the **Show It**, instruct your student to make a poster of the terms and include illustrations of examples.

• • •

Different Types of Energy

 Engage

1. As your student reads the **Read It**, ask them to identify the images for each type of energy discussed in the text.
2. Then, tell your student to read the information in the **Practice It**.

 Demonstrate

1. Now, direct your student to complete the "Different Types of Energy" activity page in the **Show It**.
2. Next, remind your student to check their answers with the **Show It AK**.

• • •

Energy Conservation

Activate

1. Begin by prompting your student to view the **Conserving Electricity - Watch It**.
2. Next, ask your student to discuss some examples of conserving energy that were presented in the video.

 Engage

1. While your student reads the **Read It**, encourage them to share how they conserve energy on a daily basis. Examples may include turning off the light when they leave a room.

 Demonstrate

1. Now, instruct your student to complete the task in the **Show It**.
2. Afterward, ask your student to evaluate their response with the **Show It AK**.
3. As an alternative to the **Show It**, challenge your student to make a public service announcement to inform their audience about ways to conserve energy. Encourage them to write a script and perform their announcement for their family or peers.

SCIENCE 4 PARENT & TEACHER GUIDE

LESSON 170

Topic Technology and Engineering

Learning Objectives

The activities in this lesson will help your student meet the following objectives:

- explain the benefits of energy conservation
- identify ways humans communicate today
- compare and contrast forms of communication

Materials

- none required

Energy Conservation Benefits

Activate

1. Have your student open the **Energy Conservation - Watch It** and ask them to make note of the username and password provided on the Discovery Education image. Be sure that they click the link for the video and enter the provided username and password to watch.
2. Then, discuss the forms of public transportation in your student's area, such as buses, trains, or subways.

Engage

1. After your student reads the **Read It**, direct them to the last paragraph about a wasteful friend? Ask your student, "How would you convince this friend be less wasteful. What tips might you give them?"

Demonstrate

1. Now, instruct your student to complete the activity in the **Show It**.
2. Then, have your student evaluate their response with the **Show It AK**.
3. To provide an alternative to the **Show It**, challenge your student to create a puppet show to convince Sam and her family to conserve energy.

• • •

Forms of Communication

 ### Activate

1. Ask your student to explain how they commonly communicate with family or friends when they are not face-to-face. Do they call, text, email, or write letters?

 ### Engage

1. As your student reads the **Read It**, prompt them to identify the types of communication represented by the images in the content.

 ### Demonstrate

1. Next, direct your student to create the communication web as directed in the **Show It**.
2. Now, remind your student to use the **Show It AK** to evaluate their work.

Morse Code vs. Cell Phones

 ### Engage

1. After your student reads the **Read It**, discuss which system is more efficient: Morse code or cell phones. (Answer: Cell phones are more efficient because a message can be transmitted immediately to the receiver.)
2. Then, tell your student to review the information in the **Practice It** about changes in technology.

 ### Demonstrate

1. Now, prompt your student to complete the Venn diagram activity in the **Show It** and check their responses with the **Show It AK**.
2. To extend learning, challenge your student to look up the Morse code alphabet and write a message to a friend. If possible, allow them to give the message to their friend to decode.
3. The next lesson is a **Mastery Assess It**. Encourage your student to review Lessons 150 through 170 in order to prepare for the assessment.

LESSON 171

Topic: Technology and Engineering

Learning Objectives

The activities in this lesson will help your student meet the following objectives:

- not applicable

Materials

- none required

Mastery Assess It 11

1. **Mastery Assess It 11** will cover what your student has learned in Lessons 150 through 170.
2. Click on the **Mastery Assess It 11** icon to begin the online assessment.
3. Have your student read the instructions before they get started. Remind them to take their time and to do their best work.
4. When they are finished and ready for their assessment to be graded, have them click the **Submit** button.

SCIENCE 4 PARENT & TEACHER GUIDE

LESSON 172

Topic | Technology and Engineering

Learning Objectives

The activities in this lesson will help your student meet the following objectives:

- describe a new form of communication
- diagram a new form of communication
- explain features and benefits of a new communication invention

Materials

- video chat computer program or app

Product System Communicator

Activate

1. Start by prompting your student to view **The Internet - Watch It** and ask them to make note of the username and password provided on the Discovery Education image. Be sure that they click the link for the video and enter the provided username and password to watch.
2. Next, ask your student to share some of the safety tips for using the Internet that were discussed in the video. They may explain that they should not give their last name or the name of their school to an unknown person. Also, they should never send a photo of themselves to someone they do not know.

Engage

1. As your student reads the **Read It**, ask them what they think about optical head-mounted displays.

Demonstrate

1. Now, instruct your student to complete the activity in the **Show It** and use the **Show It AK** to evaluate their response.
2. As an alternative to the **Show It**, have your student use a video chat program to communicate with a family member or friend.

• • •

Communication Features

Engage

1. While your student reads the **Read It**, encourage them to share how they would want to use the optical head-mounted display.

Demonstrate

1. Next, direct your student to research a communication device to complete the **Show It**.
2. Finally, have your student reference the **Show It AK** to check that they have identified another form of communication technology and labeled three features.

• • •

New Communication

Engage

1. As your student reads the **Read It**, have them compare the Comshades 2 device in the text to the Comshades device described in the previous subtopics. (Comshades 2 allows the user to play games with other people.)

Demonstrate

1. Then, have your student complete the task in the **Show It** and evaluate their response using the **Show It AK** example.
2. As an alternative to the **Show It**, prompt your student to design a new technological communication device and describe three of its features.

SCIENCE 4 PARENT & TEACHER GUIDE

LESSON 173

| Topic | Technology and Engineering |

Learning Objectives

The activities in this lesson will help your student meet the following objectives:

- create a materials list for a new communication invention
- identify a design problem for a new communication invention
- identify how a new communication design might be improved

Materials

- phone

Communication Materials

Activate

1. Instruct your student to examine a phone and determine the materials needed to make it. Some materials may include plastic, wires, or metal.

Engage

1. As your student reads the **Read It**, help them to brainstorm ideas about the ways in which each item on the materials list is used to make the Comshades device.

Demonstrate

1. Now, direct your student to complete the materials list for the activity in the **Show It**. Allow them to designate a reasonable cost for each item if they do not know the actual cost.
2. Finally, go to the **Show It AK** so your student can compare their materials list and costs to the example provided. Help them evaluate their work and determine if any adjustments need to be made.

• • •

Communication Design Problem

Engage

1. Beginning with the **Read It**, ask your student to share a time they ordered something and had to wait for its arrival. If they have never experienced this, share your own experience with them. Focus on a time when something went wrong in the process.

Demonstrate

1. Next, move on to the **Show It** and have your student complete the activity.
2. Then, have your student check their response using the example in the **Show It AK**.
3. Alternatively, instruct your student to create a news report that describes the product and states the design problems from the scenario in the **Show It**.

Communication Design Solution

Engage

1. Now, go to the **Read It** and prompt your student to identify some solutions to the Comshades design problem before reading the solutions in the text.

Demonstrate

1. Open the **Assess It** and have your student complete the activity. When they are finished, scan the document or take a photo of it and upload it to the Dropbox. For additional instructions on how to use the Dropbox, click on the paper clip icon in the upper-left corner of the **Assess It**.

SCIENCE 4 PARENT & TEACHER GUIDE

LESSON 174

Topic Technology and Engineering

Learning Objectives

The activities in this lesson will help your student meet the following objectives:

- determine the best solution to a design problem affecting a new communication invention
- identify types of transportation
- demonstrate how transportation is used

Materials

- colored pencils
- twenty feet of cotton string
- two disposable cups (paper or plastic)
- two paper clips

New Communication Invention

Activate

1. Help your student make a string telephone by completing the following steps:
    a. Poke a small hole at the bottom of each cup.
    b. Thread the string through the hole of one cup.
    c. Place a paper clip inside the bottom of the cup and tie the end of the string around it to secure the string.
    d. Repeat the steps to secure the string to the second cup.
2. Then, have your student take one cup while you hold the other. Walk to another area, as far as the string will allow. It is important that the string is straight and tight.
3. Next, test the phone and carry out a conversation with your student.
4. Discuss any problems that arose throughout the process and possible solutions.

Engage

1. After your student reads the **Read It**, have them verbally summarize the solution to the Comshades problem.
2. Next, ask your student if they would have solved the problem in the reading differently.

Demonstrate

1. Now, have your student move on to the activity in the **Show It**. Then, direct them to the **Show It AK** to compare their response to the example.
2. Alternatively, instruct your student to make a public service announcement for the scenario in the **Show It** and report the solution and its results. Remind them to report that the consumer needs to update the app for the improved version.

• • •

346 Copyright 2018 © Lincoln Learning Solutions. All rights reserved.

Forms of Transportation

Activate

1. Have your student open the **What Is Transportation? - Watch It** and ask them to make note of the username and password provided on the Discovery Education image. Be sure that they click the link for the video and enter the provided username and password to watch.
2. Then, ask your student, "What is the fastest way to transport goods or people over long distances?" (Answer: An airplane is the fastest form of transportation for long distances.)

Engage

1. Next, prompt your student to read the **Read It** and identify the types of transportation presented in the text.
2. To reinforce learning, ask your student to review the information in the **Practice It**.

Demonstrate

1. Now, direct your student to complete the activity in the **Show It**.
2. Then, have them evaluate their response using the sample paragraph in the **Show It AK**.
3. As an alternative to the **Show It**, instruct your student to make a map of three locations to which they have traveled to using different types of transportation. If they have not used different types of transportation, ask them to discuss how they could have traveled differently to their destinations.
   a. Tell your student to draw a symbol for the type of transportation used on each route.
   b. Then, encourage your student to share their map by verbally describing their adventures, focusing on how they traveled.

• • •

Travel and Transportation

Engage

1. Instruct your student to view the **Transportation and Where We Live - Watch It**.
2. Then, ask your student, "What is your favorite type of transportation? Why?"
3. Next, move on to the **Read It**. Encourage your student to share any experiences they have with flying.

Demonstrate

1. Go to the **Show It** and instruct your student to complete the activity.
2. Next, have your student evaluate their response using the example in the **Show It AK**.
3. As an alternative to the **Show It**, challenge your student to create a travel itinerary with illustrations of locations and transportation.

LESSON 175

Topic: Technology and Engineering

Learning Objectives

The activities in this lesson will help your student meet the following objectives:

- explain how a person from another state can use a transportation system to come to your community
- define the terms *domestic* and *international*
- discuss how goods are shipped domestically

Materials

- glue
- local map
- magazines
- scissors

Transportation Systems

Activate

1. Prompt your student to find images of different types of transportation in a magazine. (They may use images from more than one magazine.)
2. Then, discuss the pros and cons of each type of transportation system.

Engage

1. After your student reads the **Read It**, have them act out the mom's trip to Boston as it is described in the text. Tell them to focus mainly on the aspects of transportation in the scenario.

Demonstrate

1. Next, instruct your student to move on to the **Show It** and complete the activity.
2. Now, have your student reference the **Show It AK** for an example of transportation methods. Remind your student to check that they included two types of transportation in their response.
3. As an alternative to the **Show It**, help your student identify the nearest airport, train station, and bus station on a local map.

• • •

Domestic and International

1. While your student reads the **Read It**, allow them to share any domestic or international travel experiences they have had. Ask them to describe the transportation systems they used such as cars, airplanes, trains, etc.

1. Now, prompt your student to complete the definition activity in the **Show It**.
2. Then, ask your student to check their definitions in the **Show It AK**.
3. As an alternative to the **Show It**, allow your student to cut out letters or images from magazines that represent the terms *domestic* and *international*. Then, have them glue the cut-outs onto a piece of paper. Encourage them to verbally share their collage and explain how the letters and images relate to the terms.

• • •

Shipping Goods Domestically

1. Prompt your student to open the **Shipping Goods Domestically - Watch It** to view the video. Then, ask them to talk about any trains or tractor trailers they have seen while riding in the car.
2. As your student reads the **Read It**, ask them what types of cargo can be transported in trains or tractor trailers.

1. Then, direct your student to complete the activity in the **Show It**.
2. Afterward, have your student use the **Show It AK** to evaluate their response.
3. As an alternative to the **Show It**, help your student to look at a map and identify major freeways and/or railroads that are used to transport goods in their state.

SCIENCE 4 PARENT & TEACHER GUIDE

LESSON 176

Topic: Technology and Engineering

Learning Objectives

The activities in this lesson will help your student meet the following objectives:

- discuss how goods are shipped internationally
- compare and contrast domestic and international shipping
- explain the difference between primary and secondary manufacturing

Materials

- colored pencils

Shipping Goods Internationally

 ### Activate

1. Have your student open the **Transportation and Trade - Watch It** and ask them to make note of the username and password provided on the Discovery Education image. Be sure that they click the link for the video and enter the provided username and password to watch.
2. Then, ask your student to explain how trade is dependent on transportation. (Answer: Trade relies on transportation in order to move products from one place to another.)

 ### Engage

1. After your student reads the **Read It**, ask them if they have ever mailed a package or letter internationally. If so, ask them if they think it was shipped by boat or airplane. (It more than likely traveled by airplane.)
2. If your student has not mailed an item internationally, ask them to imagine how it would be shipped.

 ### Demonstrate

1. Now, instruct your student to complete the **Show It** activity and compare their response to the example in the **Show It AK**.
2. To provide an alternative to the **Show It**, challenge your student to create a song or rhyme about international transportation of goods.

• • •

Comparing Shipping

1. As your student reads the **Read It**, prompt them to explain the difference between domestic and international shipping. (Answer: Domestic shipping is within the country, and international shipping is outside the country.)

Demonstrate

1. Next, direct your student to complete the Venn diagram as directed in the **Show It**.
2. Then, have your student check their work with the **Show It AK**.
3. To extend learning, help your student set up an interview with a postal service worker to discuss shipping processes.

• • •

Manufacturing

1. Now, move on to the **Read It**. Ask your student to choose an item in their learning environment and determine what primary and/or secondary manufacturing processes it went through to be made.

Demonstrate

1. Then, have your student complete the **Show It** activity. Encourage them to compare their definitions to the samples in the **Show It AK**.
2. As an alternative to the **Show It**, instruct your student to draw and label a diagram that shows the primary and secondary manufacturing processes for an object.

SCIENCE 4 PARENT & TEACHER GUIDE

LESSON 177

Topic: Technology and Engineering

Learning Objectives

The activities in this lesson will help your student meet the following objectives:

- describe how raw materials are obtained
- discuss ways raw materials are refined
- define the terms *structure*, *temporary*, and *permanent*

Materials

- art supplies
- bag of chips
- dictionary
- poster board

Raw Materials

Activate

1. Instruct your student to read the ingredients in a bag of chips. Help them determine the raw materials used to make the chips. For example, potatoes are the main raw material used to make potato chips.

Engage

1. As your student reads the **Read It**, ask them if any of the resources presented in the text are found near their home.

Demonstrate

1. Next, prompt your student to complete the chart in the **Show It**.
2. Then, remind your student to check their work in the **Show It AK**.

• • •

Refining Raw Materials

Engage

1. Begin by having your student open the **Earth's Resources - Watch It** to view the video.
2. Then, ask your student to explain the phrase *Earth's resources*. They may mention that Earth's resources are a supply that will meet a need for materials or energy.
3. Now, prompt your student to read the content of the **Read It**.

Demonstrate

1. Go to the **Show It** and have your student complete the poster activity.
2. Now, have your student use the **Show It AK** to evaluate their poster. It should show how two raw materials can be refined into usable products.

• • •

Define *Structure*

Engage

1. As your student reads the **Read It**, have them describe the type of structure they are in and determine if it is permanent or temporary.

Demonstrate

1. Now, have your student move on to the **Show It** activity. When they are finished, encourage them to check their definitions with the **Show It AK**.
2. To provide an alternative to the **Show It**, instruct your student to create a graphic organizer web.
   a. First, have them write the term *structure* and its definition in the center of a sheet of paper. Ask them to draw a circle around the information.
   b. Then, have them write the terms *temporary* and *permanent* in circles coming off the center circle.
   c. Finally, encourage your student to draw images of the types of structures around the terms *temporary* and *permanent*.

SCIENCE 4 PARENT & TEACHER GUIDE

LESSON 178

Topic Technology and Engineering

Learning Objectives

The activities in this lesson will help your student meet the following objectives:

- list structures
- recognize the different parts of a structure

Materials

- marshmallows
- pieces of cardboard
- pretzel sticks
- small boxes
- tape

Types of Structures

 ### Activate

1. Give your student some pretzel sticks and marshmallows and ask them to build a structure. They can make any type of structure they would like.
2. Then, ask your student to explain why they chose to build their structure the way they did.

 ### Engage

1. Starting with the **Read It**, prompt your student to identify the images of structures in the text as either temporary or permanent.
2. Then, tell your student to open the **Beaker's Big Buzz-Structure - Play It** to play the game.

 ### Demonstrate

1. Open the **Assess It** and have your student complete the activity. When they are finished, scan the document or take a photo of it and upload it to the Dropbox. For additional instructions on how to use the Dropbox, click on the paper clip icon in the upper-left corner of the **Assess It**.

Parts of a Structure

 ### Engage

1. After your student reads the **Read It**, ask them to describe the similarities of all the structures. For example, all the structures have a foundation, walls, and a roof.

Demonstrate

1. Now, instruct your student to complete the **Show It** activity.
2. Then, have your student compare their list to the example in the **Show It AK**.
3. As an alternative to the **Show It**, challenge your student to build a structure with household items such as cardboard, boxes, paper, etc. When they are finished, ask them to name the parts of their structure.

SCIENCE 4 PARENT & TEACHER GUIDE

LESSON 179

Topic | Technology and Engineering

Learning Objectives

The activities in this lesson will help your student meet the following objectives:

- explain why some structures are temporary
- plan how to change a temporary structure into a permanent one

Materials

- colored pencils

Temporary Structures

 ### Activate

1. Have your student open the **Temporary Shelter - Watch It** and ask them to make note of the username and password provided on the Discovery Education image. Be sure that they click the link for the video and enter the provided username and password to watch.
2. Then, ask your student if they prefer a temporary or permanent shelter. Encourage them to share their reasoning.

1. Begin by prompting your student to read the content of the **Read It**. Then, ask them if they have ever been in a temporary structure. Inform them that a playhouse or a fort could also be a temporary structure.

 ### Demonstrate

1. Now, instruct your student to complete the activity in the **Show It** and compare their response to the example in the **Show It AK**.
2. As an alternative to the **Show It**, have your student draw three types of temporary structures. Then, direct them to write a sentence that describes the purpose of each structure.

• • •

Copyright 2018 © Lincoln Learning Solutions. All rights reserved.

355

Convert Temporary Structures

Engage

1. After your student reads the **Read It**, prompt them to explain some of the challenges of converting a temporary structure into a permanent one.

Demonstrate

1. Next, direct your student to complete the **Show It** activity.
2. Then, have your student refer to the **Show It AK** to evaluate their response.
3. As an alternative to the **Show It**, instruct your student to illustrate how they would change a temporary structure into a permanent one. Have them draw and label the materials they would use.
4. The next lesson is a **Mastery Assess It**. Encourage your student to review Lessons 172 through 179 in order to prepare for the assessment.

LESSON 180

Topic: Technology and Engineering

Learning Objectives

The activities in this lesson will help your student meet the following objectives:
- not applicable

Materials
- none required

Mastery Assess It 12

1. **Mastery Assess It 12** will cover what your student has learned in Lessons 172 through 179.
2. Click on the **Mastery Assess It 12** icon to begin the online assessment.
3. Have your student read the instructions before they get started. Remind them to take their time and to do their best work.
4. When they are finished and ready for their assessment to be graded, have them click the **Submit** button.